GOVERNING THE HEROIN TRADE

Law Ethics and Governance Series

Series Editor: Charles Sampford, Director, Key Centre for Ethics, Law, Justice and Governance, Griffith University, Australia

Recent history has emphasised the potentially devastating effects of governance failures in governments, government agencies, corporations and the institutions of civil society. 'Good governance' is seen as necessary, if not crucial, for economic success and human development. Although the disciplines of law, ethics, politics, economics and management theory can provide insights into the governance of organisations, governance issues can only be dealt with by interdisciplinary studies, combining several (and sometimes all) of those disciplines. This series aims to provide such interdisciplinary studies for students, researchers and relevant practitioners.

Also in the series

Islam Beyond Conflict
Indonesian Islam and Western Political Theory
Edited by Azyumardi Azra and Wayne Hudson
ISBN 978-0-7546-7092-6

Re-envisioning Sovereignty
The End of Westphalia?
Edited by Trudy Jacobsen, Charles Sampford and Ramesh Thakur
ISBN 978-0-7546-7260-9

On Abuse of Idealism
Lessons from China's Cultural Revolution
Peggy Krenn (Hui-yun Chuang)
ISBN 978-0-7546-7208-1

Measuring Corruption
Edited by Charles Sampford, Arthur Shacklock, Carmel Connors
and Fredrik Galtung
ISBN 978-0-7546-2405-9

Governing the Heroin Trade

From Treaties to Treatment

MELISSA BULL
Griffith University, Australia

ASHGATE

Published by
Ashgate Publishing Limited
Gower House
Croft Road
Aldershot
Hampshire GU11 3HR
England

Ashgate Publishing Company
Suite 420
101 Cherry Street
Burlington, VT 05401-4405
USA

Ashgate website: http://www.ashgate.com

British Library Cataloguing in Publication Data
Bull, Melissa, 1962-
  Governing the heroin trade : from treaties to treatment. -
  (Law, ethics and governance series)
  1. Heroin industry - History 2. Opium trade - History
  3. Drug control - International cooperation
  I. Title
  363.4'5

Library of Congress Cataloging-in-Publication Data
Bull, Melissa, 1962-
  Governing the heroin trade : from treaties to treatment / by Melissa Bull.
      p. cm. -- (Law, ethics and governance)
  Includes bibliographical references and index.
  ISBN 978-0-7546-7121-3
  1. Heroin industry--History. 2. Opium trade--History. 3. Drug control--International
cooperation. I. Title.

  HV5822.H4B84 2008
  363.45--dc22

                                    2008002418

ISBN 978-0-7546-7121-3

Mixed Sources
Product group from well-managed forests and other controlled sources
www.fsc.org Cert no. SGS-COC-2482
FSC © 1996 Forest Stewardship Council

Printed and bound in Great Britain by
TJ International Ltd, Padstow, Cornwall

Contents

Chapter 1

The Problem of Control

Introduction

Internationally there is a long standing and continuing government and public concern about the use of psychotropic drugs. Diacetylmorphine or heroin, as the drug is more popularly known, has consistently been at the centre of attention. In 1983 John Kaplan called it 'the hardest drug' in his book of the same title, because there are no easy answers to the problems that are linked to its use and distribution. Twenty-five years later the *2007 World Drug Report* produced by the United Nations Office on Drugs and Crime which is responsible for coordinating programs regulating illicit drugs describes how 'unsurprisingly, the main problem drugs at the global level continue to be the opiates (notably heroin)' (2007: 9). Heroin is a derivative of opium, and it is well known that opiates have the capacity to produce dependence in users of the drug, and as a result the problem of heroin is commonly thought of in terms of the pains of 'addiction'. From a governmental perspective the problem of heroin and how to govern it is usually discussed as part of the broader problem of illicit drugs which make up a set of prohibited and strictly controlled substances specified in schedules to treaties which describe an international system of control.

Heroin is listed in the schedules to the '*Single Convention on Narcotic Drugs*' (SCoND) which consolidated a world system of drug control when it was introduced in 1961. The drugs subject to the Convention (United Nations 1961, Article 2) are listed in four schedules. According to its authors, the last of these consists of a special class of drugs that are considered to be 'particularly liable to abuse and to produce ill effects, where this liability is not offset by substantial therapeutic advantages' (Article 3). They attract 'special measures of control ... having regard to the particularly *dangerous* properties of the drug' (Article 2). Furthermore, if it is the most appropriate means of protecting the public health and welfare, parties shall '*prohibit* the production, manufacture, export and import, trade in, possession, or use of such drugs' (Article 2). In 1973 Schedule IV included only four drugs – heroin was one of them.

Pharmacologically heroin has little in common with other substances included on this list; but bears a great deal of similarity to substances – like methadone – that are not subject to prohibition but are legally available albeit in highly regulated ways. What the drugs on schedule IV to the SCoND do share is their common status – their, production, manufacture, distribution and use are generally prohibited on an international scale and they are the focus of a coordinated and intensive system of global policing. These substances are collectively the subject of many authoritative reports, which often make distinctions between classes of drugs: opiates, cocaine, cannabis and amphetamine type stimulants. The *World Drug Reports* (United Nations Office on Drugs and Crime 2006; 2007) describe the problem of opiates primarily in terms of production, trafficking and use (which is defined in terms of availability and price): providing only very limited information on the demand for treatment. This implies that the governmental problem as it currently stands is predominantly one of supply. Despite optimistic claims about stabilising patterns of use (United Nations Office on Drugs and Crime 2006; 2007), the success of interdiction programs and downward trends in the areas under cultivation of opium, since 1998 global opium production has actually increased; in 2006 it 'soared to a new record high of 6,610 metric tonnes, an increase of 43 percent over 2005' levels (2007: 10). Taking this into account these reports actually document and highlight some of the failures and limits of the current international regulatory efforts (Chouvy 2006; International Drug Policy Consortium 2006; Roberts et al. 2004).

It has long been acknowledged that many of the harms associated with illicit drugs, including heroin, are linked to the control system itself. More than twenty years ago Kaplan (1983) pointed out that with widespread prohibition heroin supply reductions inevitably lead to higher street prices which force addicts to commit additional crimes to support their habits. He concluded that to some the social costs of a fully enforced prohibition out weigh the benefits. In 1988, the United Nations Conference for the adoption of the *Convention Against Illicit Traffic in Narcotic Drugs and Psychotropic Substances* was held in Vienna. It complemented the Single Convention, which was primarily directed at the control of licit activities, and was formulated specifically to deal with the growing problem of illicit trafficking. The same year Grant Wardlaw explained that the strict regulation of supply through prohibition – which the new convention promoted and reinforced:

> … itself produces many of the conditions which make the use of illicit drugs so damaging. Making the drug illegal drives up its price, which in turn forces some drug users to commit money producing crimes in order to finance their habits. The high price of illegal drugs makes the profits to be made from drug trafficking very large… and encourages more sophisticated and organised criminal individuals and groups into the market as well as increasing the amounts of violence employed within the circle of drug users and traffickers. The illegal context also means that much drug use takes place in marginal social settings, thus associating drug use with other undesirable features of contemporary life and bringing large numbers of young people [who may only ever experiment with illicit drug use] into contact with them. The necessity to administer drugs covertly contributes to the health problems (such as hepatitis and AIDS) associated with drug use. Other medical complications (such as overdose and morbidity and mortality which are consequences of using adulterated drugs) are directly associated with the illegal status of substances.

> In law enforcement terms alone, adopting an approach which over criminalizes drug use produces a myriad of negative consequences… In addition to income-generating crime, it is obvious that the policy generates a high level of associated criminal activity, much of it violent ... Undeniably, this … has lead to a whole range of derivative problems within the criminal justice system, ranging from overloading court, prison and probation systems, to encouraging deviant and corrupt official behaviour, and engendering changes to our legal system which undermine some of its basic precepts (Wardlaw 1988: 153-4).

At the beginning of the twenty-first century these problems persist. A United Nations International Drug Control Program (United Nations International Drug Control Program (1996, 1998) report lists the costs associated with illicit drug use, production and trafficking in terms of social costs like family degeneration, drug related deaths, the spread of contagious diseases like HIV/AIDS and Hepatitis C, violence, corruption and crime associated with drug markets, as well as the high economic cost of law enforcement. It notes that strong law enforcement approaches stimulate the market increasing profits and the potential that terrorist or insurgent groups will finance their operations, gain political support or undermine existing governments through the illicit drug trade. Roberts et al. (2004) highlight the significant economic costs of prohibition. For example, the United States (USA) spends about $30 billion per year on the enforcement of drug laws and it is argued that this approach is not reducing the prevalence of drug use and availability.

In addition to this very heavy financial burden these authors also point to the unintended consequences of a harsh law enforcement approach, which include health costs, and particularly an increased prevalence of HIV amongst injecting drug users. In a submission to the Canadian senate, Oscapella (2001) makes similar points explicitly arguing that prohibition itself is what makes the drug trade so profitable. Based on figures from United Nations Office of Drug Control and Crime Prevention (UNODCCP) reports the retail value of the illicit drug market is estimated to be US$400 billion a year. The production costs for a gram of heroin in Afghanistan compared to the actual retail price for the same quantity of the drug in the USA demonstrates that heroin retails for approximately 175 times more than the wholesale price in Afghanistan. Such a difference in price represents an extremely large profit margin and a huge incentive for some groups to become involved in the illicit market (Chouvy 2004c; Cornell 2006; Oscapella 2001; Stokes et al. 2000). Beyond these economic and social issues, other harms including corruption and violence are linked to the prohibitionist response. Stokes et al. (2000) describe how in Columbia three Presidential candidates, an Attorney-General, Justice Minister and more than two-hundred judges had been killed through random acts of violence designed to counter anti-narcotic programs run by the government. Beyond these deaths drug related violence has also included kidnappings, car bombings and the mid-air destruction of a Columbian jet. According to these authors the illicit drug trade impacts on the security of entire nation states, they cite examples of drug related violence and corruption in South Africa, South-East Asia, Brazil and Papua New Guinea (Chouvy 2003 on Asia). They argue that money laundering, illegal immigration, trans-national prostitution and corruption are all linked to organised crime groups who profit from illicit drugs, particularly the heroin trade. Cornell (2006) focusing on Central Asia concluded of all organised crime activity, the illicit drug trade carries the largest social, political and economic consequences, noting that recent links between terrorist groups and the illicit drug trade poses an increasing threat to regional and international security.

This book examines how the international system of drug control works, with the aim of highlighting both its strengths and limits. It makes a case study of heroin, rather than another designated illicit drug. Heroin is a derivative of opium, the drug which, as we will see, provided for the introduction of the international system of control. The regulation of opiates was initiated at a meeting in Shanghai in 1909, and provided the model for a system of global regulation which in large part has been extended to other illicit substances (United Nations Office on Drugs and Crime 2007). In describing the system of control and analysing how it works, this book begins by examining how opium and as a result heroin became a problem and then investigates how the regulatory system as it now stands came to be the answer. In short the question this book asks is: if the prohibition of heroin is the answer, what was the question? And perhaps more importantly what, once we know the question, other answers might there be? To take this approach we must begin by recognising that opium has a long history of unproblematic use. Most stories of drug regulation begin with, or at least make some reference to, its very long documented past. Even though I am mainly concerned with more recent events related to the regulation of this specific drug, it is worth rehearsing these accounts at the beginning of this book. This heritage reminds us that current social responses to this substance and its use are culturally, historically and politically situated. It should, however, be followed with a critical eye, because its lesson is not to tell us the truth of how things were or ought to be, but rather to suggest that they could have been (and they could be) other than how they are now.

The Prehistory of Regulation

It is generally reported that the poppy plant (*Papaver somiferum*) originated in the Mediterranean region. The earliest reference to it is the Sumerian's recognition, circa 4000 BC, of the *Papaver somiferum* as the 'plant of joy'. The Sumerians passed it on to the Assyrians, who also left useful descriptions of the process of collecting raw opium (circa 700 BC). The Assyrians passed the cultivation process to the Babylonians, who passed it to the Egyptians (Ashely 1972; Hess 1980; Hoffman 1990; McCoy 1980). Egyptian and Persian doctors treated patients with opium from the second century BC. Veterinary and gynaecological papyri and the Therapeutic Papyrus of Thebes of 1552 BC list opium among medically recommended drugs (Berridge and Edwards 1987: xxii). Frequent pictorial representations provide evidence of the role of opiate use in Greek culture, and Greek legends are filled with tales of how their gods and heroes used opium for mystical purposes. The healing properties of opium were detailed in the works of the Greek physician Hippocrates (466–377 BC), and the first extensive account of opium's pharmacology appears in the writings of philosopher and botanist Theophrastos (372–287 BC). These were also documented by Galen (130–200 AD), who probably recorded the first incidence of opium overdose around 140 AD (Berridge and Edwards 1987; Hess 1980; Hoffman 1990). The properties or effects of opium today associated with addiction or dependence appeared in Arabic literature in 1030 AD, however, in these more ancient times, the benefits of opium seem to have overridden any identifiable adverse side effects.[1]

---

1   For example, although early Muslims condemned the use of psychoactive substances, such as hashish, opium was valued as a medicine. It was used to treat respiratory

Arab traders brought the drug to India around the ninth century AD (Hoffman 1990), where its use spread rapidly. It was recommended for a variety of purposes: to quiet infants, as an aphrodisiac, and to give courage to soldiers. Its use also spread to China, where it was consumed in an edible form and valued for its medicinal properties. In that country, Portuguese traders introduced opium smoking in the sixteenth century. It became so fashionable in the early seventeenth century that the Emperor declared it illegal in 1729 because it offended Confusian sensibilities (Beeching 1975: 21). While this 1729 edict was popularly supported it was not strictly enforced. By that time opium trade routes had already become well established and the prohibition had little effect (Rolls 1992). In Western European medicine the place of opium was well recognised by the sixteenth century (Berridge and Edwards 1987: xxiii). The German physician known as Paracelsus (1490–1540) and his followers prepared laudanum, an opium preparation, that was to become very popular (Hess 1980: 6).[2] Platerus of Basle, a follower of Paracelsus, promoted opium's use in 1600, and Sylvius de la Boe, an important Dutch physician, declared that *without opium he could not practise medicine* (Berridge and Edwards 1987: xxiii). In the latter half of the sixteenth century Europeans also became aware of the phenomenon which would eventually be described as addiction. At that time, however, it remained a phenomenon associated with other countries (Hess 1980). It was reported by travellers to India, Turkey, Persia, the East Indies and finally China and Indonesia in the eighteenth century. These reports had little impact on the use of opium in Europe.

Opium as an Everyday Commodity

Opium's long history is closely tied to its significance as an item of trade. In the nineteenth century the main sources of supply had come to be largely controlled by European interests. This was affected either by direct political intervention, or by efficient economic penetration. Britain used both these means to extend its control over most of the world's opium supply (Parssinen 1983). With colonial victories in India in the late eighteenth century, the British East India Company took control of the opium producing monopoly of the Mogul emperors (McCoy 1991; Rolls 1992). As will be discussed in greater detail in Chapter 3, the Company increased opium production, made it more efficient, and according to Parssinen (1983) cultivated outlets for opium among Chinese smokers conniving with smugglers and corrupt officials to move it illicitly into Chinese markets. The quantities and profits involved were immense.

This British control over the production and sale of opium marked the beginning of the modern era of opium trade (McCoy 1991). Using opium to barter for Chinese

---

disease, diarrhoea, and insomnia. While the possibilities of dependence and overdose were recognised, they did not produce the condemnation of the drug (Hoffman 1990).

2   Berridge and Edwards (1987) explain that Paracelsus first used the term laudanum to describe an efficacious opium compound, probably in a solid pill form. The alcoholic tincture which is now known as laudanum was originated by the English physician Thomas Sydenham in the 1660s.

tea, silk, and porcelains, British merchants controlled a profitable triangular trade between India, China and Europe that smuggled growing quantities of opium to China. In the 1790s China's Emperor again tried to introduce a complete ban on opium. His efforts in this regard continued to have little effect on the expansion of opium smuggling by British and American merchants. The British East India Company's centralised control accelerated export of Indian opium to China from only 15 tons in the 1720s, to 75 tons in 1770 when the company began its monopoly, to 3200 tons in 1850 (McCoy 1991; Rolls 1992). During this first century of modern drug trade, British commerce had transformed opium from a luxury good into a bulk commodity of the same proportions as other commercial stimulants like coffee, tea, and cacao. In 1839 and 1856 Britain fought two wars to force the Chinese empire to rescind its opium ban. In the shadow of England's success in these wars, opium became a major global commodity in legitimate international trade.

In the nineteenth century London emerged as the centre of the international drug trade. This was in part the result of the city's commercial advantage as the centre of international shipping, finance and insurance (Parssinen 1983). Imperial expansion in the eighteenth century which gave Britain the control of the sources of many drugs – as well as other raw materials – together with the Navigation Acts of the seventeenth century, ensured that all trade in colonial goods would be channelled through London. By the 1870s Britain had become the centre of international traffic in opium (McCoy 1991; Parssinen 1983; Rolls 1992). Opiate use in England during this period was widespread. It continued largely unfettered until the introduction of the Pharmacy Act in 1868. Before this, opium was sold and used unselfconsciously throughout all levels of society. The drug was generally imported from Turkey, using legitimate trade practices of the time.[3] As a commodity it was just another item of trade, which was dealt with objectively, and rather like tea, the importer, broker and buyer's chief concern was to obtain optimum quality at the best price (Berridge and Edwards 1987; Parssinen 1983). At this time any concern about opium was with profit and quality not with controls or the dangers of the drug.

Cultivating Opium

In parts of England and Scotland opium producing poppies were indigenous.[4] Together with the push for agricultural improvement at the end of the eighteenth century and the beginning of the nineteenth century, the local availability of the plants prompted local farmers to seriously consider the commercial possibilities for opium. Enthusiastic experimentation with the cultivation of poppies continued well into the 1820s, when interest began to fade, although some cultivation did continue until the 1870s. The diminished enthusiasm was attributed to problems arising from the harsh climate or 'marauding hares' (Berridge and Edwards 1987: 13). Similar experimentation occurred on the continent, particularly in Germany and France.

---

3   Opium from Turkey was of a better quality than that from India, Egypt, China or other sources (Berridge and Edwards 1987).

4   In the Fen ditches in parts of Norfolk and Cambridgeshire, for example (Berridge and Edwards 1987).

In the USA opium was so widely used that many commentators at the turn of the nineteenth century suggested home cultivation. Early growers wanted to end reliance on expensive imported opium, and to produce a domestic variety that was both potent and predictable in its effects. By 1810 a popular dispensatory suggested that: '[s]uch is the intrinsic value of opium, and such the high price which it commands, that every method, promising to increase the quantity in the market, should be encouraged as of great importance to the community' (Morgan 1981: 2). Throughout the nineteenth century people tried poppy cultivation in many parts of the country. Strains of poppies were legally grown in Virginia, Georgia, Tennessee, South Carolina, Florida, Louisiana, Arizona Territory and California. Poppies also grew in Pennsylvania, Vermont, Massachusetts, New Hampshire, and Connecticut. Indeed, as early as 1781, a letter sent to a Pennsylvania farmer made reference to good quality opium and its seed. However, later evidence suggests that domestic crops tended to yield too little opium juice to be of value, and the cost of producing American opium made it uncompetitive with that of Turkey and the Near East (Hoffman 1990). As a result, most of the opium used in the USA was imported.[5] By 1849 north-eastern states were importing so much opium that the United States Customs Service initiated the first opium tax (Hoffman 1990: 55–56).

Australian history demonstrates similar interests. The *Transactions and Proceeding of the Royal Society of Victoria* of 1870 describes one of several efforts to compete with the steadily growing flow of imported opium.

> Two enterprising young men, Messors George and Arthur Turpin, engaged in agricultural pursuits on the Macallister River in Gipps Land, finding the expenses attendant on forwarding their cereal products to market to be very great thereby leaving no remuneration for their labour, sought out the farming of other vegetation that would give them hope for better results. One way, on my suggestion, the sleeping poppy – *Papaver somifera* – the plant which supplies the opium of commerce (cited in Davies 1986: 32).

The article observed that opium achieved 'a very ready sale in Melbourne', and then concluded that the setting aside of just one acre of ground was sufficient to cultivate an economic quantity. The crop yielded 40lb of opium to the acre. However, the labour involved in the operation was so intense that not all the plants could be worked. Some of the costs of labour were reduced by the use of children to tap the crop. Agricultural journals of the ensuing years make few references to local cultivation of opium. This is not surprising considering ultimately the Gippsland crop of 1870 yielded a return at the Melbourne market of only £84 (Davies 1986: 33).

Despite initial enthusiasm, there was never much opium grown in Australia. After the experimental Victorian crop, various small growers produced it successfully in that colony until the 1880s. Opium had also been cultivated in other parts of Australia. James Murdoch of Paradise Farm, Risdon, Tasmania, began growing opium in

---

5   The United States continued to import opium, which had two long-term social effects. Imports rose faster than the rate of population growth after the 1840s, and these statistics fortified the idea that opiate use was increasing rapidly. And in the long run imports made it appear that foreigners were adversely affecting American life (Musto, 1973; Parssinen, 1983).

the 1820s. *The Hobart Town Courier* on 3 January 1834 reported that he had just finished his opium harvest, with the 'crop abundant and of good quality'. A later article mentioned that 'he cultivated it to considerable extent', but gave no further details. J. E. Stacy, surgeon of the Australian Agricultural Company, grew opium at Booral, New South Wales (now a small town south of Stroud). In the late nineteenth century a number of unsuccessful applications were made to establish monopolies like that of the East India Company in the colonies of South Australia, the Northern Territory and New South Wales, but no opium farms eventuated as a result of these propositions (Rolls 1992: 403), and opium continued to be imported.[6]

Popular Use of Opium

These historical accounts describe the part played by opium in normal agricultural considerations, as well as the drug's role in legitimate international, national and local trade. They illustrate the customary place of opium in a number of different societies during the nineteenth century. The acceptability of opium as a commodity was also confirmed in its widespread and unselfconscious use. The widespread use of opium and opiate preparations was common in England, the USA and Australia (Davies 1986; Manderson 1993) well into the nineteenth century. In England poppy-head tea had long been known as a home remedy for soothing irritable and sleepless babies, as well as troubled adults.[7] Fomentations of opium, often with chamomile, were in regular use until the end of the nineteenth century – they were often made from recipes passed down through generations. Laudanum, the famous tincture of opium, was a palliative in most homes (Berridge and Edwards 1987; Parssinen 1983). Numerous opium preparations were stocked and sold in chemist shops. There were opium pills (or soap and opium, and lead and opium pills), opiate lozenges, compound powder of opium, opiate confection, opiate plaster, opium enema, opium liniment, vinegar of opium and wine of opium. Along with laudanum there was the camphorated tincture, or paregoric. The dried capsules of the poppy were used, as were poppy fomentations, syrup of white poppies and extract of poppy (Berridge and Edwards 1987: 24). In nineteenth century America a range of similar products was also known. Gum and powdered opium were readily available, but usually appeared in solutions – mixed with alcohol and water either formed laudanum – and

---

6   The enormous demand for morphine arising in the contest of World War II stimulated the Commonwealth Scientific and Industrial Research Organisation (CSIRO) to undertake extensive cultivation. This government poppy industry ceased at the end of the war, but cultivation was undertaken again in 1964 after the British company MacFarlan Smith extended its research base to Tasmania and commenced commercial production in the rugged north-west of the State. Tasmania is now one of the world's largest producers of legal opium (Rolls, 1992).

7   Elizabeth Pepys (1640), wife of Samuel Pepys, diarist and civil servant, unselfconsciously makes mention of 'wildpoppy' in her diary (Wednesday, 9 January 1656). 'Nicholas Culpeper says of it that "... the black seed boiled in wine, and drank, is said also to stay the flux of the belly, and women's courses. The empty shells, or poppy heads, are usually boiled in water, and given to procure rest and sleep." And "... it is also put into hollow teeth to ease the pain"' (quoted in Spender 1991: 106).

paregoric was familiar as a weapon in the battle against dysentery and as a pacifier for infants. Opium in solution was widely used in many famous cordials, syrups and elixirs, familiar companions of the nursery or medicine chest under such titles as 'Black Drop' or 'Mrs Windsloe's Soothing Syrup'. And opium's principal alkaloid, morphine, was available in powder, tablet or liquid form (Morgan 1981).

Opium was an ordinary everyday purchase. In 1857 an English pharmacist, in a town of 12,000–13,000, estimated that at least sixty people a day purchased the drug from each one of the six pharmacies in the town, and this estimate did not take into account the many and various other types of vendors. In general the entire population depended on the drug for a wide range of minor complaints, including fatigue and depression, sleeplessness, coughs, colds, stomachache, toothache, headache, flatulence, diarrhoea, and rheumatism. It was also as a liniment for piles, ulcers, bruises, sprains and chilblains. Doctors relied heavily on the drug, mainly because it was one of the few remedies that seemed to work. Opium, if not the 'cure-all', at least provided relief from pain and a period of intermission, which might aid recovery (Berridge and Edwards 1987: 70–1).

Parssinen (1983) explains that in the 1830s and 1840s opium assumed a crucial therapeutic role in English medicine. Medical journals were flooded with articles touting its expanded use. Jonathan Pereira, in his influential textbook on medicine and therapeutics,[8] echoed the dominant professional opinion when he claimed that:

> opium is undoubtedly the *most important and valuable remedy* of the whole Materia Medica. We have, for other medicines, one or more substitutes; but for opium we have none... Its good effects are not, as is the case with some valuable medicines, remote and contingent, but they are immediate, direct and obvious; and its operation is not attended with pain or discomfort (cited in Parssinen 1983: 22–3 emphasis added).

In North America, according to Morgan, during the first decades of the nineteenth century doctors prescribed opiates widely, and the early handbooks and texts were cheerful about 'God's own medicine' (1981: 4) even while warning against overdose. He quotes one author who in 1821 wrote:

> Of all the articles of the Materia Medica, this is perhaps, the *most extensively useful*, there being scarcely one morbid affection or disordered condition of the system in which, under certain circumstances, it is not exhibited, either alone, or in combination (cited in Morgan 1981: 4 emphasis added).

In the United States, dispensatories and home medical handbooks contained recipes for laudanum and paregoric, the ingredients of which were readily available in all but the most remote places (Morgan 1981). The maladies calling for opium crossed the breadth of human experience. Many home remedies contained alcohol, opium, or both; potential users at least knew that these substances had some effect in treating illnesses. Both Parssinen (1983), speaking of Britain, and Morgan (1981), with regard to the USA, explain that opium was not only effective, it was also cheap.

---

8   Pereira, Jonathan (1843), *The Elements of Materia Medica and Therapeutics* (Philadelphia: Lea & Blanchard).

This factor, together with the absence of doctors in many areas, and the uncertain efficacy of early medical practices, contributed greatly to its widespread use by all segments of the population.

The drug was widely used for both 'medical' and 'non-medical' purposes at all levels of society. It was available through a diverse range of outlets, rather than only through pharmacists – who barely existed before 1840 (Peterson 1978). Berridge and Edwards (1987) list the range of vendors as including basket makers, shoemakers, small ware dealers, factory operatives, tailors, bakers, rent collectors, undertakers and grocers as well as apothecaries and pharmacists. They explain that opium and opiate preparations were also on sale in street markets and pubs. Indeed, the drug houses, which were also wholesalers, manufacturers and retailers, sold to any dealer who chose to purchase the drug (Berridge and Edwards 1987; Parssinen 1983).

Before the introduction of regulation there were many inconsistencies associated with the sale of opium. As indicated above, the qualifications of vendors varied widely – being anything from customary use, to an apothecary's apprenticeship or pharmacy examination – and there was little guarantee that vendors had any knowledge of poisons at all. In Britain during the 1800s there were several recorded cases of manslaughter arising as a result of a grocer or general store owner's ignorance or mistake (see Berridge and Edwards 1987: 27). The quality or purity of opium and subsequent preparations varied similarly. The raw drug was often purchased in square, one-pound blocks and prepared for sale in the shop. Error could occur in the weighing or mixing of laudanum or other preparations. Again, what is notable – besides the potential for mistakes in this unregulated market – is the complete normality of open sales.

Given the free availability and the apparent extent of self-medication, dependence on opium during this period was likely to be common. Indeed, in the early decades of the nineteenth century, opium did begin to gain adverse associations. There were early warnings about the effects of overuse and overdose, and American authorities cautioned against its poisonous effects, even while praising it in normal use (Hoffman 1990; Morgan 1981). According to Parssinen (1983), however, in Britain, opium habituation cases were rarely commented upon. For the most part, this was because neither habitués nor medical practitioners considered the condition worthy of mention. To begin with, it was usually not noticeable. Opium, being a common household drug, was taken by many, perhaps most people at one time or another. Because opium was a popular medicine and widely available without a medical prescription, many persons who began taking it became habituated, lived and died without ever consulting a doctor about it. As a result, the condition of opium habituation, which would later be characterised as addiction, remained largely undetected, either by the consumers themselves or by those who sold opium to them, until the latter half of the 1800s. Some doctors, those visiting the poorhouses, hospitals and dispensaries, became aware of it during periods of short supply but saw it as a matter that did not concern them (Berridge and Edwards 1987).

Up until the beginning of the nineteenth century opium was generally not considered – by doctors or others – to be a dangerous drug (Berridge and Edwards 1987; Hess 1980; Hoffman 1990; Manderson 1988; Morgan 1981; Parssinen 1983; Scott 1969). Its use was central in the practice of medicine; its efficacy with a wide range of complaints was difficult to match. It was freely available, and relied on in most homes as a valuable remedy. However, in the late nineteenth century, attitudes to opiate use changed markedly; these changes are the foundation for contemporary perspectives on such use. They heralded a dramatic transformation, from a situation of free availability and socially accepted uninhibited use (for both medical and non-medical reasons) to one of strictest prohibition, and negative social and criminal sanctions. While today the supposedly obvious explanation for this sea-change lies in the allegedly 'inherently dangerous properties' of the drug and its supposedly free availability, the reality is much less obvious, and a great deal more complicated.

Finding Questions Where Others had Located Answers[9]

The main focus of this book is to examine the circumstances that provided for the regulation of opium and related drugs. It highlights the particular arrangements which have shaped how we govern, or try to govern heroin. In investigating the conditions of possibility for the current prohibition of this drug it does not explicitly support or condemn the prohibition of heroin, even though there is cause for criticism here, nor does it suggest new improved legislative arrangements. It does not argue that either the criminal law or medical practice should more properly have dominion over opioid use. More generally, I explore of the conditions that have given rise to, and shaped, the contemporary problematisation of heroin. My aim is to draw out the complexity and contingency of relationships which have contributed, for example, to the simultaneous possibility of methadone maintenance and refusal of heroin prescribing. Methadone maintenance treatment is an opioid drug substitution program in which illegal heroin is replaced by legally available methadone. It involves making a pure drug available to opioid-dependent individuals, under supervision, and at a minimal cost. The pharmacological characteristics of methadone provide the foundation for its efficacy as an intervention for opioid use. The technique of alleviating the problems arising from the dependent use of an opioid, or other drug, through the substitution of another dependence producing substance is nothing new. It has been a recurring feature in the modern treatment of the condition referred to as addiction: in the early nineteenth century, opium was thought to be a cure for too much drink (Berridge and Edwards 1987), in the 1860s, morphine was thought to be a cure for opium eating; and later, morphine was also used to treat cocaine addiction (Berridge and Edwards 1987; Courtwright 1982).[10] By the turn of the century,

---

9   (Dean 1994: 4).

10   Of late the term addiction has been problematised. Those working in the alcohol and drug field argue that it is morally tainted. Others suggest that it is a negative category that is socially constructed, and we should be cautious in our use of it (Bull 1996). Pat O'Malley (1999) argues that it has been replaced by the term drug dependence (which some find more palatable). He proposes that this is evidence of new ways of thinking about drug use that are linked to a conceptualisation of drug users as rational choice makers. This may well be the case in the Australian policy documents that are the subject of O'Malley's analysis. However, the process of replacement is far from complete if we take into account broader horizons. Addiction continues to be used widely as a term to describe a cluster of human behaviours that

medical practitioners promoted heroin as a safe and non-addictive drug to be used in the treatment of morphine addiction, and in the 1960s, methadone replaced them all (Gossop 1987; Krivanek 1988). In terms of their capacity for neuroadaptation, the opioid drugs are virtually interchangeable. As Michael Gossop notes, 'methadone is no more a cure for heroin addiction than heroin was for morphine addiction' (1987: 213). It seems paradoxical to prescribe methadone as part of an opioid demand reduction strategy if, as Michael Gossop (1987) proposes, prescribing methadone is pharmacologically no different to prescribing heroin. The viability of pharmacological interchangeability – heroin for morphine, methadone for heroin – begs the question of why diacetylmorphine (heroin) prescribing remains so controversial. Moreover, if there are problems associated with prescribing opioids, what makes methadone – also an opioid – a more feasible option? I begin by initially adopting an historical approach, asking: what are the chief political and governmental rationalities underlying the problematisation of opioids, their regulation, and ultimately their prohibition, in a number of contemporary societies?

Taking this approach requires avoiding historical claims to universality that construct the past as a patient and continuous development, and of any desire to know what *really* happened. It also involves rejecting histories informed by theories of social progress, and of critical theories promising emancipation (Dean 1994: 2). This helps us to move beyond what Skocpol calls 'transhistorical' generalisations and teleological schemas of grand theories and the metanarratives of modernism, development and increasing affluence, or the crisis ridden tendencies of the capitalist mode of production (1984: 2). The analysis ahead is not a traditional history of ideas, or of the progress of knowledge. It is not a search for beginnings or the origins of causes of an event which are somehow present even before the event occurs (Chartier 1994). It is not a 'total history' which attempts to draw all phenomena round a single causative centre or spirit of a society or civilisation, which posits the same form of historical influence operating on all levels – the economic, the social, the political, the religious – with the same types of transformation and influences playing on all these levels. Rather it could be described a 'general history' where the task is to determine what types of relationships can legitimately be made between the various forms of social categorisation, but to do this without recourse to any master schema, any ultimate theory of causation (Foucault 1972).

Foucault (1984a) describes this methodological orientation as genealogy, which is a type of history of the present. To write such a history is to consider the history of a problem in terms of how it is seen at present. It is founded on the conviction that the present reflects a conjunction of elements inherited from the past and current motivations. It acknowledges that our contemporary problems and practices are quite distinct from those of the past; but recognises that our present arrangements were constructed out of materials and situations which existed at earlier points in time.

---

are associated with drug use (see, for example, United Nations documents, or the vocabulary of services providers and consumers in Christie and Hil, 2000). The relationship between the terms 'addiction' and 'drug dependence' is complex and ambiguous. As a result, throughout this book I use both terms, mostly in a way that seeks to reflect the usage in documents that are cited.

Analysing a contemporary practice in this way means viewing it from the standpoint of its historical basis; it means grounding our understandings of its current structure on the series of previous transformations. The past does not repeat itself in the present, but the present is played out, and innovates, using the legacy of the past (Castel 1994).

Genealogy challenges those versions of history which uncritically accept the taken for granted components of our reality and the official accounts of how they came to be the way they are. It seeks, instead, to remain open to the dispersion of historical transformations, the rapid mutation of events, the multiplicity of temporalities, the differential forms of timing and spacing of activities, and the possibility of invasion and even reversal of historical pathways. This form of practice, according to Dean, 'has the effect of the disturbance of narratives of both progress and reconciliation, *finding questions where others had located answers*' (1994: 4). A history of the present aims to question the usual way of understanding the development of particular institutions or practices as being the result of progress or rationality. It is an examination of the way in which it has been possible to think about this or that, the knowledges and practices that have made this possible, and the tactics and strategies that have developed from this.

Generally this method of problematisation covers a long time span, and is not completely or necessarily constructed from primary sources, unpublished discoveries or historical scoops. It is largely the outgrowth of the work of historians which, however, it reads in different ways (Castel 1994). It is a technique which opens a space for the repositioning of historical work already done, while at the same time, posing new directions and aims for research. In constituting an alternative account from historical data, the aim is to contribute something to what has already been achieved; to contribute to our knowledge of a current situation derived from other approaches to the present. However, this must not come at the price of our knowledge of the past. The right to choose one's materials and refocus them in light of a current issue, to place them in different categories, is not permission to rewrite history (Castel 1994). That is, the results of research should at least be compatible with the accounts of other historians. An enormous amount of literature has addressed the subject of drug regulation. Amongst this work there are a significant number of contributions that provide well-researched and detailed historical accounts.[11] As this book is not an attempt to revise history, but rather to provide some understanding of the rationality behind the already well reported events, it is not necessary, nor particularly economical to revisit the archives. It is possible that in the light of this work, later research may require some renewed investigation. In the context of this project, however, it is appropriate to take advantage of some of the excellent histories already available in this area; and in doing so, reframe the debate in a manner which

---

11   For example: Ashley (1972); Beeching (1975); Berridge and Edwards (1987); Bruun, Pan and Rexed (1975); Courtwright (1982); Fay (1975); Inglis (1975); Manderson (1993); McCoy (1972, 1991); Milligan (1995); Morgan (1981); Musto (1973); Parssinen (1983); Rolls (1992) and Scott (1969). The numerous historical papers produced by Virginia Berridge deserve particular mention here.

is able to accommodate some of the more complex relations of contemporary drug, and specifically opioid, regulation.

Beginning from the problematisation of opium, this book is concerned with rationalities underlying the regulation of opiates and related substances. These rationalities operate through, and are intelligible in, the particular social and historical institutions and the practices, techniques, strategies and modes of calculation that traverse them (Dean 1994; Rose and Miller 1992). Political rationalities are the changing discursive fields within which the exercise of power is conceptualised, the moral justification for particular ways of exercising power by diverse authorities, notions of the appropriate forms, objects and limits of politics, and conceptions of the proper distribution of such tasks among secular, spiritual, military and familial sectors (Rose and Miller 1992: 175). They provide an intellectual framework for making reality thinkable in a way that it is open to political deliberations (Rose and Miller 1992: 179).

Governmental programs shift political rationalities into the realm of the real. They are discursive arrangements which articulate political rationalities in specific problem spaces. Programs presuppose that the real is programmable, that it is a domain subject to certain determinants, rules, norms and processes that can be acted upon and improved by authorities. They make the objects of government thinkable in such a way that they appear susceptible to political calculation and governmental intervention. They are founded upon knowledge and made operable by various technologies – intellectual technologies and technologies of inscription. In other words, it is through technologies that political rationalities and the programs of government that articulate them become capable of deployment (Miller and Rose 1990: 82).

Rose and Miller suggest that the programs of government should be analysed both in terms of their political rationalities and the governmental technologies they employ – the complex of mundane programs, calculations, techniques, apparatuses, documents and procedures through which authorities seek to embody and give effect to governmental ambitions (1992: 175). Analysing such technologies is a matter of understanding the complex relationships between diverse forces – legal, professional, administrative, for example – that shape the decisions and actions of individuals, groups, organisations and populations in relation to 'authoritative' criteria. This involves the study of the mundane mechanisms used by various authorities to initiate government: techniques of notations, computation and calculation; procedures of examination and assessment; the invention of devices such as surveys and presentational forms such as tables; the standardisation of systems for training and the inculcation of habits; the inauguration of professional specialisms and vocabularies; and building designs and architectural forms (Rose and Miller 1992: 175).

Through an analysis of the intricate interdependencies between political rationalities, programs of government, and governmental technologies, we can begin to understand the multiple and delicate networks that connect the lives of individuals, groups and organisations to the aspirations of authorities in the advanced liberal democracies of the present (Rose and Miller 1992: 175). Such networks are, however, not the simple aggregate of rationally planned technologies for shaping decisions and conduct in calculated ways. As Miller and Rose (1990) explain, the mechanisms of rule that are invented to operationalise programs and respond to political rationalities are rarely implanted unscathed, and are seldom found to have achieved what they set out to do. This is because the world of programs is diverse and contentious, and the solutions for one program tend to be the problems for another. Reality is never perfectly captured in the bodies of knowledge that inform governmental programs, and persons, things and events often fail to respond to programmatic forms of logic. Technologies produce unexpected problems, are utilised to the ends of those who are supposed to merely operate them, are hampered by under-funding, professional rivalries, and the impossibility of ensuring the technical conditions that would make them work: reliable statistics, efficient communications systems, purpose built facilities, well framed regulations etc. Unplanned outcomes emerge from the intersection of one technology with another, or from the unexpected consequence of putting a technique to work. Alternatively, techniques invented for one purpose may find their governmental role for another, and the unplanned conjunction of techniques and conditions arising from very different aspirations may allow something to work without, or despite, its explicit rationale. In short, governance needs to be considered not so much in terms of its success, but in terms of the difficulties of getting it to work (Miller and Rose 1990: 85).

The first part of this book – made up of the next two chapters – consists of genealogies of the conditions that provided for the problematisation of opioids. Chapter 2 builds on the brief prehistory of regulation above, which notes the significant position of opium, and related opiate preparations, as legitimate and relatively common, uncontroversial commodities of trade and consumption in societies of the eighteenth and nineteenth centuries. It investigates the rationalities and practices which allowed for the identification of opium as a dangerous drug, its initial regulation and subsequent prohibition. Chapter 3 traces a genealogy of the problematisation of the supply of opiates in terms of the constitution of the sovereignty of particular nation states and the capacity of nation states to self-govern. It argues that matters of state interest relating to the formation of the twentieth-century system of states played a significant role in the conditions of possibility for the international regulation and ultimately the prohibition of opium. Specific attention is devoted to the United Kingdom, United States and Australia, with some consideration of other significant European and Asian experiences.

The following chapters – 4 and 5 – investigate the translation of such political rationalities into programs that articulate them and technologies that deploy them in more contemporary settings. Chapter 4 analyses the drug control treaties that emerged out of the international system of control. It brings into focus the systems of thought that various authorities currently use to pose and specify the problem of heroin and other opiates, along with the systems of action through which they have sought to give effect to the government of this drug. In doing so Chapter 4 identifies the programs, technologies and strategies that translate the political rationalities, which provide the conditions of possibility for the regulation of opioids, into the realm of everyday life. Prominent amongst these are programs to regulate the supply and the demand for illicit drugs. Chapter 5 examines the techniques and strategies that are part of the program for the reduction in demand for illicit drugs. In doing so it considers dominant treatment trends and examines how opioid consumption is governed through methadone (and more recently an expanded range of pharmaceutical opioids). The concluding chapter discusses the nature of the governmental problems that the prohibition of heroin has addressed and considers the emerging horizon of alternative solutions.

Chapter 2

Regulating Opium

Up until the beginning of the nineteenth century opium was generally not considered to be a dangerous drug (Berridge and Edwards 1987; Hess 1980; Hoffman 1990; Manderson 1988; Morgan 1981; Parssinen 1983; Scott 1969). In the late nineteenth century, attitudes to opiate use changed markedly; these changes are the foundation for contemporary perspectives on such use. They heralded a transformation, from a situation of free availability and socially accepted uninhibited use to one of prohibition, and negative social and criminal sanctions. Today the explanation for this change is said to be the allegedly 'inherently dangerous properties' of the drug and its supposedly free availability, the reality is much less obvious, and a great deal more complicated. This chapter investigates the conditions which have initially contributed to the regulation of opium and opiate preparations. It takes nineteenth century Britain as a case study. Focusing on the British history provides insight to processes that were going in other industrialising states. As Parssinen explains similarities exist between the pre-twentieth century English and American histories of opiate use. He concludes that:

> Despite a few variations, then, the experience of nineteenth century Britons and Americans with the medical use of narcotic drugs was remarkably similar. They used opiates for almost identical purposes and took them in nearly identical form, although Americans may have taken them in somewhat greater quantity after 1860 (1983: 211).

Many of the preconditions for the regulation of opium and the recognition of a category called addiction pre-date the extensive colonisation of Australia and, in the process of colonisation, early Australian experiences of public policy, legislative and medical development, in relation to the regulation of opiate use, evolved directly from, and as an extension of, the British experience (Manderson 1988: 442). American developments did not become influential until the early part of the twentieth century; this is the subject of Chapter 3. They did not begin to shape policy or public perceptions in Australia until after World War II (Willis 1989). This chapter considers some of the institutional prerequisites for the recognition of opium as a 'dangerous' drug.

The Conditions of Possibility for the Regulation of Opiates

The Health and Wellbeing of the Population

While opium use was clearly popular, as well as prevalent, well into the nineteenth century, the extent of its use and negative effects were largely unknown. In what follows I argue that the emergence of the population as an object of governance, and the subsequent quantification of society (and social behaviour), provides the conditions for the initial recognition of opium as a dangerous drug. In the eighteenth century the good order, enrichment and health of the population in general emerged as one of the essential objectives of political power (Foucault 1980; Rose 1994). This was ensured through the multiple regulations and institutions which at that time took the generic name of police (Oestreich 1982; Pasquino 1991).[1] In relation to health the objectives of power included the cultivation of *physical wellbeing* and *optimum longevity*. It was in this context that medicine (and the problem of health) assumed a particular importance in the governance of the territorial state. Foucault suggests that the basis for this transformation was the effects of increasing population:

> The great eighteenth century demographic upswing in Western Europe, the necessity of co-ordinating and integrating it into the apparatus of production and the urgency of controlling it with finer and more adequate power mechanisms cause 'population', with its numerical values of space and chronology, longevity and health, to emerge not only as a problem but as an object of surveillance, analysis, intervention, modification etc. The project of a technology of population begins to be sketched: demographic estimates, the calculation of the pyramid of ages, different life expectations and levels of mortality, studies of reciprocal relations of growth of wealth and growth of population, various measures of incitement to marriage and procreation, the development of forms of education and professional training (1980: 278–9).

Thus, the 'population' was constituted as a problem, a target for surveillance, regulation, analysis and intervention. With this change, a particular form of 'politico-medical' regulatory arrangements came to permeate the lives of people. These arrangements were expressed through a whole series of prescriptions relating not only to disease, but also to general forms of existence and behaviour: food and drink, sexuality and fecundity, clothing, and the layout of space (Foucault 1980: 283). Bodies – those of individuals and those of populations – became bearers of new values relating to their productivity, use, and general state of health (Foucault 1980: 279). This politics of health initially figured as a problem with a number of different origins and orientations, and it was formulated as a problem of the health of all, as a priority of all. In other words, this rising concern for public health and hygiene did not simply correspond with a uniform trend of state intervention in the

---

1   Pasquino (1991) explains that police was not always understood in the present sense of the term – police having the [official] purpose of maintenance of order, and prevention of dangers. Before 1770 the interests of police were principally government and administration. The object of police was to keep the community thriving in order that 'the subjects may prosper in wealth and property and that everything hindering the common good may be prevented'. The science of police is the 'culmination of a vast, neglected literature which traverses the whole of the modern period. The body of knowledge of "police" was known in the eighteenth century as both "the science of happiness" and the "science of government" which constitutes society as the object of a knowledge and, at the same time, as the target of political intervention. The object of police is everything that has to do with maintaining and augmenting the happiness of its citizens – omnium et singularum (of all and of each); to inspect and manage the population' (Pasquino 1991:110).

practice of medicine. Rather than being a product of vertical initiative from above, a number of distinct health policies, and varying methods of addressing the medical problems of the population in general, emanated from within the social body: from religious groups, charitable and benevolent associations, and the learned societies (Foucault 1980).

Statistical measurement and analysis emerged in the late eighteenth and early nineteenth centuries as a means of measuring, classifying and monitoring characteristics of the population (Hacking 1990; Rose 1988). Nowhere else was statistics pursued with quite the level of fervour as it was in Britain. The characteristic institution of statistical enthusiasm in that country was the private statistical society (Hacking 1990; Porter 1986). A proliferation of statistical societies at the beginning of the nineteenth century was stimulated by the gathering pace of urbanisation and industrialisation, as the changes in the mode of production and population density aggravated problems of health, overcrowding and a lack of recreational space (Bulmer et al. 1991; Cullen 1975; Janes Yeo 1991; McGreggor 1957). An increasing concern regarding these social transformations was reflected in a perceived need to investigate society more 'scientifically' on a systematic basis. In the opening decades of the nineteenth century this interest was expressed in the use of statistics as a tool to bring together 'facts' which would 'illustrate the condition and prospects of society' (Janes Yeo 1991: 49). Public hygiene, health, housing, family life and employment were key topics of extensive investigation.

Out of this activity grew embryonic town councils and new state departments (Hacking 1982; Janes Yeo 1991; Porter 1986). For example, the distinguished London Statistical Society, formed in 1834, included among its membership a number of notable public servants: Adolphe Quetelet, whom Hacking describes as a 'master statistical informant and creator of national bureaucracies and international congresses of the nineteenth century' (1982: 24); Edwin Chadwick, who combined social inquiry with the process of government policy-making in his preparation of *The Poor Law Report* of 1834, and the *Report on the Sanitary Conditions of the Labouring Population* (cited in Bulmer et al. 1991); and, not insignificantly, Dr William Farr, who was an important figure in the development of medical and demographic statistics. For forty years he was the effective head of the Registrar General's Office, one of the first central government agencies to be established (in 1837). This office was the dominant fact-gathering institution of its time. It set the style for official statistics for many nations, including Australia (Forster and Hazlehurst 1988).[2]

Despite the intention of systematic scientific reform, the early collection of information, by the state or the statistical societies, was not conducted from a strong methodological base – or even with a specific purpose in mind (Bulmer et al. 1991; Eyler 1979; Janes Yeo 1991; Lazarsfeld 1961). Available resources were mainly

---

2   William Farr was responsible for the institutionalisation of British vital statistics (regularly published in *The Lancet*); his system of reporting and analysis of the incidence of birth, life and death became the model for the world. Two things were important:

1) nosology (Farr helped revolutionise the classification of diseases) and

2) counting according to the new nosology (Hacking 1991:53).

devoted to conducting door-to-door surveys which, as Janes Yeo (1991) explains, provided an important opportunity for surveillance. The state investigators, and later the advocates of the movement to improve public health, were quite happy to select relevant facts, from the social statistical information only then becoming available (Hacking 1982), to create the knowledge they wanted.[3] To be more precise, early investigations were not stimulated by already-identified social problems like addiction.

Ian Hunter (1994) makes a salient point in relation to this apparently haphazard approach. He reminds us that this knowledge of life, of the population, was supplied by social statistics as an intellectual technology, and that knowledge of mortality rates, incarceration frequencies, literacy levels or national productivity is not available to human perception without such a technology. That is to say, knowledge of morbidity rates, for example, is not something that human consciousness can acquire independently of the practical existence of the technique of probability calculation or of the governmental arrangements which gather the sick together and subject them to uniform observational procedures. Similarly, life tables could not be calculated in the absence of the same techniques and the pertinent governmental arrangements which provided for the collection and ordering of bills of mortality. Hunter's view is founded in the work of Ian Hacking; in particular Hacking's argument that while statistical laws that looked like facts were first found in human affairs during the nineteenth century, they could be noticed only after the social phenomena had been enumerated, tabulated and made public (Hacking 1982; Hacking 1990; Hunter 1994). That role was served by the 'avalanche of printed numbers' at the start of the nineteenth century.[4]

The statistics most commonly studied were those of birth, life and death. In Britain the institution of a regular census of the population and systems of notifying births and deaths to a central body (the Registrar General's Office) in the first half of the nineteenth century allowed the construction and publication of *Vital Statistics*.[5] Statistical research on populations led to findings that drew attention to differences in mortality rates, identified the illnesses and diseases causing the greatest mortality, and nominated groups that were found to be particularly vulnerable to certain illnesses or early death. These figures played an important role in the early identification of opium as a dangerous drug. They were significant on at least two fronts. Opium related death first became visible as a problem in relation to life insurance in the early 1830s, and then as a more general concern in the context of the broader public

---

3   In the 1820s an immense amount of data was not only accumulating, it was beginning to be analysed. This could not have occurred without the many new bureaucracies, which were created to collect information about the people and to arrange populations into a well organised databank (Hacking 1982). By 1850 there were six distinct types of agency carrying out social investigation: royal commissions, parliamentary committees, government officials, the Registrar General's Office, private individuals, and statistical societies. Between 1832 and 1846, over 100 royal commissions were set up (Janes Yeo 1991). The enormous number of inquiries conducted collectively by these agencies produced an avalanche of information which had not been previously available.

4   Hacking (1991) identified the period 1820–1840 as significant.

5   These figures were regularly published in *The Lancet* during the nineteenth century.

hygiene campaign of the middle of the nineteenth century (1830s–1860s). Each of these two developments is discussed in greater detail below.

Life, Longevity and Opium

The practice of selling life insurance first developed in England in the late eighteenth century (1750–1780). It involved speculation on the longevity of the insured according to criteria established by a series of expert knowledges: medical, statistical and actuarial. The rates of payment were determined in accordance with the general table of mortalities drawn up by the state actuary (Defert 1991). Insurance is primarily a schema of rationality – a way of breaking down, rearranging, and ordering certain elements of reality. It is formalised by the calculus of probabilities. One of the effects of insurance is the invention of risks. In the domain of insurance, risk is less associated with danger and peril; rather it is bound together with ideas of chance, hazard, probability, eventuality or randomness on the one hand, and those of loss or damage on the other. Ewald (1991) explains that these two series come together in the notion of accident. One insures against accident, against the probability of the loss of some good – including loss of life. Insurance, through the category of risk, objectifies every event as an accident. The insurer's activity is not just a matter of passively registering the existence of risks, and then offering guarantees against them. The insurer produces risks, that is, makes risk appear where each person had hitherto felt obliged to submit to the blows of fate. Insurance is a technology that involves the calculation, according to various combinations of life events, of the probability of a particular 'accident' occurring. The development of life tables, in the seventeenth and eighteenth centuries, as a means of predicting the life span of males and females in certain populations at different ages, led to a new way of conceptualising death. In this context death was transformed from a random event striking anyone at any time, into a calculable and patterned occurrence, subject to the laws of probability, striking populations rather than individuals, resulting in 'an actuarial vision of human existence' (Prior and Bloor 1993: 355).

It was the matter of life insurance that initially forced nineteenth century English society to confront the social issue of opiate use (Berridge 1977; Berridge and Edwards 1987). The question of the relationship between opium eating and longevity first arose in the context of a life insurance claim, and the refusal to pay out on that claim. In 1826 the Earl of Mar had taken out several insurances on his life. In 1828 he died of jaundice and dropsy. Investigation revealed that he had been an opium eater of thirty years standing, taking a tablespoon before going to bed. At one stage he had informed his housekeeper that he was taking forty-nine grains of solid opium and an ounce of laudanum each day. The insurance company refused to pay out on the policy, arguing that opium eating was a habit affecting health and longevity, which should have been revealed. The case went to the Scottish courts where, in the course of two trials, in 1830 and 1832, the value of opium eating and its effects *on health and longevity* were extensively discussed. The medical witnesses were equivocal, but tended to agree that the lord's excessive indulgence in opium eating would render 'his life more than usually hazardous' (cited in Berridge 1977: 372).

While the case went against the insurance company on a technical point, it was significant because it inspired further investigation of the matter.

Dr Robert Christison[6] took up the issue and concluded, after conducting a series of case studies,[7] that 'a certain number of opium eaters may attain a good old age'. He found that in 'many instances, when an opium eater is under the influence of the drug no one could suspect the fact' (Berridge 1977; Berridge and Edwards 1987: 84–6). Christison himself was dubious of his results saying:

> I cannot bring myself to think that the habitual use of a drug which procures such permanent effects as opium, which greatly disorders the digestive functions, leaves those who use it in so miserable a state during the intervals of using it, and leads to an early worn out appearance, can be consistent in general with the enjoyment of health, and the prolongation of life (cited in Berridge 1977: 372).

He appealed for further evidence, and so the controversy began. While others took up the opposing view, Christison's initial point held ground, and in 1832 he repeated it in more definite terms in his textbook on poisons: 'the practice of eating opium is not so injurious, and an opium-eater's life not so uninsurable as is commonly thought'. He did not believe that the habit could not shorten life, but held that it was not so deadly to life as might be thought. Frequent references to Christison's work led Virginia Berridge (1977) to conclude that such views did much to shape medical opinion on opiate use. Elsewhere Berridge suggests that John Pereira's more moderate conclusion about the longevity question was perhaps the most generally adopted:

> some doubt has recently begun to be entertained as to the alleged injurious effect of opium eating on the health, and its tendency to shorten life; and it must be confessed that in several known cases which have occurred in this country, no ill-effects have been observable … we should be careful not to assume that because opium in large doses, when taken by mouth is a powerful poison, and when smoked to excess is injurious to health, that therefore the moderate employment of it is necessarily detrimental...(cited in Berridge and Edwards 1987: 86).[8]

Christison's, and Pereira's, ideas about opium eating, although influential in the medical profession, did not make much impact on the insurance world. In this area, with exceptions, attitudes towards the opium habit contrasted sharply with the apparent tolerance of much of the rest of society (Berridge 1977). De Quincey who was famously, or infamously, associated with opium eating by his own *Confessions*[9]

6　　Dr Christison was Professor of Medical Jurisprudence at Edinburgh, the first British authority on medical jurisprudence (Berridge and Edwards 1987).

7　　Initially he considered ten English cases, later these were supplemented with another four (Berridge 1977).

8　　Published in his influential text: *Elements of Materia Medica* (1839-1840) (Berridge and Edwards, 1987).

9　　In 1821 the *London Magazine* published Thomas De Quincey's autobiographical *Confessions of an English Opium Eater*. Parssinen summarises the reaction to the widely read *Confessions* as follows:

(Berridge and Edwards 1987; Parssinen 1983), found the attitude of insurers a problem:

> Myself in particular they regard, I believe as the abomination of desolation. And fourteen officers in succession, within a few months, repulsed me as a candidate for insurance on that solitary ground of having owned myself to be an opium-eater (1856, cited in Berridge 1977: 375).

So far as the insurance companies were concerned, the official attitude to opium eating was one of disapproval. Insurance companies took a fairly harsh line towards overt use. The development of actuarial science led to the institution of differential premiums for those with intemperate habits; but, reflecting broader social views, attention was generally concentrated on the drinker rather than the opium eater.

In the nineteenth century life insurance was a significant factor in the early problematisation of opium eating and, as noted, the case against the Earl of Mar initiated the first serious medical and legal consideration of the dangers of the drug. Medical debates about opiate use and health, and about methods of treatment, which arose in the context of the case, foreshadowed broader controversies that would become more prominent in the last quarter of the century (Berridge 1977). The hostile attitude of the insurance companies towards the opium eater was an indication of coming changes in both medical and public opinion.

Perhaps it is more salient, however, that through the technology of life insurance the use of opium first began to be identified as an unacceptable risk – something to be avoided. In the Earl of Mar's case the insurance company argued, in effect, that death in combination with opium use is more than a quirk of fate that anyone might fall into; rather it was a probable outcome. Taking this view also involved the adoption of a moral stance: according to the insurers the consumption of opium is linked to a risk which threatens life and, thus, it is the responsibility of the insured to conduct him or herself in a way that such danger is avoided.

The Public Hygiene Movement

The public hygiene movement was a further nineteenth century expression of the concern for the *health* and *physical wellbeing* of the population which emerged as part of the governmental domain during the seventeenth and eighteenth centuries

---

In revealing his opium habit, De Quincey introduced the subject of drug addiction to nineteenth-century Englishmen in a way that was both personal and intense. He made it clear that opium may have elevated his consciousness, but it had crippled his life. Yet the reaction of his contemporaries to this unique confession was benign, even bemused. De Quincey's career did not suffer from his revelation. To the contrary, the *Confessions* was the springboard to success and even a modest prosperity. The reaction to De Quincey is indicative of the early Victorian attitude towards opium and opium addiction generally. It was, for the most part, a non-issue. Medical men wrote about it rarely; popular writers almost never. And when people thought about it at all, they thought that addiction was a relatively infrequent, if unfortunate, by-product of the therapeutic use of an important drug (1983:7–8).

(Lupton 1995). In nineteenth century Britain it was led by reformers concerned with the problems of the towns in the wake of rapid industrialisation and urbanisation. During the 1840s the renowned reformer Edwin Chadwick became a prominent figure in the campaign for public health. His aim, and the aim of other like-minded reformers, was 'to rationalise the principles of government, to remove waste, inefficiency and corruption' in order to make the free market more effective and to maintain and improve national prosperity (Jones 1986 cited in Lupton 1995: 28). The reformers used comparative statistics to study the spread of illness and death within geographic space. In the course of this reform the open availability of opiates and the rate of associated poisoning became a minor, yet significant, social issue. The protagonists of the movement did much to publicise opium as a dangerous drug, noting, in particular, the high rate of accidental death from opium (Berridge and Edwards 1987).

The public health case for the regulation of opium began in the first half of the nineteenth century. It was founded in the social surveys conducted by organisations like the London Statistical Society and the Association for the Promotion of the Social Sciences as well as in the official statistics of the Registrar General's Office (Berridge and Edwards 1987; Parssinen 1983). In the middle decades of the nineteenth century, official statistics from the Office of the Registrar General, together with a number of public inquiries, reflected a high rate of accidental poisoning. Opium and opiate preparations were identified through procedures for the registration of deaths, and coroners' reports, among the substances responsible for the apparently growing number of fatalities. Other substances identified included prussic acid, belladonna, arsenic, strychnine and carbolic acid (Berridge and Edwards 1987). As a result of the keen interest in the condition and size of the population at that time, deaths from poisoning were widely reported in the medical journals of the day.[10] It is arguable, however, that the perceived increase in poisoning was quite possibly an artefact of the introduction of the then new reporting strategies, or that many of these fatalities were largely a function of the lack of available health care. Furthermore, given the widespread nature of use, and lack of quality control, the mortality rates due to opium overdose were probably not unusually high (Berridge and Edwards 1987; Parssinen 1983).

Parssinen (1983) cautions that the statistics referred to were unlikely to be accurate. Before 1863 the Registrar General's Office kept figures on poisoning only sporadically, and until 1874, it was optional for medical practitioners to furnish a certificate for the cause of death. William Farr complained as late as 1870 that 'numerous cases are returned simply as murder, suicides or injuries, without any information as to whether poison or any other instrument was employed in the deed' (Parssinen 1983: 73). Moreover, poisonings were often difficult to detect; opiate poisoning, in particular, resembled death from natural causes and was probably consistently understated in the vital statistics throughout that period. Nevertheless, regardless of their accuracy, the collection of statistics in itself was significant in the identification of opium as a dangerous drug. As Parssinen concludes: '[t]he very act of keeping statistics drew attention to certain causes of death – such as accidental

---

10   See *The Lancet* between 1830 and 1860, for example.

poisoning – which could seemingly be altered by government action' (Parssinen 1983: 74).

Along with the dangers of the drug, the official opium poisoning statistics provided evidence of extensive adulteration. From the usually Turkish poppy plantation, to the retail outlet, there were many opportunities for adulteration to occur, making the strength of opium and opiate preparations variable and their effects uncertain. This increased the risk of opium poisoning, or overdose, significantly. Adulteration was part of a general deterioration in both food and drugs that resulted from the transition to an urban society (Berridge and Edwards 1987; Parssinen 1983). Throughout the nineteenth century adulteration became widespread. While this was to some extent associated with commercial fraud and the desire to increase profits, it was more the result of the changing methods of food production, and in the case of opium, of popular drug use. Urbanisation increasingly deprived the labouring classes of the opportunity to produce their own food, and denied them access to the herbs and plants that could be freely picked to make up their rural remedies. For example, the age-old remedy of wild poppy-head tea was replaced with commercially produced laudanum. As a result of urbanisation and industrialisation the poor were less able to control the strength or quality of the opium in the remedies they now consumed; overdose became a greater risk. Together with these changes the traditional methods of control also deteriorated; the guilds that regulated quality and sale lost impact in the changed conditions of the early nineteenth century, when the medical and pharmaceutical societies were only beginning to effectively assert their influence (Berridge and Edwards 1987).

Another public health concern was the doping of young children with opiates. The parliamentary inquiries, and *Reports of the Medical Officer to the Privy Council*[11] which highlighted the issue of opium poisoning and adulteration, together with the statistics of the Registrar General's Office and voluntary social surveys, brought the problem into view. They showed that the major proportion of opium poisoning deaths occurred among infants (Berridge and Edwards 1987). Numerous soothing syrups for children that contained the drug were on the market. The best known included Godfrey's Cordial, Dalby Calmative, Daffy's Elixir, Atikinson's Infant Preservative, Mrs Winsloe's Soothing Syrup and Street's Infant Quieteners. In rural areas such tonics, made up in the home with recipes passed down through the family, were common. Mothers working in factories, in cottage industries or in agricultural gangs were most often accused of the practice. Parssinen explains that the use of opium as an infant quietener was a part of the stark reality of life for the labouring classes in the nineteenth century – the economic arrangements of the day that forced women to work long hours, often outside the home, motivated the practice. Opium was a cheap

---

11   For example, PP 1862, XXII: *Fourth Report of the Medical Officer of the Privy Council*, Appendix 5, 'Dr Greenhow's report on the circumstances under which there is an excessive mortality of young children among certain manufacturing population', and PP 1864 XXVIII: *Sixth Report of the Medical Officer of the Privy Council*, Appendix 14, 'Report by Dr Henry Julian Hunter on the excessive mortality of infants in some rural districts of England', and Appendix 16, 'Professor Alfred S. Taylor's report on poisoning and the dispensing, vending and keeping of poisons' (cited in Berridge and Edwards 1987:77, 297).

solution to the noisy demands of children: ill paid nurses and childminders found that they could cope with ten or more children by drugging them, and women who had been working all day found that they could buy some much needed rest at night for as little as a 'ha'penny's worth of infant sedative'(1983: 45-6).

Berridge and Edwards argue that the campaign against infant doping expressed class interest and a desire to remould popular culture into a more acceptable form – that while opium was the immediate concern, the campaigning against it criticised basic patterns of working class child rearing (1987: 104). These authors suggest, in addition, that the movement was culturally and economically insensitive and that it was silent about the extent of the practices outside the working class, even though there was clear evidence of the use of infant quieteners in the nurseries of the 'well-to-do'. Indeed, as Parssinen (1983: 44) explains, the practice of feeding opiates to children crossed class and geographic boundaries.

Whereas Berridge and Edwards (1987) position the reactions to the use of children's quieteners as a class concern, a governmental perspective furnishes a less conspiratorial interpretation. From the middle of the eighteenth century the family unit emerged as fundamental to the government of the population (Foucault 1991: 100), and with this the problem of 'children' emerged: their number at birth, the relation of birth to mortality rates and their survival to adulthood. An 'infrastructure of prevention' was erected around the child and a series of inquiries and programs were set in motion to protect him or her (Donzelot 1979: 97). The problem of childhood was expressed through a new set of obligations for parents and children, including the control of bodily hygiene, diet, housing, clothing, physical exercise and familial relations. The family unit was charged with the responsibility for developing and maintaining the child's body: 'health and principally the health of children, becomes one of the family's most demanding objectives' (Foucault 1980: 280). In this context the concern in relation to child dosing can be understood within the broader frame of the governmental relationship between the child, the family and the population. Rather than being simply another example of class conflict it was a measure concerned with the responsibilisation of parents. It amounted to an expression of anxiety regarding the apparent failure of the family unit to fulfil governmental ends in relation to the health and wellbeing of the population by jeopardising the survival of children into adulthood. Mothers who worked, in particular, were construed as shirking their responsibilities by either leaving their children with hapless childminders who – devoid of maternal bonds – callously dosed infants with opium in the interests of increasing profits. Or worse still, they (the working mothers) dosed their own children, selfishly putting their own need to rest above the welfare of the child.

The public health inquiries and the related statistics also reported the widespread popular use of opiates and, in particular, the use of opium as an adjunct to alcohol. Nineteenth-century social reformers feared that the poor were turning to opium for non-medical or stimulant purposes, and not for medical reasons, and that they used the drug as a cheap alternative to drink.[12] This concern was yet another signal of changing perceptions of opiate use at the time.

Public Health, Professionalism and Reform

In the eighteenth century doctors held some authority in relation to public health. They had acquired the task of teaching individuals the basic rules of hygiene, which they must respect for the sake of their own health and that of others. As a result medical practitioners became prominent players in the observation, correction and improvement of the 'social body' (Foucault 1980). Social reformers rather than doctors, however, led the public hygiene movement in nineteenth century England. A range of experts, including doctors, pharmacists, chemists, veterinarians, sewage engineers, architects, scientists and administrators, collaborated in the push for social change. The concern for public health was just one aspect of a much broader movement. As part of this, however, there was a call for the reform and regulation of the medical and pharmaceutical professions (Berridge and Edwards 1987; Petersen and Lupton 1996).

It was only in the early part of the nineteenth century that the medical profession – along with a number of others, for example, the legal profession and even the clergy – began to assume its modern form. Peterson (1978) argues that it was impossible to talk of the medical profession as a consolidated entity prior to the Medical Act of 1858. Before that time, medical care had been characterised by a hierarchical social structure of three distinctly organised, legally defined groups practising the profession of physician, the craft of surgery, and the apothecary's trade. Physicians held university degrees. Surgery was considered more of a craft (historically associated with barbers) and training was by an apprenticeship system. Apothecaries were linked with trade, having been part of the Grocers' Company until 1617. During the seventeenth and eighteenth centuries apothecaries gradually expanded their territory – initially only dispensing, they began to provide medical advice (Willis 1989: 38). The task of providing care for the bulk of the population fell to the lower order practitioners, especially the apothecaries whose inexpensiveness secured a practice. The three arms of what became the profession were unified by the 1858 Act, however differences remained in training. While the physicians relied heavily on their privileged social position and connections, the rank and file of the general practitioners, who became prominent at this time, were very much in competition and much pressure for health and professional reform, backed by legislation, came from them (Jacyna 1994; Porter 1991; Willis 1989).

For the general practitioner, science was the vehicle of reform for medicine. Lacking the social breeding and subsequent access to genteel and wealthy patients of the physicians, they used the concept to promote themselves. They argued for the superiority of their own kind of medicine by calling it scientific and seeing

---

12   This link was largely a misunderstanding on the part of the investigators, or an artefact of their moral bias. Opium, rather than being a cheap substitute, was widely used as an antidote for too much drink in the labouring classes (Berridge and Edwards 1987; Levine 1978).

it as a means of substituting meritocracy for social rank. While medical men in the seventeenth and eighteenth centuries had been reluctant to adopt quantitative methods,[13] in the nineteenth century reformers were keen to emulate the objective approach of the physical sciences (Shyrock 1961). Pathologists, for example, began to use quantitative measures in the early part of the century. Once it was possible to identify diseases, attempts were made to record the number of cases of a supposed disease that exhibited a particular symptom. This prepared the way for the development of a belief in the real existence of disease and its ontological autonomy from the perception of both the doctor and the patient. It showed that disease was present in the environment and could invade and infect people. From the late 1830s the emerging profession recorded the value of clinical statistics. Henry Holland of London (1839) stated that 'through medical statistics lies the most secure path into the philosophy of medicine', and in 1855 W. P. Alison of Edinburgh assured British scientists that many of the most important questions in medicine could be investigated by statistics 'and in no other way' (Shyrock 1961: 101).

In the wake of this 'new order' medicine came to be characterised by more meritocratic principles, expressed in certified standards of training, knowledge and qualifications, the emergence of the general practitioner or family doctor, the parliamentary enforcement of minimum requirements for the licence to practice, the marginalisation of the unqualified, the establishment of the Medical Register (of qualified practitioners), the General Medical Council (as a professional self-regulating body) and the emergence of professional associations like the British Medical Association and professional journals like the *British Medical Journal* and *The Lancet* – all of which helped processes of both reform and professionalisation along.

The professionalisation of medical and pharmaceutical practice coincided with the movement against adulteration and calls for restrictions on the sale of poisons, including opium. In this context doctors and pharmacists lobbied to restrict the availability of poisons to accredited professionals, arguing that this would reduce the opportunity for adulteration and guarantee the high quality of drugs. In the middle of the century this was realised in a number of medical and pharmaceutical Acts (Parssinen 1983; Willis 1989). Opium came under the Sale of Poisons Act, and after 1857 it was to be kept under lock and key. In 1868 it was included in the Pharmacy Act, which limited availability to professional practitioners.

In many respects the practical operation of the new Acts had no effect on consumption levels, only serving to alter the sources of availability of certain drugs. These regulations were explicitly concerned with the sale of certain so-called poisons, and not their patterns of use. They were intended to ensure that such poisons were properly labelled and dispensed, and thus, that people were not killed by accidentally taking a wrongly labelled drug. Indeed, the United Kingdom Select Committee on the Sale of Poisons Bill 1857 apparently sought to ensure that habitual use could

---

13 Ivan Illich explains that doctors who applied measurements to sick people during the seventeenth and eighteenth centuries were liable to be considered quacks by their colleagues who depended on their own clinical experience. He suggests that this early reluctance was largely the result of poor qualitative understandings of physiology and anatomy (1975: 16).

continue unhampered. 'Lord Talbot de Malahide expressed concern during the hearings that if provisions of the Poisons Bill were made too stringent inconvenience would be given *to persons of certain habits* for whom laudanum *is a necessary of life*' (Manderson 1988: 443 emphasis added).

Many features of the pre-1868 popular culture of widespread opiate use remained undisturbed. It is significant, however, that together the effect of these Acts finally established that the availability of opiates must be subjected to some form of professional control. A shift in attitude had taken place, and it had received official legislative support.

Vital Statistics and the Science of Government

The seventy years up until the middle of the nineteenth century was a period of reform. In Britain it was stimulated by a desire to avoid destructive social unrest of the type seen on the continent, and particularly in France in the twilight of the eighteenth century (Porter 1986). To a degree then, the impetus for change (and the regulation of opiates), emanated from the fear that a failure to reform key social institutions could result in violent uprisings. Reformers found the language of science, and statistics, in particular, a useful vehicle for comprehending and acting on what they perceived to be the sources of social disarray. The emergence of statistics as a form of organising knowledge was vital for governmental practices to render an 'unruly population' manageable and amenable to rational forms of administration (Rose 1989: 7). The social reformers believed that through the quantification of life it was possible to identify statistical laws in relation to the distribution of particular characteristics of the population – crime, deviancy, death and illness received special attention. Furthermore, in their view, one could change the boundary conditions and so change the laws under which the population would evolve (see the account of the work of William Farr in Hacking 1991). Following this vein the protagonists of the public health movement initially used social statistics to identify issues for the social agenda, and by the middle of the nineteenth century they harnessed these figures as support, or evidence, to support calls for government intervention in the form of a permanent set of regulations and measures to prevent the spread of death and disease. They lobbied for legislative intervention that would regulate their concerns under the aegis of state authorities (Porter 1986).

The rhetoric of reform was full of appeals to the public interest: the poor and the ignorant as well as the rich and knowledgeable would benefit (Hacking 1990; Porter 1986). This, together with the pivotal role played by social statistics, was compatible with the liberal temperament of the nineteenth century. I am not referring here to interpretations of liberalism which portray human beings as instrumentally rational and naturally self-regarding, or rational maximisers (cf. Holmes 1995). Rather the classical liberal view was that most human behaviour is non-calculating, habitual and heatedly emotional and that these passions and habits of all individuals – the ruled and the rulers – need to be constrained. According to Holmes (1995), the classical liberal desire was to bridle destructive and self-destructive passions and to induce people, so far as possible, to act rationally instead of hot bloodedly. The insight, formulated in antiquity that 'cruelty arises more often from non-calculating passions than from calculating interest' became a central premise of classical liberalism. As John Stuart Mill remarked: 'it is not from the separate interests real or imaginary of the majority, that minorities are in danger; but from the antipathies of religion, political party or race' (cited in Holmes 1995: 3). While statistics provided bureaucracies with some of the knowledge that is indispensable to power, they also suggested certain limitations to this power. These limitations were not constitutional ones, but constraints which, through the quantification of social behaviour, seemed to exist independently of any particular arrangements of government (Porter 1986).

The discovery of statistical laws in relation to the population transformed its government into a matter of calculation. From the liberal reformers' point of view, the 'science of government' based on statistics could discover guiding principles which 'lay outside the realm of partisan dissension and arise from the accumulation of simple irrefutable facts' (Eyler 1979: 6). These facts could be used to inform official policy. This view was well represented in the writings of the political philosopher George Cornwall Lewis: '[i]t is the essence of the statistic that its object is scientific, not practical, that it is intended to represent the truth of the facts, not to subserve some immediate purpose of administration or legislation'. At the same time, however, he held statistics indispensable for the practical statesman: '[i]t is by comparing the number of a subject under consideration that his practical judgement ought to be formed'; without numbers legislation is ill informed or haphazard (cited in Porter 1986: 36–7). William Newmarch, a member of the Statistical Society of London, interpreted the laws of statistics in a similar way. Writing in the *Economist* newspaper, he explained how governments had begun to learn that legislation could only accomplish its aims if it was formulated in accordance with the 'natural principles' of these things. Official support for statistics embodied a need to understand the condition of society. In 1860 he proposed that '… now, men are gradually finding out that all attempts at making or administering laws which do not rest upon an accurate view of the social circumstances of the case are neither more nor less than imposture in one of its most gigantic and perilous forms … ' (cited in Porter 1986: 59). Earlier, Charles Morgan, in a review of Quetelet published in 1835, also explained how legislation need not take account of numbers' individual nature, but could instead be founded upon a knowledge of the 'abstract being man' which can be attained through statistics (cited in Porter 1986: 66). According to these liberal ideals, the legislator would not try to impose his will on the social system, but would seek first to measure the direction and magnitude of secular social evolution. While statistics did not eliminate the need for an active state, neither did it give the state much control over the autonomous domain(s) of society. As Porter summarises:

> Statistical investigation was not the product of sociological fatalism, however, but of cautious hopefulness for improvement. Statistics reflected a liberal temperament and a search for reform that flourished not during the first years of repression following the Congress of Vienna, but the late 1820s and especially the 1830s. The statists sought to bring a measure of expertise to social questions, to replace the contradictory preconceptions of the interested parties by the certainty of careful empirical observation. They believed that the *confusion of politics* could be replaced by an orderly reign of facts (Porter 1986: 27 emphasis added).

Thus, the regulation of opiates in nineteenth-century Britain was contingent on the convergence of (at least) three key trajectories: the quantification of life, the professionalisation of medical expertise, and the emergence of liberal rationalities of rule. The quantification of life constituted the population as a describable and hence manageable domain that became the object of the practices of medicine which relied on science, and statistics in particular, in its reformulation as a modern profession. This was possible in the context of an era of reform where those eager to avoid revolution drew on liberal principles and rationalities in the pursuit of governmental ends. The quantification of the population, however, had effects beyond providing for more calculating modes of governance.

Enumeration demands kinds, or categories, of things to count. Thus, it requires the classification of people and their behaviour. As I have argued, many of the facts presented by the newly formed bureaucracies and the philanthropic and statistical societies of the nineteenth century did not exist ahead of time. Categories had to be invented into which people could conveniently fall in order to be counted (cf. Hacking 1990; Hunter 1994). Indeed, many of the categories we now use to describe people are the by-product of this need.[14] Another effect of counting which arose, according to Hacking (1986), with the quantification of people and their habits was a new type of law, analogous to laws of nature, but pertaining to people. These new laws were expressed in terms of probability, and they carried with them the connotations of the normal and the deviant or pathological. The effects of these types of distinctions within the population – the classification of individuals and behaviour, as well as the differentiation between the normal and the pathological – had a significant impact on the ongoing development of the medical regulation of opiates and their use. This is discussed in more detail in the section below.

Addiction as Disease

Variations on a Theme

Like today, accidental overdoses (or opium poisoning) in the nineteenth century were due to misjudging tolerance, inexperienced use, or adulteration. Because opium use was so widespread, such accidents were a fact of everyday life. Opium poisoning was a commonplace matter generally dealt with in the home. Most people were familiar with opium poisoning (overdose) and knew what to do; it was not usually considered to be a matter that required any formal medical attention or even medical concern (Berridge and Edwards 1987). Physical dependency on the drug was seen in much the same way. The medical profession's involvement in the longevity debates and subsequent public health discussions on opium poisoning and regulation marked the beginnings of sustained medical intervention in this area. Opium poisoning was translated into a medical matter through the regulatory Acts, which provided for the

---

14 Farr's nosology is the basis for contemporary World Health Organization (WHO) classifications (Hacking 1991).

closer involvement of doctors (and pharmacists) in the definition and ultimately the treatment of the condition.

The identification of addiction as a disease originated in the last quarter of the nineteenth century, when doctors became more closely involved in the way opiates were administered and used. The concept of inebriety was central in its formulation. As a term 'inebriety' had been initially used in the early part of the century to address undesirable patterns of alcohol use. It later became the foundation for the more general 'disease' model of addiction.[15] In 1877, Norman Kerr, the Chairman of the Society for Study of Inebriety explained: inebriety is 'an undoubted disease, a functional neurosis' that could be classified with reference to the intoxicating agent. 'We thus have alcohol, opium, chloral, chloroform, ether, chlorodyne and other forms of the disease' (Berridge and Edwards 1987: 154). As a concept it was a vehicle for the application of medical criteria to behaviours formerly regarded as much a social problem as a vice (Garton 1987).

While popular use of opium continued and the sale of non-medical patent remedies containing opium remained high well into the twentieth century, it was mainly the increased medical use of morphine (an opium derivative), which inspired the development of clinical interventions. This was intrinsically related to the increased visibility of opium users who, following the passage of the 1868 Pharmacy Act, were obliged to present to doctors and pharmacists in order to obtain their supply. Morphine first became known in the 1820s. After the hypodermic technique was developed in the mid-nineteenth century, hypodermic morphine to some extent replaced opium in medical circles as the most valued remedy. 'Morphia' injection was advocated for a wide range of complaints; it was specifically recommended as a treatment of confirmed opium eaters. The efficacy of the drug was reported in the medical journals of the day (for examples, see *The Lancet* between 1870–1890). The new drug and new method were strongly supported by that section of the medical profession which saw the development of more exact scientific means of treatment as a way to elevate the status, and develop the expertise, of doctors as a professional body (Berridge and Edwards 1987).

In the 1870s doctors wrote enthusiastically to the medical journals reporting the good results they had obtained by using hypodermic morphine. However, warning signs were apparent – the first acknowledgments of the possibility of drug dependence arising from morphine injection began to appear in the 1860s. British doctors became increasingly aware of the problem. Case histories, which had appeared only sporadically in the medical press in the 1870s, were by the end of the decade, greatly increased in quantity and prominence.[16] By the late 1880s doctors were busy elaborating the dimensions of morphinism and morphinomania,[17] and

---

15   This was the case in both the USA (Levine 1978) and England (Berridge and Edwards 1987).

16   For examples, see *The Lancet* between 1860 and 1880.

17   Morphinism was the condition of dependence on morphine experienced by patients who wanted to be cured, thus they cooperated with treatment and were viewed positively. Morphinomania was the condition of dependency on morphine experienced by patients who

delineating the outlines of the typical morphia *habitué*. Case histories of morphine addicts largely replaced studies reporting the value of morphine use.

Well-defined views were held on the origin and incidence of the disease. Most accepted the belief that morphine dependence was vastly increasing and that many had acquired the habit through lax medical prescription, and through eventual self-administration of the drug. Women were said to be peculiarly susceptible to 'morphinism' and the medical profession itself was also recognised as highly prone to the condition. Berridge and Edwards (1987) suggest that while the accuracy of this stereotype remains uncertain, it seems likely that the medical profession was myopically exaggerating the dimensions of a situation it had helped to create. While there is evidence that use of opium and opium preparations remained widespread, and morphine was a valued tool of the medical profession, there was nothing like the epidemic of rising consumption which the medical accounts suggested. Indeed, it is probable that there was no comparison between the numbers dependent on morphine and those on opium. However, it was primarily the use of morphine, visible in the doctor's consulting room, and to some extent the dispensaries, that stimulated medical discussion of opiate dependence as a disease. 'The quite small numbers of morphine addicts who happened to be obvious to the profession assumed the dimensions of a pressing problem – at a time when, as general consumption and mortality data indicate, usage and addiction to opium was tending to decline' (Berridge and Edwards 1987: 149).

Through the new direction taken by medical discourse then, opiate consumption came to be regarded as a disease. Somewhat paradoxically, however, the cure for this disease remained the responsibility of the individual patient. Berridge (1979) reminds us that the disease theory of addiction was never an autonomous, scientifically elaborated entity; it was always accompanied by a strong moral overlay. In 1864, for example, Dr Anstie's influential text *Stimulants and Narcotics* described the condition as a product of both 'physical necessity' and of 'a debased moral nature' (Berridge 1979: 72). In the latter part of the nineteenth century a hybrid theory of the disease, incorporating both medical and moral formulations, emerged. Addiction was disease and vice, a form of 'moral bankruptcy', 'disease of the will',[18] or a 'form of moral insanity'. Dr Thomas Clouston described it as the product of 'diseased cravings and paralysed control'; other authors also stressed moral rather than physical symptoms: implausibility, disorderliness, no standards of truthfulness and a complete disregard of time (Berridge 1979: 77). Norman Kerr described the condition as a disease of the nervous system allied to insanity and characterised by an overpowering impulse of craving for the oblivion of narcotism. He recognised the physical dimensions, in 1880, distinguishing between the predisposing and existing causes of inebriety. Heredity, together with sex, age, race, climate, education, pecuniary circumstances, marriage relations, and temperament were grouped as predisposing characteristics.

---

did not really wish to be cured; they were uncooperative, and therefore had to be treated as lunatics (Berridge and Edwards 1987).

18   See Mariana Valverde's (1998) *Disease of the Will* for an excellent analysis of significance of this 'disease of the will' formulation in the context of the problematisation and regulation of alcohol consumption.

As the eugenic trend evident in scientific thinking towards the end of the century intensified, later works reflected the increasing concern with the 'enfeeblement of the race' by explaining 'chronic intoxications' as more directly the result of hereditary defects. In 1906 Albutt and Dixson – two influential writers – explained in a prominent medical text[19] that 'hereditary craving for intoxicants', with sometimes also nervous disease or insanity in the family tree, was predisposing to an urge for narcotics and, as late as the 1920s, Harry Campbell's claim in the *Medical Press and Circular*, that most addicts were congenital neurotics and therefore difficult to cure, was still typical (Berridge 1979: 78). With addiction, like so many other socially troubling conditions of the day,[20] it was a degenerative constitution which was identified as the predisposing factor.

With the development of the disease theory, ideas about addiction (opium inebriety) became more rigid. The moderate stable addict accepted earlier in the century by Christison and others (involved in the longevity debate) was largely a casualty of the 'disease of the will' formulation. Addiction came to be seen as an exclusive condition rather than, as previously believed, a bad habit which anyone might fall into (Berridge and Edwards 1987; Garton 1987; Levine 1978). Its formulation as a disease was closed to the possibility of other patterns of use. Non-dependent or recreational patterns of use could not be accommodated or tolerated. Through the medical discourse that developed, these practices were excluded from any consideration as a possibility in relation to opiate consumption.[21]

The development of the disease model influenced the institutionalised response to the condition. Pre-formulation treatment methods varied according to the doctor's personal preferences; they were diverse and haphazard. Immediate withdrawal, gradual withdrawal, maintenance and substitution were all well accepted responses. With the development of disease theory the more absolute methods (immediate withdrawal) fell out of favour. This change was accompanied by a strong institutional trend, and a desire to segregate the addict, which had its parallel in the custodial treatment of the insane. Indeed, there is a strong argument that addiction can be understood as an extension of this latter category (Bull 1991) – a variation on the theme of 'unreason' (Foucault 1967). This was reflected in the perceived need for the physical confinement of the addict[22] and disciplinary treatments evident in most

---

19   Albutt T. C. and Rolleston H. D. (eds), *A System of Medicine* , Vol 2, London, 1906.

20   Similar trends were apparent with regard to criminality, insanity, homosexuality and poverty, which were also reclassified as biologically determined at this time (see Foucault 1973; Foucault 1977; Garland 1985; Hacking 1986, 1992; Marshall 1981; Weeks 1981; Wiener 1990).

21   It is noteworthy that it has only been during the last three decades that the possibility of use, which is not abuse, has re-entered the mainstream discussion in this field.

22   On page 471 of *The Lancet* 1888 vol II a medical practitioner made the following suggestion: 'there is one way of dealing with habitual drunkards which has not yet been noticed – that is, to send them for a voyage in a teetotal ship. If a "retreat" could be established on a small island there would be no difficulty from neighbouring public houses, and no necessity to send a guide with the patient when he goes out.' This is striking particularly in the context of Foucault's description of the Narrenschiff, the Ship of Fools, a strange 'drunken boat' (Foucault 1967: 7) that, during the Renaissance, conveyed a cargo of madmen from town to

discussions of the condition from the 1880s.[23] In the closing decades of the nineteenth century addiction specialists were virtually unanimous in advocating the need for greatly increased medical control; it now became rare to find one who argued against the use of retreats or asylums (Berridge and Edwards 1987). In England, control was initially achieved through Section 116 of the 1890 Lunacy Act, which allowed a form of guardianship for imbeciles and habitual drunkards; on occasion this was applied to drug addicts. Throughout the 1890s and early 1900s addiction specialists lobbied for the formal extension of such provisions to explicitly address the addict. This was eventually achieved with amendments to the Inebriates Act in 1908. However, insanity and habitual intoxication with alcohol and other drugs, were later reunited in the 1913 Mental Deficiency Act, which formerly provided for such 'moral imbeciles', that is, addicts, to be sent to an 'institution for defectives', or placed under guardianship (Berridge and Edwards 1987).

In treatment, the straightforward physical side of addiction increasingly took second place to a strong psychological emphasis, and the disease was defined, not so much in physical, as in mental, terms. Emphasis was placed on the cultivation of self-control as part of the treatment regime (Garton 1987; Levine 1978). Health was equated with self-discipline. It was the 'voluntary renunciation' of the morphia habit and the 're-education of self-control' which were important. For example, Jennings referred to the importance of 'control', 'moral orthopaedics' and the 're-education of the will' (Berridge 1979: 77). Addiction was identified as deviation from the norm, and had social connotations of personal failings; that is, the addict was abnormal in the literal sense that he or she deviated from the generally accepted norms of conduct and thought (Berridge and Edwards 1987).

Expertise as Vocation

At this point it is worth reflecting for a moment on the preceding discussion which describes the complex of intellectual technologies, knowledges, actors, powers, institutions and social arrangements which begin to crystallise around the phenomenon of 'life' during the nineteenth century. It draws our attention specifically to the complex role played by expert knowledges (statistical, actuarial and medical), by technologies of recording (births, deaths and marriages), by insurantial technologies,[24] by statistical societies and nascent bureaucracies (the Register General's Office and public health inquiries) and by the processes of the professionalisation of medical practice (accreditation, legislation, journals, specialisation, treatments) in the identification of opium as a dangerous drug and the recognition of the *persona* of the opium inebriate or addict. That is, it describes the development of an identifiable

---

town. 'Confined on the ship, from which there is no escape…And the land he will come to is unknown – as is, once he disembarks, the land from which he comes. He has his truth and his homeland only in that fruitless expanse between two countries that cannot belong to him' (Foucault 1967: 11).

23   This is still evident today, for example, see chapter five below.

24   The insurance debates forced the issue by bringing in doctors on both sides of an adversarial court system.

network of expertise concerned with the consumption of opium and its derivatives. In this context expertise is the authority arising out of a claim to true and positive knowledge of humans, and to neutrality and efficacy.

A number of authors have explored the process by which expertise and, in particular, the expert – embodying neutrality, authority and skill in a wise figure operating to an ethical code *'beyond good and evil'* – have become significant in society. From a Foucaultian perspective, Rose (1993; 1994) and others (Armstrong 1994; Johnson 1993) have argued that the rise of expertise is linked to a transformation in the rationalities and knowledges of government; that expertise emerged as a possible solution to a problem that confronted liberal mentalities of government in the eighteenth and nineteenth centuries. Through expertise it was possible to link socio-political objectives in relation to the population and the minutiae of daily life. Rose (1993) explains that for liberal modes of governance the truth claims of expertise were highly significant. Through the powers of truth, distant events and persons could be governed 'at arms length': political rule would not itself set out the norms of individual conduct, but would install and empower a variety of normalising professionals, investing them with authority to act as experts in the forums of social regulation. As a result, liberalism's claim to legitimate government was not arbitrary (see pp.29–31 above), but based upon intelligence concerning those whose wellbeing it is mandated to enhance. He argues that liberal forms of government have depended for their possibility upon the power of experts and the allegedly neutral and objective authority of truth.

From this perspective the grand inquiries into the health of the population, local and municipal collections of information, case studies and diagnosis amounted to a positive knowledge of the population and individuals in relation to opiate use. This knowledge came to be recognised as a form of truth regulated by rationalities proper to codes of scientific reason that could constitute and inform specialised medico-administrative expertise. Through these processes opium consumption was problematised and medicine – through practices of differentiation formed in relation to the normal and pathological – provided a vocabulary which rendered the opium inebriate, in the form of the morphinist or morphinomanic, thinkable, governable and in need of specialised expert intervention.

In the nineteenth century the differentiation between the normal and pathological came to distinguish particular types as persons to be problematised in medical terms. Normalcy was conceptualised in terms of 'health', and the inebriate,[25] described earlier in this chapter as a manifestation of a degenerative constitution, was a clear exemplar of the pathological. According to Rose (1993; 1994), the secular value of health replaced older non-corporeal or theological virtues. Health replaced salvation in our ethical systems, and the doctor supplanted the priest. The discourse of medicine became increasingly concerned with the meaning of life, and there was an apparent loss of faith in the sanctity of moral codes. Medicine seemed to offer a rational, secular and corporeal solution to the problem of how we should live our lives for the best – how we should govern ourselves. Clearly, this genealogical analysis of expertise is important as well as instructive in relation to

---

25 Along with other socially troublesome categories.

understanding the regulation of opiates; but to focus on it alone could be to overlook other possible explanations. The risk in following Rose too closely, therefore, is that our concern with expertise and government in the form of the emergence of the medico-administrative domain could be seen as the only significant trajectory in the regulation of opiate consumption.

Typically, historical accounts of the regulation of opium have tended to give a great deal of credit to the nineteenth century professionalisation of medicine. These accounts have had various foci: the activities of the public health campaigners that provided the conditions for the identification of opium as a dangerous drug; the rise of medical and pharmaceutical professions and their desire to establish a monopoly over the control of opium in order to consolidate their position; or the professions' medicalisation of a condition which had previously been considered little more than a bad habit. Indeed all of these positions have been touched on in the preceding discussion. There are, however, other lines of investigation which are significant in the development of institutionalised and legislative control. For example, Johnson (1975) argues that it was the moral claims of the nineteenth century anti-opium movement and their agitation against opium which provided the basis for modern policy. Harding, as well, proposes that addiction as a category was identified as an issue of public concern 'due largely to the "moral crusade" launched by the Victorian anti-opium movement against the non-medical use of opium' (1986: 75). Virginia Berridge, one of the most prolific historians of the place of opium in British society, also explored the role of morality and the anti-opium movement in regulation (1979; Berridge and Edwards 1987).

The anti-opium movement had its beginnings in the first half of the nineteenth century. It had links with the temperance movement, which in the early part of that century expressed considerable concern in relation to stimulant use by the labouring classes. In the wake of the opium war (from 1839–1842)[26] anti-opium movement sentiments condemning the trade with China as immoral were heard in Parliament, and organised anti-opium agitation began to appear. However, anti-opium activity at that time had little public support (Berridge and Edwards 1987). It was only in the last quarter of the century that such agitation had any effect.

The first well-led and well-financed anti-opium organisation, the (Anglo-Oriental)[27] Society for the Suppression of the Opium Trade (SSOT) was established in 1874. It was the most prominent organisation in the Victorian anti-opium movement. Its founding members without notable exception were Quakers and its initial funding came from the Pease Quaker family (Berridge 1979; Harding 1986; Johnson 1975). The SSOT was based on a series of beliefs, which were clearly laid out in the inaugural issue of its newsletter (*Friend of China*). Britain, it was argued, forced opium on China, and revenue was the sole reason for continuing the trade. Prohibition except for medical purposes was the Society's long-range goal. Everyone (except the British government's India Office) agreed that opium is evil, that it could not be consumed in moderation and that it physically and morally destroyed the user (cited in Harding 1986: 81; Johnson 1975: 304). The SSOT regarded the exploitative

---

26 The British-Chinese opium wars are discussed in greater detail in chapter three.

27 'Anglo-Oriental' was subsequently dropped from the name.

practices endorsed by British colonial policies as distasteful, and particularly abhorred the use of force to export opium to China. Objections to the trade lay in the belief that opium when consumed for non-medical purposes was evil, and that the Chinese government, recognising this, had the right to block its importation on moral grounds. Yet despite the Chinese protestations, the opium trade was enforced by the British who believed it to be a legitimate commercial and exportable commodity.

Johnson argues 'that the anti opium crusaders deserve much more credit than they have received for ending the major obstacle to international control of opiates – the financial stake of powerful governments in the legitimate commercial production and sale of opiates for non-medical use' (1975: 318). Moreover, he proposes that this 'moral crusade' was at least partially responsible for development of widely held beliefs about opium. He suggests that while the political goals of the movement aimed at eliminating the commercial opium trade, the crusaders had to educate and convince the public that opium use was *bad and evil* in the fullest religious sense. Despite considerable opposition, they were so effective in their arguments with regard to the 'evilness of opium smoking' that today their nineteenth-century views are the commonly accepted 'facts' about opiates and their derivatives. That is, people continue to believe that opium cannot be consumed in moderation, and that opiate dependence causes physical deterioration, mental damage, deviant behaviour, leads to crime and is worse than alcoholism. Johnson concludes that the crucial legacy of the crusade is that opium policy is 'now based solely upon considerations of moral righteousness, which tolerates no variation from an ideal' (1975: 318–19).

Harding's argument similarly highlights the significance of this 'moral crusade' (1986). However, this author suggests that the legacy of the anti-opium movement lies not only in its opposition to the trade, but also in its influence on medical views, principally its formulation of a 'moral-pathological' model of addiction. He begins by explaining, fairly conventionally, that the concept of opium addiction is a relatively modern one. During the first half the nineteenth century opium dependence was popularly known as a 'habit' which, when it was recognised, constituted nothing more than an unfortunate side effect of the drug. In other words, when dependency occurred it was thought that it was the result of an intrinsic pharmacological action of opium. People did not deliberately 'addict themselves' to opium, rather it was opium's imputed pharmacological properties that were thought to be responsible for getting them addicted. With rising concern in the middle of the century in relation to stimulant use, the anti-opium lobby agitated for a response directed not at the user, but at the supply of the drug. He claims that *this* was the precursor to the first legislative measure designed to regulate opium's availability – the 1868 Pharmacy Act (Harding 1986: 79). This point of view contrasts rather starkly with accounts that identify the influence of the public health campaign or the rise of the medical and pharmaceutical professions as the impetus of legislative intervention (Berridge and Edwards 1987; Morgan 1981; Parssinen 1983). Harding goes on to explain that later in the century understandings of dependency changed. The new model conceived of addiction as a deviation from normal functioning and located its origin, not in the drug, or even the body of the addict, but in the 'incorporeal moral faculty of the addict's soul' (Harding 1986: 82). He argues that this model, and the control measures which flow from it, owe their existence to the religiously inspired founders of the SSOT.

Central to the success of the SSOT was the constitution and promotion of the 'moral-pathological' model of addiction. There are two important elements in this model that combined to provide the SSOT's evidence that opiate addiction was a vice. First, that opium, with its tendency to foster a gradual and increasingly strong craving, was inherently bad; and second, that its use for non-medical purposes was, therefore, indefensibly wrong. According to Harding these propositions were based upon the rationale that opium, as a sensual indulgence or vice, was extensively injurious to the 'soul' (1986). This view was derived from the Quaker doctrine of the SSOT's founders. It had at its core a conception of the spiritual domain occupied by the individual's soul, which was conceived of as being physically comprised of a material constitution. The path to righteousness was marked not by prayer, but by pursuit of those activities which nourished the soul's morality, and avoidance of those that adversely affected it. Quaker doctrine directed its members to the avoidance of luxuries, exhibiting pride, undue expenditure and self-indulgence; it stressed the need for simplicity, industriousness, moderation in all things, and the recognition of one's material as well as spiritual responsibilities (Harding 1986: 83).

Harding (1986) describes how the 'moral-pathological' model of addiction is indebted to the metaphor of the material soul. Such a model enabled the SSOT to implicate the functioning of opium's pharmacological effects in a metaphysical, incorporeal realm. As a result by the end of the century the addict could be cast not as a victim of opium, but as an irresponsible individual adopting a course of self-destruction – fully aware of the probable consequence, but unable to resist the drug-induced craving. He demonstrates how this model came to influence medical thinking on opiate use and shaped the disease model emerging in the late nineteenth century. It was reflected in advice about medical treatment; for example, an 1877 issue of *The Lancet* reported in its editorial the belief that addiction to morphine 'degenerated the moral character' and advocated 'moral treatment, by urging the patient to some form of steady work' (Harding 1986: 85), and Norman Kerr recommended treatment within the confines of an institution – an asylum or nursing home – on the grounds that it provided '… everything which can contribute to the improvement of the soul and spirit' (Kerr 1884: 298 cited in Harding 1986: 85). Harding concludes that these formulations were made possible by medicine's ability to affiliate itself to that distinctive feature of the Quaker model – a moral faculty, the health or illness, development or retardation of which, could be analysed as if it were constituted materially. The material soul could be diagnosed as 'normal' or 'pathological' and, as a result, medical knowledge and practice was able to accommodate the Quakers' model of addiction. Moreover, it could support its application in medical practice (Harding 1986). Harding turns the medicalisation thesis on its head, suggesting that this was a moral and spiritual victory where science had failed. When medical men had been unable to locate the physiological basis of addiction, it was the SSOT Quaker model that made the conceptualisation of opiate use as a disease possible.

Berridge agrees that the earlier 'moral' view of addiction/inebriety retained a place in disease theory, and owed much to the pressures of the temperance and anti-opium campaigns (1979; Berridge and Edwards 1987). She explains that from the early part of the century medical concepts of opium eating could be linked with agitation concerning opiate use in the Far East. While some medical writers, like Christison, drawn into debate about opium in the context of the longevity debate, based their views on domestic case histories, others who discussed the issue – and opposed Christison – tended to quote the Far East experience. Lord Shaftesbury (then Lord Ashley), as early as 1843, spoke against the opium trade in Parliament, using the evidence of the latter group to support his case (Berridge 1979; Berridge and Edwards 1987). He cited an eminent group of doctors[28] who were of the opinion:

> However valuable opium may be when employed as an article of medicine it is impossible for anyone who is acquainted with the subject to doubt that the habitual use of it is productive of the most pernicious consequences – destroying the healthy action of the digestive organs, weakening the powers of the mind, as well as those of the body, *and rendering the individual who indulges himself in it a worse than useless member of society* (Berridge and Edwards 1987: 175 emphasis added).

Thus, an embryo inter-relationship between the medical and anti-opium movements for the regulation of opium was established by mid-century.

Berridge (1979), like Johnson and Harding, goes on to explain that in the latter part of the century the anti-opiumists were more organised. Moreover, the SSOT had leading medical men and addiction specialists among its supporters. These included the likes of Norman Kerr, Professor Arthur Gamgee, Benjamin Ward Richardson, Risdon Bennett and Brigade Surgeon Robert Pringle.[29] She suggests that the moral emphasis of its 'propaganda' influenced English thinking on addiction through the agency of medical specialists. The involvement of such men in the moral campaign strengthened the moral bias within the medical concept of addiction and ensured the medical influence in the anti-opium campaign. According to Berridge and Edwards (1987), the views of the anti-opium movement supported the medical exclusiveness of disease theories, and this relationship served both the moral interests of the Society and the professional interests of medical men. They propose that the moral emphasis of the SSOT's arguments was successfully translated into 'scientific respectability through the medium of doctors active in both spheres', while for the emerging

---

28   Twenty-five medical men including Sir Henry Halford, President of the Royal College of Surgeons, and Sir Benjamin Brodie also a noted surgeon.

29   Norman Kerr was President of the Society for the Study and Cure of Inebriety, and spent many years as a member and Chairman of the Inebriates Legislation committee of the British Medical Association. He was active in both the temperance and the anti-opium movements, establishing a total abstinence society while a student at the University of Glasgow, and later as an active supporter of the SSOT. Professor Arthur Gamgee was Dean of the Medical School at Owen's College, and a writer on the treatment of morphine addiction. He spoke publicly for the Society. Doctor Benjamin Ward Richardson was also an influential writer on the treatment of morphine addiction and a Vice-President of the Society. Other medical representation on the SSOT's Council included Risdon Bennett, President of the Royal College of Physicians and also a Vice-President of the Society, as well as Brigade Surgeon Robert Pringle, a prolific writer and speaker on addiction, who was a paid official of the SSOT. He was a regular speaker at gatherings of both the SSOT and the Society for the Study of Inebriety (Berridge 1979).

medical profession, the anti-opium movement was, 'in much of its propaganda, a further justification for the medical control of opiate use being established at the time' (Berridge and Edwards 1987: 193).

Each of these alternative accounts alerts us to a network that extends beyond the relations between the medico-administrative complex and a positive knowledge of the population. Clearly the anti-opium movement was of some import. These representations, however, also have limitations. The first two implicitly argue against the influence of medical and other types of expertise in the regulation of opiates, proposing that the basis of such regulation is not really the development of medical science or some positive knowledge but rather less legitimate religiously based moral views. Each wishes to instate some type of replacement narrative telling it like it really was – to fill the gap with their own preferred teleology. This is done with the intention of undermining the legitimacy of contemporary drug policy and legislation, by exposing its unobjective (non-medical or unscientific) historical roots. Johnson, for example, acknowledges 'that the moral crusade was at least partially responsible for development of widely held beliefs about opium'. Somewhat paradoxically he concludes, however, that the 'crucial legacy is that opium policy should be based *solely* upon considerations of moral righteousness'; and that the British anti-opium crusade has left an important and enduring legacy to the twentieth century, 'a fact which needs to be *restored* to its proper prominence' (1975: 319 emphasis added). Harding draws our attention to the 'relational' nature of the forces that contributed to regulation and the formulation of the disease model of addiction. However, his tendency to overstate the influence of the anti-opium movement in the enactment of the 1868 Pharmacy Act alerts us to his project. Here he clearly ignores the broader social relations contributing to changing perceptions important in the regulation of supply. Ultimately he proposes that the SSOT (anti-opium movement) model of addiction rescued the medical profession from its inability to account for the condition in properly scientific terms. For him, it is the Quaker formulation of the material soul that makes the identification of the disease model of addiction possible. In contrast, Berridge's (1979; Berridge and Edwards 1987) account dutifully acknowledges the existence of the anti-opium movement, but is careful to circumscribe its significance. In a later edition of the same argument she highlights the limited scope of its influence:

> The anti-opium movement can hardly be said to have disseminated views hostile to opiate use throughout the British public even by the end of the century, only in the early 1880s did it gain a wide degree of public support – and this did not extend very far down in society (Berridge and Edwards 1987: 193).

According to Berridge (1979; Berridge and Edwards 1987), the movement had little real effect. But in avoiding one danger she falls into another, reinstating, albeit in a relatively subtle version, a medicalisation thesis through her analysis of the movement, which in the end is harnessed as more evidence of the medicalisation of the condition. After all, the movement is only successful when its arguments can be translated into 'scientific respectability through the medium of doctors active in both spheres', for whom the movement was simply a 'further justification of medical control' (Berridge and Edwards 1987: 193).

These criticisms are not intended to exclude these accounts, but rather to temper their claims, and to open the possibility of retaining their contribution to an analysis of regulation. Such accounts are possible because of an intellectual tendency to separate the moral and the religious from the technical and the scientific, where medicine is exclusively bound to the latter. The *persona* of the doctor, or the moral crusader for that matter, is conceptualised simplistically as contiguous with a particular positive knowledge or discourse; this makes any sophisticated analysis, which is able to accommodate converging, entwining, overlapping or competing trajectories, impossible. From such a position, how are we to understand, or fully appreciate, the persona of the doctor, who is clearly active in both fields? Berridge's (1979; Berridge and Edwards 1987) account tends to imply a somewhat conspiratorial colonisation by doctors of the anti-opium movement, which is motivated by a desire to medicalise a condition which had previously been considered a sin or a vice. Johnson avoids consideration of the influence of medicine by ignoring it altogether. Harding notes, but fails to consider, the significance of the presence of medical expertise, in the persona of doctor, in the religious and moral domain of the anti-opium movement. He never gives a thought to the possibility of accommodating the apparently divergent authoritative discourses. He seems to gloss the issue in terms of the implied inadequacies of then emerging medical knowledge.

Jeffrey Minson's paper 'What is an expert?' (1997) points to a way of accommodating these apparently divergent discourses which, at the same time, allows us to more fully appreciate the complexity of the *persona* of the doctor. He argues that the expression of expertise is more than the diverse statuses and institutional effects associated with the 'expert function' and the representation of the persona of the expert as a 'purely robotic terminal through which pass a network of functional obligations and positive knowledges'. Minson suggests that by invoking the sense of the 'multiplex' and discontinuous character of personhood implied by Foucault's (1984b) concept of *pluralite 'd'ego* it is possible to recognise that the same individual can in some circumstances acquire the habits of thinking and capacities for being affected which are appropriate to apparently conflicting ways of comporting oneself. 'In other words it is possible to describe experts as *amalgams* of institutionalised types of ethical character or persona, no less than as bearers of technical knowledge and the terminals of formal institutional roles and statuses' (Minson 1997: 407).

This provides for a reformulation of governmental expertise that does not revolve exclusively around 'the monotonous theme of the ethically blind, instrumentalist technical knowledgeability' (Minson 1997: 410). From this point of view the valorisation of competence based on positive knowledge, which was promoted in the context of the reform of the medical profession, does not simply equate with the neutral delivery of expertise. Indeed, as Osbourne (1992) points out, it promoted the development of a type of 'charismatic status ethic' amongst clinicians.

> If clinical rationality is 'modest' in so far that it is restrictive of doctrine, the valorisation of competence and personal attributes correspondingly promotes the 'immodesty' of the clinician himself. The doctor becomes as if by definition something of an arrogant

man. Somebody all the more willing to convert clinical power to social power, somebody whose clinical power is embodied in his social power (cf. Bourdieu 1988: 63 in Osbourne 1992: 36).

Thus, the general practitioners' (that is, medical reformers') appeal to competence as a liberal antidote to the privilege historically held by physicians in effect enhanced the status of the general medical persona. The identity of the doctor came to embody professional values centred upon the 'ideal-typical gentleman' whose relation to medical acts is based not only upon reason and science but upon aesthetic criteria: probity, tact and competence (Osbourne 1992). This type of analysis problematises the tendency of some authors to simply identify expertise with a will to truth, and promote an image of the neutral objective expert, who makes decisions and is valued on the basis of his/her access to/understanding of positive knowledge in the field of human sciences.

Using Foucault's work in the way that Minson (1997) suggests allows us to recognise the complexity of the formation of medical expertise in the nineteenth century. Moreover, it does not try to privilege the moral or the scientific, but rather allows for an *amalgam* of these apparently conflicting ethical values to coexist in the persona of the doctor as well as in the expression of medical expertise relating to opiate use. It also allows us to see the medical presence in the anti-opium movement, not as a conspiracy to colonise or medicalise a previously moral domain, but as an example of doctors self-consciously constituting themselves as ethical subjects. This provides an alternative account to Berridge and Edwards' (1987) view, that the anti-opium movement was only successful when doctors active in both spheres translated its arguments into scientific respectability. Such respectability may not hinge on the scientific, embedded in the claim to true and positive knowledge, but rather on the newly found (or recognised) social status of doctors as men of honour who were able to convert their clinical power to social effects (Osbourne 1992). Clearly the persona of the doctor as medical expert is not simply the embodiment of a neutral or objective authority, operating to an ethical code '*beyond good and evil*'. Moreover, the governmental power of expertise does not reside simply in an appeal to truth, and the functional transmission of positive knowledge. The diverse modes of ethical comportment which converge in the persona of the doctor suggest a much more complex genealogy of the regulation of opium use than can be described by the investigation of the medico-administrative domain alone.

Opium and Cultural Consciousness

One other set of relations is also worthy of closer consideration in this investigation of the regulation of opium. These relations revolve around the use of opium by the Chinese. In the preceding discussion this has been a persistent theme. In the early part of the nineteenth century, opium addiction, where it was recognised, was considered to be a feature of Eastern/Far Eastern use. This view was reinforced by the investigations associated with the longevity debates of the 1830s. While medical men drawing on British case studies failed to concede that the condition warranted serious intervention, evidence to the contrary was consistently presented by those with experience of the East or Far East. From the beginning of the century the anti-opium movement was opposed to the British trade in the drug, and concerned about Chinese opium use in China. As the century drew to a close its members expressed increasing alarm with regard to Chinese opium use in Britain (Berridge and Edwards 1987). In 1883 the Reverend George Piercy, a former missionary to Canton, and a member of the SSOT warned rather dramatically that as retribution for Britain's dishonourable trade the Chinese would enter, colonise and conquer the English social body in the form of a 'contagion' enabled by opium:

> With great pain of mind, I now must say, clearly and strongly shows that we really have a new habit, prolific of evil, springing up amongst us … It is coming close to us with a rapidity and spring almost undreamt of even by those who dreaded its stealthy and unseen step… There have been warning voices in the air, but they have been little heeded. Those who have been claiming justice for China relative to the opium traffic at the hands of our government have not been silent on this point – the reflex action and retributive consequences of our own doings … What could all this grow but to the plague spreading and attacking our vitals? If I speak again of what has been seen of the Chinese who smoke opium in London it must be understood that it is to raise a warning voice against the evil they have brought. It begins with the Chinese, but does not end with them! (*Friend of China* cited in Milligan 1995: 82).

The anti-opium movement stimulated popular concern by drawing public attention to the growing number of Chinese immigrants in the British community,[30] and by advertising the evils of the East End opium den. Berridge and Edwards claim that 'the most obvious legacy of the anti-opium movement was the image of the opium 'dens' and the image of Chinese opium smoking in East End London which it helped to form'(1987: 195). However, these authors (along with others like Parssinen 1983) suggest that this phenomenon and its associated risk was far less prevalent than the anti-opiumists (and journalists, as we will see) made out. In the current discussion the 'real' magnitude of the risk is of little consequence. What is important is that this was a clear expression of a relationship that had increasingly become a significant part of British cultural consciousness. Milligan's (1995) work, using literary analysis to investigate a number of widely consumed culture products, supports this conclusion. He argues that the subtle Anglo-Oriental references evident in the work of Coleridge and De Quincey become increasingly more resonant and specifically China-focused by the century's end. In the last third of the nineteenth century a new literary genre evolved, consisting of narratives about mysterious and evil opium dens in the East End of London. The authors who typified this genre included Dickens, Wilde and Conan Doyle. Readers were also made familiar with these particular East End establishments, and the dangers of opium smoking, through countless magazines, newspapers and books presenting reports from 'roving

---

30   The number of Chinese settling in London began to expand relatively rapidly in the 1860s. In 1861 there were an estimated 147 Chinese in the whole country; by 1881 there were 665 – most lived in London. In 1891, 582 were resident there, mainly living in the East End (Berridge and Edwards 1987:195).

correspondents' who had taken the then fashionable police-guided tour of the East End and its dens (Milligan 1995; Parssinen 1983).

The genre and its products followed a formula, which reflected Piercy's anxieties about oriental infection as insidious invasion (Milligan 1995; Parssinen 1983). Such infection was more often than not construed as being communicated by inhalations of opium smoke – a metaphor that draws on the miasma model of disease. Orientalness is portrayed as a transmittable disease (Milligan 1995). The practice of opium smoking was construed as being so essentially Chinese that it was was portrayed in the narratives as having the capacity gradually to render Britons more Chinese in their customs, attitudes and physical appearance. For example, in Dickens' unfinished *The Mystery of Edwin Drood* (1870), an English woman is described as having 'opium smoked herself into a strange likeness of the Chinaman. His form of cheek, eye and temple, and his colour are repeated in her' (Milligan 1995: 97). Another reporter, with regards to a Chinese opium master's English wife, finds her so extensively transformed that:

> It was only by her speech that her nationality could be so readily decided. A small lean woman, with such a marvellous grafting of Chinese about her, that her cotton gown of English cut seemed to hang awkwardly on her sharp shoulders. Her skin was dusk yellow, and tightly drawn at the nostrils and the cheekbones; and evidently she had, since her marriage, taken such an Oriental view of life, that her organs of vision were fast losing their European shape, and assuming that which coincided with her adopted nature. She was very ill, poor woman. It was killing her, she said, this constant breathing of the fumes of the subtle drug her husband dealt in (cited in Milligan 1995: 90).

Two characteristics were standard features of the genre: an almost superstitious dread of 'Orientals' and a tendency to portray them as animals and vampire-like, living dead parasites; and, a preoccupation with the role of English women in the opium den accompanied by the suggestion that they are being orientalised. According to Milligan, such narratives tended to depend upon the portrayal of the seductiveness and *will-usurping* quality of the drug, which enabled Oriental and specifically Chinese men to gain sexual power over English women. This set the stage for anxieties about racial purity, fears that were exacerbated by growing apprehensions that the increased mixing of cultures and races in the British Empire would dissipate the British Identity and undermine England's control of the empire (Milligan 1995). Milligan also suggests that the anxiety surrounding the union of British women with Chinese men was not only driven by fear of genetic contamination, it was concerned with the threat it posed in relation to the household and family as the backbone of English character. Citing Samuel Smiles' view:

> The Home is the crystal of society – the very nucleus of national character; and from that source, be it pure or tainted, issue the habits, principles and maxims, which govern public as well as private life. The Nation comes from the nursery; public opinion itself is for the most part the outgrowth of the home (cited in Milligan 1995: 93).

Milligan unwittingly alludes to the governmental significance of this particular concern. As explained earlier (see p.26 above), during the eighteenth and nineteenth centuries the family unit emerged as fundamental to the government of the population (Foucault 1980). In the nineteenth century campaigns to medicalise the family sought to transform it into a quintessentially 'private space', yet ensure that it accepted the responsibility for securing the public objectives of social health (Rose 1994). Women in particular took on new roles in relation to the protection and cultivation of the health and wellbeing of their children and spouse. They were the main point of support for all the actions that were directed towards this reformulation of family life. They worked in partnership with the medical and teaching professions in order to disseminate their principles and to win adherence to new norms within the home (Donzelot 1979). Thus, Milligan's cultural analysis, in his assessment of the position of women in Victorian society, as well as other themes, is consistent with the governmental perspective pursued in this chapter. Clearly concern with invasion, contagion and racial purity are issues that are tied up with the health and wellbeing of the social body, and the problem of population (see pp.17–21 above).

It is worth noting here that Milligan's account has its parallels in various analyses of the cultural products and consciousness of both the USA and Australia (Davies 1986; Hoffman 1990; Manderson 1988, 1993; Morgan 1981). In respective histories of opium use and regulation in the USA, Courtwright (1982), Morgan (1981) and Duster (1970) all draw their readers' attention to press stories of the late nineteenth century that often reported about the 'frightening opium dens' where Chinese 'yellow fiends' forced unsuspecting white women to become enslaved to the drug (cited in Hoffman 1990: 57). Manderson (1988; 1993), while admitting that Australia had no equivalent of Coleridge or De Quincey, analysed the content of the popular press as well as parliamentary debates to arrive at similar conclusions. He explains that *The Bulletin* in particular provided colourful accounts of the Chinese in Australia. It was a leading force in the anti-Chinese crusade, unambiguously stating its editorial view: '[w]here ever the pigtailed pagan herds on Australian soils they introduce and practice vices most detestable and damnable vices that attack everything sacred in the system of European civilisation' (in Manderson 1988: 455).

The anti-Chinese crusade was a successful precursor to Chinese Restriction Acts, which were introduced in different States towards the end of the 1880s in order to limit or stop migration. Henry Parkes, on the second reading of such a Bill in the New South Wales Parliament urged:

> Support us in this effort to terminate a moral and social pestilence, to preserve to ourselves and our children, unaltered and unspotted, the rights and privileges which we have received from our forefathers… to preserve the soil of Australia that we may plant upon it the nucleus of a future nation stamped with a *pure* British type (cited in Manderson 1988: 444).

Clearly expressed here is a concern for the emerging nation, and the maintenance of a *pure* British stock, mirroring the concerns in relation to invasion and racial contamination evident in Milligan's analysis described above.

Manderson's research reveals that the Chinese were painted as living squalidly and in filth, their habits depraved, and their life degraded (Manderson 1988). The absence of Chinese women was seen as a threat to the honour and chastity of innocent

European girls. Opium in particular was one of the many vices that contributed to the evilness of the Chinese. The effect of the drug was to enable 'the criminal and sensual Chinese' (1988: 444) to seduce white women. Mr Johnson, in the Commonwealth Parliamentary Debates of 1905, adopted the defining characteristics of the literary genre described by Milligan (1995):

> One case in Melbourne struck me as being particularly abhorrent, for on one opium couch, smoking the one tray was a shrivelled up, decrepit-looking old Oriental resembling nothing so much as a revivified Egyptian mummy, and a young European women of scarcely twenty very scantily clothed … (cited in Manderson 1988: 450).

Again concerns for the maintenance of racial purity and sexual morality coalesce. Opium was feared as a tool for miscegenation. In Australia, like Britain, contagion was also a dominant theme. Following Manderson's interpretation, the issue was 'to protect white people.' 'White men and white women' were to be isolated from any contact with the drug by legislation; and if as a result 'the Chinkey will get deleterious opium,' too bad. To quarantine the clean you must make the dirty suffer (Manderson 1988: 450).

It seems that these types of views were more forcefully expressed in the USA and Australia than they were in Britain. In both these countries such concerns received legitimate expression in the enactment of anti-Chinese laws, like the various Australian Chinese Restriction Acts (Hoffman 1990; Manderson 1988). The greater numbers of Chinese immigrants and resulting visibility of the supposedly invading aliens inspired this type of government intervention. Between 1852 and 1879 more than 70,000 Chinese workers immigrated to America. Immigration to Australia peaked in the 1870s, with 9,616 Chinese in Australia in 1878, and 800 of these living in the town of Ballarat. Clearly the magnitude of this settlement is much greater than that in the East End of London.[31] In its wake both the USA and Australia were subsequently motivated to enact laws *absolutely* prohibiting smoking opium, a form of use practised almost exclusively by and associated with the Chinese. These laws explicitly were not concerned with opium prepared for other purposes – for example, laudanum or popular patient remedies which were widely used by the rest of the population. As Mr Bosisto, a druggist, and resident 'opium expert' to the Victorian Legislative Assembly explained in 1893: it was desired 'to see a Bill introduced to restrict and regulate the importation, sale and use of Chinese opium… We should not legislate for the other opium at all' (cited in Manderson 1988: 448). Such strong forms of regulation contrasted starkly with the more liberal styles of regulation introduced throughout the nineteenth century. Their form is the subject of analysis in the next chapter.

---

31   For more discussion on social relations relating to Chinese in Australia in the nineteenth and early twentieth centuries see also the work of McCoy (1972; 1991) and Walker (1999).

Conclusion

The preceding discussion has provided an historical account of how opium was transformed in the nineteenth century from a legitimate item of international trade and a popular palliative, the use of which was widely accepted, into a dangerous substance and a corruptor of international economies and individual morality alike. It described how the complex of technologies, knowledges, actors, powers, institutions and social arrangements which began to crystallise around the phenomenon of life during the nineteenth century provided the conditions for the initial regulation of opium and its derivatives. Highlighting the role played by expert knowledges (statistical, actuarial and medical), by technologies of recording (births, deaths and coroners' reports, and vital statistics), by statistical societies and nascent bureaucracies (the Registrar General's Office, and public inquiries) and by the processes of reform and professionalisation of medical practice (accreditation, legislation, journals, specialisation and treatment practices), it demonstrated how the development of an identifiable 'network' of expertise concerned with the consumption of opium and its derivatives contributed to the identification of opium as a dangerous drug and subsequently the constitution of the persona of the opium inebriate (addict). Acknowledging the relationship between the religiously founded anti-opium movement and medical expertise, embodied in the persona of the doctor, it warns us against interpreting expertise too narrowly, and alerts us to a complex social network – contributing to regulation – that extends well beyond the medico-administrative complex and a positive knowledge of the population.

This genealogy corresponds with Foucault's claims that at the end of the eighteenth century the good order, enrichment and health of the population emerged as one of the essential objectives of political power. The population was constituted as a problem, a target for surveillance, regulation, analysis and intervention. A particular form of 'politico-medical' regulatory arrangement came to permeate the lives of people. These arrangements were expressed through a whole series of prescriptions relating not only to disease, but to general forms of existence and behaviour. They were focused on individuals and population. Such regulation of life did not amount to state interventions from above, but rather emanated from within the social body: from religious groups, charitable and benevolent associations and the learned societies (Foucault 1980).

In relation to health, Foucault suggests that the objectives of power included the cultivation of *physical wellbeing* and *longevity*. These concerns were clearly expressed in the longevity debates initiated by the life insurance claim of the Earl of Mar. The insurance company refused to pay out on the policy arguing that opium eating was a habit affecting *health* and *longevity,* which should have been revealed. The ensuing court case, and the debate that followed, forced nineteenth-century English society to confront the social issues of opiate use. Moreover, through the technology of life insurance, the use of opium first began to be identified as an unacceptable risk which threatens life, making it the responsibility of the insured to conduct him or herself in a way that such dangers are avoided. The public hygiene movement was another unambiguous expression of the concern for the *health* and *wellbeing* of the population. It used the intellectual technology of comparative statistics to study the spread of illness and death. These statistics – mainly available through the Registrar General's Office – played a significant role in the problematisation of the open availability of opium and its initial regulation.

The coalescence of regulation, social reform and the associated professionalisation of medicine provided the conditions of possibility for the constitution of opium consumption as a disease and the identification of the opium inebriate – the addict. With this shift, opium consumption was transformed into a category of unreason; it was homogenised into a single negative entity – a pathology to be contained and rectified. It became the subject of the disciplinary practices – surveillance, normalisation and examination (cf. Foucault 1977) – of medicine. In the shadow of madness the addict crossed 'the frontiers of bourgeois order of his own accord and alienate[d] himself outside the sacred limits of its ethic' (Foucault 1967: 57–8). However, for the addict, unlike the lunatic, there was the possibility for redemption (cf. Valverde 1998). The hybrid formulation of the disease of addiction was characterised in terms of a degenerate constitution as well as a moral failing of the will. The weakening of the will and the surrender of responsibility, however, was not total and irrevocable. Doctors recommended treatment methods that relied on the inebriate's own moral capacity – his or her will to reform. In doing so they presupposed the existence of at least some residual rationality, autonomy and self-control. The very idea of sending inebriates to reformatories or retreats necessarily involved an assumption that at least a good proportion of them could – unlike lunatics or mental defectives – reform themselves. Unlike these other categories of patient in state institutions, inebriates necessarily were required to participate actively and sincerely in their own cure (Valverde 1996a; 1998). Thus the free will – that key technical requirement of liberal government – was not wholly lost in the inebriate/addict. Inebriates were potentially reformable, and reform necessarily consisted in strengthening the will. The formulation of the concept of addiction and inebriety in the late nineteenth century as a contemporary technique for the government of conduct reflected the inseparability of discipline and freedom in the domain of medicine – being governed from above and becoming free through governing oneself (Sedgwick in Valverde 1996a).

The regulation of opium and its derivatives and the identification of the addict in the nineteenth century was bound to rationalities concerned with the government and preservation of life – the life of the population and the life of individuals. By the end of the century such rationalities had become well entrenched where opium was concerned. Not only were they expressed in the knowledges and technologies that represented medical expertise, as Milligan's work demonstrates, they had come to permeate popular culture. A widely consumed literary genre emerged which rehearsed concerns regarding the *health* and *wellbeing* of the population and the moral fortitude of individuals (particularly women). The genre abounded with medical metaphors of infection and contagion relating to the evil of opium smoking. It blurred the distinction between this practice and the Chinese, confounding the source of threat and danger. Employing what was to become a familiar formula, the narratives described how the seductiveness and *will-usurping* quality of opium was used by Chinese men to gain sexual power over English and European women. This was an expression of fears relating to racial purity which, at that time, was a significant consideration in relation to the strength and wellbeing of the population. This, however, could also be construed in terms of an attack on the family as the backbone of English society, as well as an attempt to dissipate the British national identity and undermine England's control of the empire (Milligan 1995). According to Milligan, the threat of mixing the races is all the more problematic when the groups in question were at odds – as the British and Chinese were – because it would make it impossible to sort family members from enemies (Milligan 1995: 92). In this light, while health and longevity remained important, it is apparent that a new consideration had begun to emerge. In popular discourses opium smoking clearly came to represent the threat of an alien invasion and conquest (Manderson 1988, 1993; Milligan 1995). Opium was constituted not only as a problem for the health and wellbeing of the population, but for national stability and security, and thus sovereignty as well. This disjuncture heralds an important shift, which is the subject of the analysis to follow.

Chapter 3

Preserving the Nation State

The genealogy described in the last chapter identified a governmental rationality concerned with the good government – especially the health and wellbeing – of the national population as underlying the initial regulation of opium in nineteenth-century England. It concluded with a reflection on the extent to which this rationality came to permeate the cultural consciousness of Britain, as well as the USA and Australia. In doing so it highlighted an important disjuncture that could easily be overlooked or accounted for in terms of prejudice or xenophobic hysteria (see for example Manderson 1993: 302). This disjuncture was subtly articulated in the conflation of the dangers of opium smoking with the presence of Chinese men. According to popular discourses, 'Chinamen' employed the seductiveness and will-usurping quality of opium to gain sexual power over European women. This was portrayed in literature at that time as an attack on the family, seen as the backbone of English society, as well as an attempt to dissipate the British national identity and undermine England's control of the empire (Milligan 1995). This articulation of the threat posed to the nation by the Chinese and their use of opium is both important and ironic. It is important because it signals the emergence of a novel rationality directed towards the control of the drug – a rationality that has subsequently gained considerable support throughout the twentieth century. It is somewhat ironic because, as will be argued below, from the late eighteenth century, opium had increasingly come to represent foreign domination of the Chinese by the British and was blamed for the degeneration of the once powerful Manchu Dynasty and the Chinese empire (Fay 1975).

This chapter investigates the historical conditions that made such a situation possible. It argues that matters of sovereignty, state formation and preservation, characteristic of those described by Hirst and Thompson (1996), in relation to the formation of the modern system of states, played a significant role in producing various forms of opiate regulation in the international domain. It begins by briefly rehearsing the points made by Hirst and Thompson (and others: Hindess 2000b; Hunter 1998), noting in this context the particular significance of the political rationality of reason of state. Drawing on the extensive body of historical literature concerned with international drug control,[1] it discusses how international as well as domestic systems regulating the supply of opium emerged in the context of a range of competing governmental trajectories.

---

1 For example: Bean (1974), Beeching (1975), Brecher (1972), Fay (1975), Greenberg (1951), McCoy (1991), Musto (1973), and Rolls (1992).

Reason of State

The idea of reason of state has a long and at times ambiguous history – a particularly significant reformulation of this political doctrine emerged towards the end of the sixteenth and the beginning of the seventeenth centuries. Tuck (1993) suggests that this significant revision occurred in an intellectual environment influenced by the psychological orientation of skepticism reinforced with the ideas of the neo-stoics. By drawing parallels between *ataraxia* and *apatheia* in relation to the importance of a detachment from passion and from belief which causes emotion, he argues that both philosophical orientations were fundamentally concerned with the notion of self-preservation: the preservation of individuals not only from external attack but also from passions which might leave them open to attack (Tuck 1993).[2] Tuck proposes that these ideas were translated into a political theory of reason of state in which the population had to be disciplined in the interests of the preservation and the security of the state (1993: xiv). In the late sixteenth and early seventeenth centuries the political theory of the neo-stoics (Tuck cites the work of Lipsius and Montaigne) centred on the necessity for the prince to preserve himself as the head of the state at all costs. The prince's own interests were bound up with those of his republic, but if the preservation of political order was at stake, then the rules of justice or constitutional proprieties had to take second place.[3]

Hunter (1998), tracing developments in Germany – rather than Italy, as is the case with Tuck (1993; see also Viroli 1992) – describes a similar trajectory regarding the shift in the ends of politics. He describes the elaboration of several novel doctrines of sovereignty and reason of state emerging in the seventeenth century, the object of which was to separate politics and the state from religion and community, in effect the 'moral neutralisation of politics' (Hunter 1998: 253). In support of this claim Hunter cites a number of seventeenth-century authors for whom the end of politics was not the moral and economic wellbeing of the community, but political order (Hunter 1998). According to Henning Arnisaeus, for example, the statesman was required to attend to the economic and moral welfare of the population only to the degree necessary for the preservation of order. His task was not to lead his people to salvation, or function as an executor of natural law inscribed in communal will. It was simply to preserve the empirical political order against various political

---

2   Support for this argument is also evident in Viroli's discussion of Botero (1992: 256), where moderation of the passions of the subjects is similarly seen as important to the preservation of the prince and the state.

3   Lipsius, for example, argued that rulers ought to privilege the cause of civil peace and, when necessary, sacrifice all other principles for it:

As for me I should be of this opinion that the prince in desparat matters should always follow that which were most necessarie to be effected, not which is honest in speech. Then I say let him decline gently from the lawes, yet not except it be for his own conservation, but to inlarge his estate. For necessitie which is the true defender of the weakness of men, doth breake all lawes. And as the Poet sayth, he doth not hurt, who hurteth against his will (cited in Tuck 1993: 57).

pathologies arising from estate society and international rivalry (Hunter 1998).[4] This could be done whatever his religious or moral proclivities. Hunter explains, given that any community requires the exercise of power to preserve order, it is possible to arrive at a morally neutral conception of politics. Thus, law-making was governed by reason of state. Moreover, the prince was free to commit supra-legal acts in the interests of preserving the state, but not in his own personal interest. For Arnisaeus, the pursuit of personal satisfaction and aggrandisement meant the neglect of politics as the expert technical preservation of order.

These ideas of putting self-preservation first, and the influence of skepticism/ stoicism, have resonance in contemporary understandings of sovereignty and theories of the modern state; they were influential in the formation of the system of modern states. Hirst and Thompson (1996) explain how the doctrine of reason of state was important in the formation of the early modern state and the rise of national sovereignty. Prior to the seventeenth century there was no singular relationship between authority and land or populations. Political authorities and other forms of functionally specific governance (like religious communities and guilds) had existed in complex and overlapping relations that made parallel and often competing claims to the same territorial areas (Greik 1900 in Hirst and Thompson 1996: 171). This provided a volatile environment of civil unrest and disorder, which made government impossible. Hunter (1994) explains that it was these circumstances – in particular the overlay of the territorial state with the confessional state – which ignited the Thirty Years War. This religiously based civil war was driven by supra-mundane politics of conscience that claimed to derive government from absolute moral principles expressed by the prince as God's representative on earth. Religious passion made states vulnerable to attack. In the wake of the staggering carnage, principles of moral righteousness and justice gave way to a more pragmatic concern for the survival and security of the state itself as the principal directive of political thought and action. The state came to be recognised as the absolute political authority with exclusive possession of a defined territory. It became the dominant form of government accepting no other agency as rival authority (Hirst and Thompson 1996). Thus, it stood above religion as a governing authority. It did so not in the name of a new political philosophy but as the circumstantially driven instrument for ending religious slaughter and preserving civil peace (Hunter 1994; Koselleck 1988).

The objective of the various doctrines of state that emerged at that time (the seventeenth century) was the moral neutralisation of politics – achieved by separation of politics from religion and community (Hirst and Thompson 1996; Hunter 1994; Tuck 1987). The end of politics was the preservation and management of the state as an empirical entity. Politics was concerned only with the maintenance of an empirically given form of rule or domination regardless of the moral and economic orientation of society. The specific goal of politics gave rise to the concept of sovereign as absolute power, because the preservation of political order could only

---

4   The same principle is evident in Hobbes' theory of the absolute state, where what mattered was the citizen and his survival in this world, not the man and his redemption in the next (in Saunders 1997, see also Koselleck 1988).

be achieved by domination over competing estates and powers. This necessitated the deployment of a power superior to all others (Hirst and Thompson 1996).

In sum, the conceptualisation of the political rationality of reason of state that is relevant in this context had its genesis in the principle of self-preservation; preservation not only from external attack but also from passions which might leave it open to attack. This translated into a political theory concerned with the regulation of the population in the interests of state preservation. In this formulation preservation of political order stands above all else; rules of justice or constitutional proprieties take second place. Laws can be broken for the preservation of the political order but not for any other reason. Preservation of the state hinged on the recognition of sovereignty – absolute political authority – with exclusive possession of a defined territory, and the state as the dominant form of government accepted no other agency as rival authority (Hirst and Thompson 1996).

The Degeneration of the Dynasty

Beeching (1975) explains that at the end of the eighteenth century China was strong, self-contained and self-sufficient. Any exchange of goods with foreign representatives was based on principles of good will and benevolent diplomacy rather than considerations of necessity or profit (Greenberg 1951; Rolls 1992). For example, in the eighteenth century, Britain – through the East India Company – attempted to initiate trade with China. The Emperor's response to the British representative who, in 1793, made approaches in this regard was short:

> Strange and costly objects do not interest me. As your Ambassador can see for himself we possess all things. I set no value on strange objects and ingenious, and have no use for your country's manufactures (cited in Greenberg 1951: 4).

While the Chinese had no desire or need for British goods or to cultivate external trade, the same was not the case for the English. China offered tea, a valued commodity, which in those days could not be acquired elsewhere. By 1785 the East India Company – which enjoyed a legal monopoly of trade between Britain and the East – was buying and selling fifteen million pounds weight of China tea per year (Beeching 1975: 19). The quantity of tea taken from China could not be matched by imports and the gap in the balance of trade grew. The Indian administration[5] was anxious for revenue; England was desperate – the Seven Years War with France ending in 1763 and the American War of Independence had been very expensive (Beeching 1975). In view of China's indifference to European goods, ever-increasing amounts of silver (and some gold) were being paid for Chinese tea, and some cotton and silk. For years a very high proportion of British cargoes to China, sometimes almost the whole of them, consisted of silver (Fay 1975; Greenberg 1951). The reliance on bullion, however, was an unsatisfactory way of trading. For England and the Company the problem was to find commodities that would be acceptable to the Chinese, which would pay for teas, and perhaps themselves bring a profit.

---

5   Which was the East India Company.

With the conquest of India in the mid-eighteenth century the British, through the East India Company, had acquired and cultivated what grew to be a monopoly on opium (Rolls 1992). In 1781 Warren Hastings, then the governor of Bengal, attempted to promote trade in opium with China by sending a cargo of the drug to Canton.[6] There was little interest. This should have been no surprise, as it was well known that the use of opium was prohibited by an Imperial decree (see p.5 above). The East India Company developed more aggressive marketing. In 1794 another British cargo of opium sailed from India to Guangzhou, and a Hong merchant bought it. Two years later energetic and corrupt trading practices had lifted China's consumption to 4,000 chests, and sales continued to increase (Rolls 1992: 385–6). Opium became the only ready money article sold in China. Nothing else could be counted on for the resources needed for buying teas. While the East India Company produced the opium and enjoyed its returns, it did not take the drug to China. A complex system of consignment to independent traders – French, English, American, Portuguese, Dutch – handled the direct exchange with the Chinese. As a result, the Company, which was also the government of India and represented the interests of Britain, claimed that it did not engage in illicit trade or smuggling itself (Fay 1975; Greenberg 1951). Nevertheless, it was this trade in opium that underwrote the whole of the Far Eastern trade.

After 1804 the Company sent very little silver from Europe to China. The balance of trade began to shift. Both Indian and British administrations, as well as other countries, enjoyed the benefits.[7] In the nineteenth century the trade in opium yielded one-seventh of the total revenue of British India (Greenberg 1951).[8] By 1830 the opium trade was probably the largest commerce of its time in any single commodity anywhere in the world (Greenberg 1951). Sales continued to increase, amounting in 1836 to 26,000 chests, and in 1837, with a rumoured prospect of legalisation, reached 40,000 chests worth $25 million (also see Greenberg 1951: 113; Rolls 1992).[9] By the 1830s the previous balance had been completely reversed. A contemporary pamphleteer wrote:

> From the opium trade the Honourable Company have derived for years an immense revenue and through them the British Government and nation have also reaped an incalculable amount of political and financial advantage. The turn of the balance of trade between Great Britain and China in favour of the former has enabled India to increase tenfold her consumption of British manufacture; contributed directly to support the vast fabric

---

6   Foreigners were allowed access to trade with China only through the port of Canton.

7   There were powerful national interests behind the drug trade and not all of them British – the USA and Portugal as well as other countries were heavily involved. If the Chinese had not bought opium from Americans, then the United States' imports of silk, porcelain and tea would have had to be paid for in silver coin. In 1819 there was not enough American silver available. The House of Representatives Committee on Currency reported that the 'whole amount of our current coin is probably not more than double that which has been imported in a single year to India, including China in the common term'. Opium smuggling was as good for the American dollar as it was for the English pound (Beeching 1975: 36).

8   Friman estimates its magnitude at approximately $50 million per annum (1996: 6).

9   Where unspecified currency refers to American dollars.

of British dominion in the East to defray the expenses of His Majesty's establishment in India, and by the operation of exchanges and remittances in teas, to pour an abundant revenue into the British Exchequer and benefit the nation to an extent of 6 million pounds yearly without impoverishing India. Therefore the Company has done everything in its power to foster the opium trade (Warren 1839 in Greenberg 1951: 106–7).

So much had the balance of the China trade altered that between 1829 and 1840 only $7.33 million of silver was imported while nearly $56 million of treasure – dollars, sycee[10] and gold – was sent out of the country (Greenberg 1951: 142). The drain of silver caused a shortage of the circulating medium and sent up local prices. This was noted by local officials and reported to the Emperor. It caused considerable alarm. Given how little silver was mined in China such an outflow threatened the entire monetary system. Major transactions were always made in silver; taxes, for example, could not be remitted to Peking in any other form. Opium was considered the source of other problems as well: brigandage, corruption of the army and the civil service,[11] and the ruin of increasing numbers of ordinary Chinese (Beeching 1975; Fay 1975; Greenberg 1951).

From the beginning of the increase of opium trade with India in the late eighteenth century, the Emperor had regularly responded with new and ever more stringent Imperial decrees condemning the growing traffic.[12] While the wretchedness of the users was often mentioned, the outflow of silver increasingly became the key focus of concern. By 1838 the situation had become critical, and an Imperial edict appointed Lin Tse-hsu Special Commissioner to destroy the opium trade. It was phrased very clearly in economic terms:

> Since opium has spread its baneful influence through China the quantity of silver exported has yearly been on the increase, till its price has become enhanced, the copper coin depressed, the land and capitation tax, the transport of grain and the [salt] gabelle all alike hampered. If steps be not taken for our defence. …the useful wealth of China will be poured into the fathomless abyss of transmarine regions (Fay 1975: 128).

Lin's title was Imperial Commissioner, President of the Board of War, and Viceroy of Hoo Kwang (Fay 1975: 128; Rolls 1992: 393). Imperial Commissioner was an exceptional appointment in China, which was created to meet an emergency and granted special powers (Beeching 1975: 74). Lin carried the rarely given Imperial

---

10   Uncoined shoe-shaped ingots of pure silver (Greenberg 1951).

11   Greenberg (see also Beeching 1975) describes the often blatant exhibition of corruption:

Two obstacles in the way of any effective suppression on the Chinese side were a corrupt Mandarinate and naval weakness. Corruption went to such lengths that the 'smug boats' which delivered the opium were often Mandarin boats whose function it was to prevent smuggling. Likewise a favourite means of conveying opium to the northern provinces was the annual Imperial junks, which left Canton for Peking river loaded with presents for the Emperor (Greenberg 1951: 111).

12   In 1780, 1796 and 1799 and pronouncements after that of almost one a year (Beeching 1975).

seal which gave him almost equal powers to the Emperor himself (Rolls 1992: 391).
On 18 March 1839 he issued a proclamation in Chinese and English announcing that
he was 'specifically appointed as Imperial Commissioner with great irresponsible
(translators error) authority ...' He more forcefully repeated the monetary theme.[13]

> Formerly the prohibition of our Empire might still be considered indulgent, and therefore
> it was that from all our ports that Sycee leaked out as the opium rushed in. Now, however,
> the great Emperor on hearing of it, actually quivers with indignation, and before he will
> stay his hand, the evil must be completely and entirely done away with. ... it is computed
> that the loss of silver of China during the period of several years past, by exportation
> beyond sea, has not been less than some hundreds of millions. The imperial commands
> have been repeatedly received in reference to the importation of opium and exportation
> of pure silver reproving all the officers of every degree in most severe terms. Yet these
> Hong merchants have continued in the same course of filthy and disgraceful conduct to
> the great indignation and gnashing of teeth of everyone. I, the High Commissioner, in
> obeying the Imperial commands, in accordance with which I have come to Canton, shall
> first punish the depraved natives. And it is by no means certain that these Hong merchants
> will not be within the number. ...I have given commands to the foreigners to deliver up
> to Government all the myriads of chests of opium which they have on board their vessels
> and called upon them to subscribe a bond in the Chinese and foreign language jointly,
> declaring that thenceforth they will never venture to bring opium...these bonds are to be
> obtained by the Hong merchants, and the same reported to the High Commissioner within
> three days, on penalty of death (cited in Rolls 1992: 390).

His language was threatening and the edict was backed, according to Elliot
(the British Chief Superintendent at that time), by an 'unusual assemblage of
troops, vessels of war, fire ships and other menacing preparations'. Moreover, 'the
communication by the command of the Provincial Government, that in the present
posture of affairs the foreigners were no longer to seek for passports to leave Canton
according to the genius of our own countries, and the principles of reason, if not an
act of declared war, was at least its immediate and inevitable preliminary' (see also
Fay 1975: 142-52; Rolls 1992: 390).

Lin was true to his word. He restricted all British trade and movement in Canton to
demonstrate that now the Chinese were serious about prohibition. In the course of the
confrontation some 20,000 chests of Indian opium were confiscated and destroyed,
and the lives and safety of British subjects in Canton were threatened (Inglis 1975).
Britain sent troops to reopen trade. The fear that England might take China, and
Peking in particular, raised considerable alarm. In the end the Emperor's negotiators
were instructed to make peace no matter what the cost should be; *preservation* of
the dynasty was to be their primary concern (Fay 1975: 357). The Treaty of Nanking
was signed after some delay in August of 1842. China agreed to open more ports to
unrestricted trade, to cede the island of Hong Kong to Great Britain, and to pay the
equivalent of approximately 10 million pounds in reparation for loss of trade and
destruction of opium (Rolls 1992: 397). The legalisation of the opium trade was not
mentioned, and smuggling continued unhindered, much as it had before. In the mid-

---

13   In China 'Commission Lin was "one of the shrewdest economists of his time"'
(Greenberg 1951: 143).

1850s another incident brought the British navy. The resulting second war ended with the occupation of Peking and the Treaty of Tientsin, which finally established that imports of opium be legally permitted on payment of a duty (Inglis 1975).

These confrontations, referred to as the Opium Wars, were fought by the British to force China to accept the 'normal' practices of Western trade, which included the importation of opium. Britain claimed that the legalisation of trade in the drug would be in China's best interest. This was a point of view with which a string of Emperors – and the balance of trade – consistently disagreed (Rolls 1992). On the other hand, the legalisation of opium would clearly have been in Britain's interest. At a more subtle level, however, these conflicts were fought over Chinese sovereignty: China's right or capacity to govern its own affairs, to regulate trade in its own interests, and specifically to legislate against the sale and use of opium. As a result of defeat the Chinese experienced a humiliating reduction in sovereignty, and opium was to become a constant symbol of the downfall of the empire and the beginning of an external – particularly British – domination.

Reason of state mentalities are clearly evident here. The Imperial decrees and actions to prohibit the trade in opium sought to preserve China from a growing passion that opened it to external attack. The continuing illicit trade in the drug undermined the dominion of the Emperor. For China this came to constitute an emergency, which challenged the very existence of the Imperial dynasty. The failure of both Chinese and foreign traders to observe Chinese law relating to the prohibition of opium eroded the Emperor's claim to absolute political authority, and the drain of silver pushed China dangerously towards the possibility of economic collapse. The opium trade was also unambiguously associated with the corruption of the army and the civil service (Beeching 1975). The urgency of the problem was confirmed by the appointment of Lin, who was sanctioned by Imperial decree to put a stop to the trade. The appointment of a High Commissioner was exceptional in China. The post held special powers – almost equal to those of the Emperor – which were granted only in the face of an emergency. Lin responded by imposing extraordinary (or supra-legal) limitations on usual trade practices and the movement of non-Chinese in Canton in order to bring the problem under control and preserve political order. In Britain, the Indian-Chinese opium trade was considered by some[14] to be immoral (p.37 above). Others, having an eye to the needs of the Indian and British administrations, as well as the balance of trade, considered it regrettable but necessary. Despite ongoing pressure to end the trade throughout the nineteenth century, the *pragmatics* of economic necessity persistently won out. This conflict of interest between the Chinese and the British resulted in war. Britain exercised superior power in gaining the domination of China, and the Chinese acquiesced to British demands in the interests of preserving the dynasty and saving the empire. Both sides had a stake in the preservation of their respective 'states'.

By the end of the nineteenth century China had been transformed from a strong and self-sufficient empire into a society characterised by serious economic, social and political degeneration (Taylor 1969). The Chinese, and those affiliated with the anti-opium movement, believed that this was a direct result of the opium trade. In

---

14 Anti-opiumists, and in particular members of the SSOT, as discussed in chapter two.

China, opium was accused of sapping the strength and initiative of the nation so that it lagged in education, science, technology and military effectiveness (Musto 1973). In the first decade of the twentieth century a number of factors combined to enable the reintroduction of a ban on the drug. During the nineteenth century domestically produced opium captured an increasing proportion of the Chinese market (Berridge and Edwards 1987; Musto 1973; Parssinen 1983). Together with the growth of other types of trade in India, this development translated into a reduction in the importance of opium revenue for the Indian and British administrations. Towards the end of the century the Anglo-Oriental Society for the Suppression of Opium Trade (SSOT) became more influential, securing international as well as domestic parliamentary support (Berridge and Edwards 1987; Bruun et al. 1975). In Britain, 1906 saw the Conservative party replaced in government by the Liberal party which included among its candidates a considerable number of supporters of the anti-opium cause. They wasted no time introducing a resolution declaring the Indo-Chinese opium trade 'morally indefensible' and requesting that the government 'take such steps as may be necessary for bringing it to a speedy close' (Bean 1974; Friman 1996: 7). The same resolution had been introduced in 1891 but then had been defeated. In May of 1906, however, it was supported by the government and passed unanimously. The British placed the burden of ending the trade on China. In September 1906 the Chinese government released an Imperial declaration pledging a renewed attack on the opium problem, including new restrictions on opium use and the proposal for a ten-year phased reduction of opium imports. Britain offered to abolish the trade to the extent that China decreased the cultivation of poppies and use of opium. Agreement was reached in 1907 to reduce, under inspection, both the Chinese consumption and Indian shipments of opium by 10 per cent of the export annually, so that the whole trade could end in 1917 (Bean and Wilkinson 1988; Friman 1996; Musto 1973; Rolls 1992).

There was much popular support in China for this renewed restriction. It was fuelled by anti-foreign and anti-Imperialist sentiments. This, however, was not the end of the problem (Musto 1973). Less bulky – more readily smuggled – opium derivatives like morphine and heroin began to be illegally exported to China. The large number of the Chinese population already dependent on opium provided a ready market that was hard to suppress. While Britain had entered into a bilateral agreement not to import opium to China, and by 1901 arrangements preventing direct export of morphine from Britain, the United States, France, Germany and Portugal had been secured, a loophole – transshipment – allowed smuggling to continue (Friman 1996). Drugs produced in Britain, Germany, Switzerland and the USA were shipped to China through countries which did not regulate the cargoes which passed through their ports en route to other destinations.[15] Despite various measures and agreements implemented by China, and other countries, the narcotics

---

15   These included the United States, Switzerland, France, Siberia, Turkey and particularly Japan. Japan figures conspicuously in this surreptitious trade, taking no action against transshipment, despite appeals by Chinese and United States consular authorities, until 1908. Japan's reluctance was allegedly related to its successful manufacture and export of syringes. Moreover, the Japanese saw no reason to impose restrictions on itself when China

traffic continued. At Shanghai, opium smuggled from the north and from Hong Kong was constantly being detected and seized, well into the twentieth century (Bruun et al. 1975).

Bringing China in

Only at the beginning of the twentieth century did the USA take an interest in the anti-opium movement. This was motivated by national economic interests and anti-European sentiments, as well as a growing perception of problems with the domestic consumption of morphine and opium preparations (Bean 1974; Musto 1973). During the nineteenth century, the Americans, like the British, had been active in the opium trade with China. The United States government formally withdrew support for American involvement during the 1880s. When the British had not followed suit by the early 1900s, the Americans were concerned that they were being shut out of trade with China. Adopting an anti-opium stand was seen as one way of eroding the European or Anglo-Indian domination of trade. As Taylor (1969: 329) explains, the US's interest in the opium question may be understood against the background of its China policy:

> As is well known, the object of American policy with reference to China was the *establishment and preservation* of a strong, stable and prosperous nation which would be able to *resist the encroachments of foreign powers* and at the same time provide opportunities for mutually profitable commercial relations with the West. As the opium habit was believed to be largely responsible for the political, social and economic degeneration of China, its suppression was considered indispensable to China's revivification and to the development of her commercial potential (also Bruun et al. 1975: 134; 1969: 329 emphasis added).

Paradoxically, despite the desire to promote China as a strong trading partner, Chinese living in the USA at the time received some of their worst treatment. Tension between China and the USA reached a climax over the determination of Congress to exclude Chinese labourers. Brutality in the USA against Chinese travellers and immigrants did not go unnoticed in China (Hoffman (1990) and others cited in relation to the anti-Chinese legislation referred to in Chapter 2, p.47 above). It generated a fierce response which upset the equation for calculations of national and inter-state interests. Chinese merchants protested by organising a voluntary embargo against American goods in 1906. Although not formally supported by the Chinese government, the embargo was popular and in certain trading areas effective. The growth of the embargo, and the fear of total cessation of trade, upset American traders who needed to find a market for a growing surplus of manufactured goods (Musto 1973: 30).

This conflict of interest coincided with the period of American expansion in the Far East. In 1898 the Philippines had been ceded to the USA at the conclusion of the

---

had not yet introduced its own domestic regulations against morphine (instituted only in 1909) (Friman 1996: 45).

Spanish American War (Bruun et al. 1975; Musto 1973). Opium was widely smoked by the Chinese living in the Philippines (Platt 1986). The Spanish had operated a government opium monopoly that permitted sale of the drug to this group alone. With the end of the Spanish monopoly and a cholera epidemic in 1902,[16] opium use became widespread among the indigenous population as well. A War Department Commission of Inquiry was established to assess the availability of the drug in the Philippines. In its view, opium smoking was a serious problem, and domestic legislation prohibiting the import of non-medical opium was an ineffective means for reducing what it described as an illicit trade (represented by the use of opium amongst the indigenous population). It advised that domestic legislation had to be complemented by international action (Brecher 1972; Bruun et al. 1975; Platt 1986). To this effect, Bishop Brent – the Chair of the Commission – wrote to Theodore Roosevelt urging an international meeting of representatives of the United States, other great powers with interests in the Far East, and Japan, to help China with its opium struggle. In his view, this type of action alone could shut off the flood of opium into China and make effective the opiate prohibition in the Philippines (Musto 1973: 30–1; see also Renborg 1964: 2). Roosevelt recognised this proposal as timely. It provided an opportunity to ease Chinese-American relations and challenge European domination in the Far East. As Musto explains:

> A humanitarian movement to ease the burden of opium in China would help his (Roosevelt's) long-range goals: to mollify Chinese resentment against America, put the British in a less favourable light and support Chinese antagonism against European entrenchment (1973: 30–1).

US diplomacy worked towards this end and, in February of 1909, an international opium conference opened in Shanghai with the participation of thirteen countries: Britain, America, Germany, France, Italy, Siam, Russia, Persia, Portugal, Austria-Hungary, Netherlands, China and Japan (Bean 1974; Fox and Matthews 1992). Britain, China and the USA dominated the proceedings (Chatterjee 1981). The conference ended in the adoption of nine resolutions, some of which were based on Chinese propositions, others on American or British proposals, and yet others on compromises struck between the representatives of these groups. The resolutions called for the suppression of opium smoking (no mention was made of opium eating), and the recognition of the non-medical use of opium as a matter for 'prohibition' or 'for careful regulation'. Participants, having strict laws aimed at preventing the smuggling of opium and its derivatives into their respective territories, confirmed their intention to adopt measures to prevent, at ports of departure, the shipment of opium to any country which prohibited the entry of the drug or its alkaloids, derivatives and preparations. Regulation of the manufacture, sale and distribution of morphine and other derivatives of opium was also provided for. It was proposed that each government represented in the Shanghai Commission assist every other government in the solution of its internal opium problem. And, finally, a number of resolutions specifically addressed the problems faced by China. They directed

---

16 The constipating qualities of the drug were thought to be life saving in relation to this illness.

those governments which had concessions and settlements in China, and which had been trading in opium with China, to take effective and prompt measures for the prohibition of the trade and manufacture of substances containing opium or its derivatives. While these recommendations indicated that the governments concerned should apply their own respective pharmaceutical laws to their respective subjects, in the Consular districts, Concessions and Settlements in China, they stressed the importance of having stringent pharmaceutical laws controlling the traffic in opium and allied drugs (Bean 1974; Bruun et al. 1975; Chatterjee 1981: 39; Friman 1996; Musto 1973).

The focus of the Commission was clearly on what was perceived largely as a Chinese problem. Participants – the USA and Britain, at least – saw opium smoking as a particularly Chinese practice, and other modes of consumption (like opium eating) were not regulated. The agreement to endeavour to prevent the shipment of opium to any country that prohibited it, was a response intended to address problems of the nature faced by China – that is, external interference in drug regulation – since the Indian trade in the drug began. This conclusion is only confirmed by the resolutions that directly addressed the Chinese situation. The regulation of morphine proposed by the British, and received favourably by the Americans, acknowledged growing concerns in relation to smuggling, as well as the perception of domestic drug problems in both these countries. Morphine use, in both Britain and America, was said to be increasing, even though, as Berridge and Edwards (1987) and Brecher (1972) explain, there was little empirical evidence to support these claims. The resolution, put by the Americans, that each government assist every other government in the solution of its internal opium problem provoked resistance from the British delegation which claimed that such a resolution amounted to an infringement of national sovereignty (Chatterjee 1981; Friman 1996; Musto 1973).

On reflection it seems that most of the Shanghai resolutions – as well as being directed towards the control of opium – were concerned with just this matter. They amounted to an international agreement to recognise and respect the sovereignty of China by assisting with the promotion and preservation of Chinese dominion. The agreement to endeavour to prevent the shipment of opium and its derivatives to any country that prohibited it (as China did), along with those resolutions formulated specifically in relation to problems faced by the Chinese, and relating to diplomatic behaviour in Chinese territories, support such an interpretation. In short, the Shanghai resolutions amounted to an expression of international commitment to non-intervention in Chinese governance, and mutual respect of Chinese dominion, of a similar nature to that described by Hirst and Thompson (1996) and Hindess (2000b) in relation to the Treaty of Westphalia and the formation of the modern state system.

Hirst and Thompson (1996) and Hindess (2000b) argue that the modern state did not acquire its monopoly on power by its own internal efforts; rather is was the Treaty of Westphalia[17] that allocated exclusive control over populations and

---

17   With the Treaty of Westphalia, and other agreements which followed the Thirty Years War in 1648, governments ceased to support co-religionists in conflict with their own states. The mutual recognition by states of each other's sovereignty in relation to religion meant

territories. According to these authors, the capacity for sovereign domination came from without, being a function of agreements between states. It required the mutual recognition by states of each others' sovereignty, that is, the recognition that each state was the sole political authority with exclusive possession of a defined territory. The rise of the modern state as a territorially specific and politically dominant power, thus depended in part on international agreements that recognised that each state was sovereign within its territorial border, where it alone determined the nature of internal and external policies. The possibility of imposing sovereignty depended upon non-intervention from other states (or bodies). The principle of non-intervention established by the Treaty was an expression of reason of state doctrine directed at the preservation and security of the states. Westphalia recognised that this would reinforce sovereignty – the exclusive control of the territory by one principal political body (Hirst and Thompson 1996). The Treaty granted supreme political authority to territorial rulers within their domains and recognised that the maintenance of political order within the territory of a state requires that there be no significant interference of a disruptive kind by powerful outside agencies (other states or religious groups) Hindess (2000b).[18]

In sum, Hirst and Thompson (1996) and Hindess (2000b) argue that the prospects for maintenance of order within the territory of a state – and thus the opportunities for the state to practise and develop the modern arts of government – depend in a large part on the conduct of other influential states and non-state agencies. Taking this into account, the Shanghai meeting and The Hague Convention that followed it can be understood as the mutual recognition by other states of Chinese dominion or sovereignty. This had the governmental effect of constituting China as a member of the modern state system; in other words, it amounted to the induction of China into the modern system of states. This conclusion is consistent with Taylor's (1969: 109) assessment of The Hague Convention as the first conference and treaty in which China was accorded equality with other foreign states (see also Musto 1973: 256). It was the first international meeting dealing with Chinese problems in which China did not participate under threat (Taylor 1969: 79).

The International System of Control

The Shanghai Commission is commonly regarded as the starting point of international drug control (Bruun et al. 1975). Thus, international drug control was initiated in response to a specific problem in a specific area of the world – opium in China and the problems that the unrestricted import of the drug posed for that country's

---

that states were willing to forgo certain political objects in return for internal control and stability (Hirst and Thompson 1996). With autonomy from external interference, sanctioned by a mutual and international agreement, states were able to impose sovereignty on their societies. The Treaty of Westphalia and other agreements which ended the Thirty Year War in 1648 are conventionally taken to mark the emergence of a new European order of independent sovereign states.

18   This point was also made by Hobbes: for civil peace a single jurisdiction must be sovereign and absolute (in Saunders 1997).

sovereignty. The Commission had no power to make binding resolutions but lead to The Hague Convention which did. The Hague Opium Convention of 1912 was the first international convention in which an attempt was made to regulate opium and related substances. The preamble of the Convention read that it was 'Desirous of advancing a step further on the road opened by the international Commission of Shanghai of 1909' (Bean 1974: 25; Bruun et al. 1975: 11; Chatterjee 1981: 45).

Initially there was reluctance on the part of all the Shanghai participants – with the exception of the Americans and Chinese – to attend The Hague Convention (Bean 1974; Musto 1973). While there was a general interest in regulation, there was as yet no sense of urgency, and in some cases like Britain and Germany (which were large producers of morphine and other drugs) industrial concerns were at stake. The Americans engaged aggressive diplomatic persuasion to encourage attendance; eventually all of the previous delegates, with the exception of Austria-Hungary, were represented (Bean 1974). After the convention had begun, the German delegates manoeuvred a ratification procedure that prevented the convention coming into force before World War I. They protested that it was an unusual practice to frame a world convention with only twelve powers represented and that some provisions must be made for the signatures of other states. Until those states took unanimous action, the delegates argued, there was no point in any one nation acting against its own industrial or agricultural interests (Musto 1973). Hamilton Wright – one of the American delegates – retorted that 'it would seem most unusual to decide that what had been accomplished by the conference must wait for the adhesion of Powers not represented' (Chatterjee 1981: 50). Provision was made to obtain signatures for all the powers in Europe and the USA not represented at the conference by the end of 1912. Despite considerable efforts to obtain the signatures, two more conferences had to be convened in the interest of securing this end. By the second conference in July of 1913, thirty-four nations had signed leaving only twelve in abeyance. When the third Hague conference closed in June of 1914, forty-four governments had signed the convention, less than half had ratified it, and in the following five years only seven nations put it into effect (Bean 1974: 26; Bruun et al. 1975: 12; Musto 1973: 52–3). This protracted process was indicative of the difficulties of obtaining any type of agreement with regard to the control of traffic in opium and the regulation of associated drugs.

The Hague Convention consisted of six chapters, which dealt with opium (raw and prepared) and related substances (cocaine, morphine, medicinal opium, heroin, and any new derivative that could be scientifically shown to offer similar dangers), devoting a special chapter (VI) to the issue of China, giving effect to some of the Shanghai resolutions (Chatterjee 1981). It made provisions for the enactment of 'laws or regulations for the control of the production and distribution of raw opium', and for the prohibition of the export of prepared opium to countries which decree to restrict its entry (Chatterjee 1981: 46). Signatories agreed that they 'shall take measures for the gradual and effective suppression of the manufacture of, internal trade in, and use of prepared opium, with due regard to the varying circumstances of each country concerned'. The agreement also stipulated that the contracting powers 'shall use their best endeavours to adopt or cause to be adopted, measures to ensure that morphine, cocaine and their respective salts shall not be exported from their countries, possessions and colonies…', and that efforts would be made towards the limitation of manufacture, sale and use of morphine, cocaine and their respective salts, by the enactment of pharmacy laws or regulations (Chatterjee 1981: 45–8).

The text of The Hague Convention was by no means a strong one: the contracting powers agreed to 'endeavour' to control their own traffic in opium and associated substances (Renborg 1964: 3). It left the interpretation of control to the individual governments, and the regulations it called for on production and distribution were domestic rather than international. Responsibility for the enactment and form of relevant laws and regulations lay with the contracting powers. Thus the convention placed the major burden of narcotics control on domestic legislation. The matter of securing the relevant domestic legislation and regulations in some cases proved to be almost as difficult as gaining universal ratification of The Hague Opium Convention – even for countries actively involved in the promotion of regulation. Both Britain and the USA – for different reasons – resorted to supra-legal strategies, justified not necessarily by the reality, but clearly by the rhetoric, of reason of state, to achieve what was considered to be adequate control. Both these cases are discussed in more detail below.

Prohibition in Defence of the Realm

American pressure had coerced an initially unwilling Britain to attend the Shanghai Commission (Friman 1996). Berridge (1978; 1984) explains that, contrary to some historical accounts, Britain's reluctance had less to do with any potential loss of revenue from the Indian-Chinese opium trade than it did with the view that any responsibility regarding this matter was already being addressed by the Anglo-Chinese opium agreement of 1907, and no other action was necessary. Tension was evident between the British and American camps in relation to the USA's proposals for a unilateral approach. Rather than withdraw from negotiations, however, the British Secretary of State of Foreign Affairs, Sir Edward Grey, insisted that it was better to have a deciding voice within an international conference than to 'stand out alone and obstruct the convening of the proposed conference'. He called for an interdepartmental meeting to discuss the British response (Friman 1996: 9).

Indeed, a series of meetings was called to discuss the British response to the international agreements. The first was in 1911, before the initial Hague Convention. The basic details of proposed legislative changes and developments were not discussed with any great urgency. At this stage it was quite unclear what form of regulation The Hague agreement would lead to. It seemed that any resulting legislation would be little more than an extension of existing pharmacy laws which provided for professional self-regulation. Between 3 March and 7 May 1914, six meetings were held to lay down the British version of The Hague requirements (Berridge 1984). The controls proposed emphasised a continuing reliance on professional medical and pharmaceutical expertise. Those dealing with raw opium and opium prepared for smoking were more stringent than the Convention required,[19] while those dealing with medical opium, morphine and cocaine were more liberal. Proposed control of retail sales under the new system was very similar in form to the already established system of pharmaceutical self-regulation.

Opium sales had been subject to the minimal restriction, by the 1868 Pharmacy Act, of sale through a pharmacist's shop. Regulation in the early part of the twentieth century was still concerned only with availability and sale, not possession or use of the drug. The only charge which could be brought under this legislation was selling a scheduled poison which was not properly labelled. The pharmaceutical profession was under the general supervision of the Privy Council Office, and that department had the responsibility for adding new poisons to the Schedule. The main focus for control lay with the pharmacists themselves, and there was minimal state intervention. It was likely, following the meetings, that there would be no significant change to this system; the everyday retail sale and use of narcotics would not be greatly restricted. No government department was eager to take a leading role in the control over narcotic drugs. As a result, until 1914, there was no palpable urgency directed towards activities in this area. According to Berridge (1978; 1984), many civil servants were unconvinced of the necessity for further extensive legislation.

The impact of war changed all of this and the focus of narcotics policy shifted substantially. The perceived needs of the war effort allowed the passage of more stringent regulation and brought the Home Office into a central controlling position (Berridge 1978; 1984). Two issues promoted this about face: an ongoing problem with smuggling, and concerns in relation to army efficiency. Smoking opium and morphine were being smuggled to China, and cocaine to India, on British ships (Bean 1974). Clearly the unsanctioned passage of opium to China was not a new problem, but this type of movement of drugs under the emergency conditions of war became a more serious matter as well as a source of some embarrassment (Berridge 1978; Bruun et al. 1975; Friman 1996). Throughout 1915 and 1916 the volume of protests about opium smuggling grew in intensity. Pressure from anti-opiumists, their parliamentary allies and shipping companies (which were the unwilling carriers of smuggled drugs) became impossible to ignore (Berridge 1978). An interdepartmental meeting was called in June 1916 to discuss 'legislation for the strict control of traffic in opium' (Berridge 1984: 20). Malcolm Delevingne, who represented the Home Office, made a decisive stand in relation to what must have seemed like a relentless issue. He was frank and pragmatic in his analysis of the problem as well as in his proposed solution:

> The most convenient way of dealing with the question would be by regulation under the Defence of the Realm Act [DORA], which would give power to control dealings in opium etc. similar to the power which has been given to controlling dealings in war material... if this method is adopted, Regulation 51 would give the Police the necessary powers of search and seizure... (cited in Berridge 1984: 20).

He went on to admit that:

---

19   This reflected domestic concerns regarding the presence of the Chinese in London described in chapter two.

The difficulty of dealing with the question in this way is that its bearing on the 'Defence of the Realm' is neither very direct nor important ... the only alternative method would be legislation which might be difficult to get and would possibly not be regarded as uncontroversial (cited in Berridge 1984: 20).

The emergency conditions of war provided an opportunity for a supra-legal response, which positioned the Home Office more clearly in a controlling position and, at the same time, secured some of the wider aims of international narcotics control.

Growing concern in relation to drug use amongst members of the armed forces provided added impetus for the successful passage of Delevingne's proposal. This matter first arose through an infringement of the Pharmacy Act by well known London retail stores. In February of 1916, Harrods and Savory and More were fined small amounts for selling morphine and cocaine without observing proper regulations. Savory and More had advertised small packets of the drugs in handy cases in *The Times* as a 'useful present for friends at the front' (Berridge 1978: 294). This raised considerable alarm. As Sir William Glyn-Jones, Secretary of the Pharmaceutical Society and prosecuting council in the Harrods case pointed out, 'it was an exceedingly dangerous thing for a drug like morphine to be in the hands of men on active service...It might have the effect of making them sleep on duty or other serious results' (Berridge 1978: 295).[20] The selling of cocaine to soldiers on leave in Folkstone added to the sense of emergency. The problem in official eyes assumed threatening proportions (Bean 1974; Berridge 1978: 296). Fears that drug use would compromise national security led to stricter controls in the form of an Army Council Order that prohibited the supply of cocaine and other drugs to any member of the forces unless ordered by a doctor (Bean 1974). The medical reaction to this restriction was supportive. The following editorial view was published in *The Lancet*:

The order was 'yet another instance of an innovation long advocated in the years of peace being secured without controversy under the stimulus of the great war' (cited in Berridge 1978: 297).

The author urged the extension of regulation to the broader population, arguing that:

... If we wait until the war is over we shall find ourselves confined with all those pettifogging controversies and clamouring of vested interests which always put the brake on progress (cited in Berridge 1978: 297).

There was mounting pressure from an expanding array of stakeholders – the press, anti-opiumists, parliamentarians, police and army – for immediate action. In the newspapers there were demands for an absolutist response. A *Times* correspondent, in a manner reminiscent of cultural-nationalist reasoning regarding the Chinese in London, described in the last chapter, saw the so-called epidemic as a 'Hunish plot to destroy the British Empire' (Berridge 1978: 299). Sir Frances Lloyd, General Officer

---

20 This view agrees with that of J. S. Mill, who argued strongly against the prohibition of opium, except in relation to use by the armed forces (Bakalar and Grinspoon 1984).

Commanding the London District (Police) maintained that 'Special legislation is imperatively needed... Protective measures are not the less needed in the interests of the civilian population, at present gravely menaced...' (Berridge 1978: 299). The Commissioner of the Police for the Metropolis – supporting the General Officer Commanding the London District – said in a letter of 20 July 1916 that it was necessary

> To stamp out the evil now rapidly assuming huge dimensions [and that] special legislation was imperatively needed... the necessary powers may be obtained with the least possibly delay... Great as is this need, however, in my judgement protective measures are not less needed in the interests of the civilian population at present gravely menaced...I wish to urge to the utmost of my ability, that it will be of no value in any restrictive measures merely to deal with illicit sales; it is essential if the problem is to be seriously grappled with, that the unauthorised possession of the drug shall be an offence punishable at least in certain circumstances with imprisonment without the option of a fine (cited in Bean 1974: 28).

On 28 July 1916, DORA 40B came into operation. It made the possession, sale or distribution of raw and powdered opium and cocaine an offence for anyone except medical and pharmaceutical professionals. Now these drugs could only be supplied on non-repeatable prescriptions. Coinciding with the introduction of this more stringent legislation was the publication of a proclamation prohibiting the import of all opium and cocaine except under licence (Bean 1974).

In the year following the enactment of this stricter legislative control, evidence emerged that the drug crisis had been greatly over-stated. Police and court reports, together with a 1917 report on the use of cocaine in dentistry, indicated that there was little substance to claims made by the proponents of the legislation regarding the threat cocaine posed to the army or the civilian population. The committee that produced the report, initially interested in the use of cocaine by unregistered dentists, had extended its frame of reference. In questioning those involved in the drawing-up of DORA 40B, it found that there was little evidence to support its enactment (Berridge 1978: 302–3). In relation to concerns regarding the threat of cocaine to national security it concluded:

> We are unanimously of opinion that there is no evidence of any kind to show that there is any serious, or perhaps, even noticeable prevalence of the cocaine habit amongst the civilian or military population of Great Britain. There have been a certain number of cases amongst the overseas (sic) troops quartered in, or passing through, the United Kingdom, but there is hardly any trace of the practice having spread to British troops, and apart from a small number of broken down medical men, there is only very slight evidence of its existence amongst the general population (cited in Berridge 1978: 303).

Despite these revelations, DORA 40B continued in operation until the Versailles Peace Settlement passed responsibility for the supervision of international narcotics agreements to the League of Nations in 1919. Article 295 of the Settlement finally brought The Hague Convention into operation (Chatterjee 1981). This international commitment prepared the way for the 1920 Dangerous Drugs Act, the foundation of all subsequent British legislation, which simply extended the wartime controls of

DORA to a wider range of narcotic drugs – morphine and other opium preparations (Bean 1974; Berridge 1978; 1984; Parssinen 1983).

With this sequence of events, pre-war controls, established on the basis of professional self-regulation, with little government involvement, were replaced by more extensive and centralised controls. These controls, introduced under the rationale of wartime expediency, were extended and made permanent in the post-war period. War conditions had led to a degree of state intervention and stricter regulations that would have been difficult to achieve at any other time (Berridge 1978, 1984).

The post-war years were characterised by tension between medical professionals and the Home Office approach to drug control. Despite a limited recognition of the right of professional bodies to secure their own position, the Home Office remained firmly in favour of a policy that subordinated them to an absolutist approach. The grass roots of the profession thought that any increases in regulation were unnecessary. In particular, general practitioners resented the intrusion of government policy into the area of the doctor-patient relationship, particularly since the number of addicts was small, and most doctors had never even seen an addict (Berridge 1984: 25).

In 1924 the Home Office established the often cited Rolleston Committee to:

> consider and advise as to the circumstances, if any, in which the supply of morphine and heroin (including preparations containing morphine and heroin) to persons suffering from addiction to these drugs, may be regarded as medically advisable and as to the precautions which it is desirable that medical practitioners administering or prescribing morphine or heroin should adopt for the avoidance of abuse, and to suggest any administrative measures that seem expedient for securing observations of such precautions (cited in Berridge 1984: 28).

The epidemiological evidence presented in the Committee's report unambiguously led to the conclusion that addiction was a very minor problem, confined to a large extent, to the medical profession itself. Moreover, there was no reason for the disease model to be replaced, or for stricter state control (Berridge 1984). The final report concluded '[t]he condition [of addiction] must be regarded as a manifestation of disease and not a mere form of vicious indulgence...' (cited in Berridge 1984: 26). This contrasted starkly with the assumption made by Delevingne, and other Home Office notables, that the findings of the Committee would support Home Office control of drug issues. Delevingne, when initiating the Committee's investigation, had anticipated that its findings would be:

> an authoritative statement which we could use in dealing with practitioners, and to which we could refer the courts, that regular prescription of the drugs on the ground that without them the patient will suffer or even collapse... is not legitimate and cannot be recognised as medical practices... (cited in Berridge 1984: 26).

The report failed to deliver on this expectation. Indeed it had the opposite effect; it re-asserted the importance of the role of medical expertise. The Home Office was no longer in a position to demand absolutism, but rather was now seeking medical advice.

The findings of the Rolleston Committee to an extent restored an approximation of the pre-war system based on professional judgment (Bean 1974). This was possible because of the limited nature of the problem. The overtly repressive response of 1916–1924 was abandoned in part because the amount of drug use it proposed to contain was slight. British controls did not lead to small numbers of drug dependent persons – they were the result and not the cause of them (Berridge 1984). However, in the post-war years, the Home Office retained a central position in drug control, and there was a much greater degree of state intervention in relation to the use of opium than would have been possible in the past. War provided the conditions of possibility for the development of stricter drug controls. The rhetoric rather than the reality of risk to national security was harnessed as a rationale for the implementation of stricter legislation, which would shape Britain's drug legislation for years to come.

The American Case: From Harrison to McCarthy

The USA, as we have seen, both instigated and largely organised both the Shanghai Commission and The Hague Opium Convention. Why did they go to these lengths? In the literature, several motives emerge. Firstly, there was the desire of American statesmen to secure the nation's position as an international power. Added to this was the already noted objective of establishing China as a strong and prosperous state in order to provide opportunities for mutually profitable commercial relations (Taylor 1969). And finally, there was the assumption that if other nations controlled their internal growth, manufacture, and export of opium, the USA would be free from any problems associated with use, since the poppy (and the coca leaf) had never been grown in significant commercial quantities in that country (Musto 1973: 39). In short, drugs like opium and cocaine were perceived as a foreign threat to the American way of life.

The US authorities and delegates to the Shanghai Commission saw it as the responsibility of the convening nation to have exemplary laws regulating opium and its derivatives (Friman 1996; Musto 1973). While a number of cities and states had passed local ordinances and laws regulating smoking opium, and Congress had attempted to limit the importation of the prepared drug in the last quarter of the nineteenth century, the USA had no national laws limiting or prohibiting importation, sale, use or manufacture of opium (or coca leaves) and any derivatives (Brecher 1972). This situation reflected the USA's constitutional reservation of police powers to the states. Nevertheless, it was a source of embarrassment for the Commission officials who, as a result, pushed hard for the enactment of federal anti-narcotics[21] legislation before the 1909 Shanghai meeting (Brecher 1972; Musto 1973).

In the interests of expediency a fairly uncontroversial approach was pursued. The proposed bill was a combination of the form of legislation pertaining to the importation of opiates passed for the Phillipines (Brecher 1972; Musto 1973) and the standard statute used for the prevention of illegal imports. The Phillipines legislation

---

21 The term narcotic refers to the sleep inducing properties of certain drugs – like opiates. Much drug legislation does not acknowledge this and, failing to distinguish between the different properties of drugs, uses the term more generally to refer to all illicit drugs.

was modified to make it possible for citizens to import opiates other than smoking opium. It introduced no new methods of enforcement, and only the importation of opium for smoking was prohibited. The new law was actually superfluous: Section 11 of the Pure Food and Drug Act already made provision for banning any imported drug that was dangerous to the health of the people of the USA (Musto 1973: 34–5). In the eyes of the Commission participants, and their supporters, however, the established legislation was not considered sufficient to adequately demonstrate the nation's sincerity in relation to drug control in the international forum.

Following Shanghai, and with the prospect of The Hague Opium Convention, the delegates pushed for more stringent and thoroughgoing legislation for the control of opium, morphine, cocaine and the derivatives of these drugs. Hamilton Wright, who was particularly enthusiastic, drafted legislation and eventually secured agreement from Representative David Foster to introduce it to the House. The Foster Bill was designed to uncover all the traffic in opiates, cocaine, chloral hydrate and cannabis, no matter how small the amounts involved. Its focus was on sale and availability, rather than the modes of drug use. The Bill sought to control traffic through federal taxation regulations. It would require every drug dealer to register, pay a small tax, and record all transactions. The drug container would be required to carry a revenue stamp; interstate traffic would be prohibited between individuals who had not paid the tax. There were heavy penalties, and possession of drugs other than those specified in the Bill would constitute evidence for convictions (Musto 1973: 41).

While the medical and pharmaceutical professions endorsed the goal of the law, they forcefully expressed the view that it was too cumbersome: '…what we want is a simple law, one that can be enforced and will not inflict too much hardship on trade' (Musto 1973: 45). As it stood, however, the Foster Bill's uncompromising provisions posed a great threat to everyday routine and sales in the drug trade. The druggists, who were most vocal, clearly spelled out a number of requirements: provision for exemption of proprietaries (patent medicines), simple record-keeping, and softer penalties. Wright and the other delegates quickly discovered that while it was relatively easy to secure legislation to deny smoking opium for the Chinese, the regulation of opium consumption for the rest of the population would prove to be much more of a challenge (Musto 1973). The Bill was defeated. At the time of The Hague Convention other nations already had more stringent domestic legislation than the United States. Germany challenged the American delegation on its country's lack of legislation, making it into a matter of international embarrassment (Musto 1973: 51).

After the first Hague Convention the matter became increasingly urgent, particularly if American diplomatic efforts in this area were to retain any credibility in relation to drug control. Nevertheless, meaningful federal control continued to prove difficult to secure. In 1912, Francis Burton Harrison agreed to shepherd anti-narcotics legislation through the House of Representatives. The first Harrison Bill did not differ greatly from the previously defeated Foster Bill of 1910. It contained no provision for exempting small amounts of narcotics in patent medicines. Revenue stamps, record keeping and various details such as bonds, licence fees and severe penalties were also retained. The professional and trade response again was unenthusiastic; the Bill, as far as they were concerned, was still too complex (Musto

1973). Representative Harrison, being more concerned with the political viability, than the specific form or philosophy of the legislation, was prepared to negotiate. The final Bill to go before the House incorporated many compromises. Record-keeping procedures were simplified and numerous patent medicines containing less than permitted amounts of morphine, cocaine, opium and heroin could continue to be sold by mail order and in general stores. Everyone dealing in narcotics, except the consumer, would have to be registered. Retail dealers or practising physicians could obtain a tax stamp for one dollar a year. No bond was required and chloral hydrate and cannabis were not included (Musto 1973: 59). In December of 1914 the Bill was passed and the USA had, in the minds of state officials at least, fulfilled its international obligations.

On 1 March 1915 the Harrison Act came into operation. Its enforcement was assigned to the Bureau of Internal Revenue of the Treasury Department. This, however, was not the end of the matter; for at least the next thirteen years the Act remained controversial (Ashely 1972; Musto 1973). To begin with there was considerable disagreement about how the Act would work. Conflict arose over whether the Act opened the way for the extension of federal police powers into the control of drug use itself and the regulation of medical and pharmaceutical practices; or whether it was simply an information collecting device that left the policing of drug use and professional practices to the states. The original proponents of the Harrison Bill had said little about this matter in the congressional debates. They had focused more on the need to implement The Hague Convention of 1912 (Brecher 1972). On its face, the Act was merely a law for the orderly marketing of opium, morphine, heroin, and other drugs – in small quantities over the counter, and in larger quantities on physician's prescription. The right of the physician to prescribe seemed to be specifically protected in unambiguous terms:

> Nothing contained in this section shall apply... to the dispensing or distribution of any of the aforesaid drugs to a patient by a physician, dentist or veterinary surgeon registered under this Act *in the course of his professional practice only* (Harrison Act 1914 cited in Brecher 1972: 49).

It did not appear to be a prohibition law. Registered professionals were required only to keep records of drugs prescribed or dispensed. However, as Nikolas Rose and Peter Miller so cogently remind us, 'government is a congenitally failing operation: the sublime image of a perfect regulatory machine is internal to the mind of the programmers'. Moreover, '[t]he world of programmes is heterogeneous, and rivalrous. ...[and] techniques invented for one purpose may find their governmental role for another...' (Rose and Miller 1992: 190–1).

In January of 1915 the Treasury Department promulgated regulations for the enforcement of the Harrison Act. A number of these addressed sensitive professional and trade issues. They made the Act much more demanding than the professional groups had expected. Registered professionals became the only source of supply, and detailed record keeping provisions indicating the number of prescriptions and the amount of narcotics sold by doctors, made it possible to monitor and discipline prescribing and dispensing practices. There were heavy penalties for errors or omissions, and the regulations drew a distinction between a normal dose and maintenance supply (Brecher 1972; Musto 1973). Druggists were instructed to examine each narcotics prescription submitted to determine whether it was forged or had been altered, but also in order to provide some review of the prescribing practices of physicians. On this last point a druggist from Montana complained to the Attorney General that having technically correct prescriptions for six users 'the revenue agents who are neither lawyers nor physicians tell me that these prescriptions are in excessive amounts' and since the prescribing physician insists that the doses are not excessive for the users, the druggist was placed 'in an anomalous position'. The Attorney General's reply predicted that this aspect of the Harrison Act 'was a proper matter for the determination of the judiciary' (Musto 1973: 123).

The Treasury Department attempted to rectify this problem with the introduction of specific regulations dealing with prescriptions for unusually large quantities. The new requirements stipulated that in such cases the medical professional should indicate on the prescription the purpose for which the drug is to be used, and '[i]n cases of the treatment of addicts the prescriptions should show the *good faith* of the physician *in the legitimate practice* of his profession by decreasing dosage or reduction of the quantity prescribed from time to time' (Musto 1973: 123). As Musto (1973) explains, this regulation was based on particular assumptions about what should be regarded as the legitimate practice of medicine; something which in the eyes of the Treasury Department, clearly did not include maintenance prescribing (see also Brecher 1972). It was through phrases like 'good faith' and 'in the legitimate practice of medicine' in this regulation and 'in the course of his professional practice only' in the words of the Harrison Act proper, that the Bureau of Internal Revenue sought to regulate the practice of medicine. Its particular concern was to prohibit prescribing to an addict with the intention of maintaining an addiction (Ashely 1972; Musto 1973).[22]

The judiciary had trouble with the Treasury Department's interpretation of the Act; that is, with the assertion that registered physicians could not prescribe as they wished, to anyone they wished. The Federal Court's assessment of this attempt by the Treasury to prohibit maintenance prescribing was that any federal regulation of medical practice was unconstitutional (Ashely 1972; Musto 1973). Numerous district judges expressed this view in the first few months of enforcement.[23] The Act was interpreted by the lower court as strictly a revenue Act. If it was used to address matters other than revenue and interstate commerce powers it could violate

---

22 Brecher (1972: 50) explains that the prosecution of registered physicians rested on the assumption that maintenance of addiction was illegitimate medical practice and could not be conducted in good faith. Addiction was not a disease; so the argument went, therefore, that the addict was not a patient, and opiates dispensed or prescribed for him or her by the physician were not being supplied 'in the course of his professional practice'. Thus a law apparently intended to ensure the orderly marketing and regulation of the distribution of narcotics was transformed into a law prohibiting the supply of certain drugs to addicts, even from a physician's prescription, in effect closing off the only legitimate source of drugs.

23 Musto (1973:297) cites Montana: *US v Woods*, 224 Fed Rep 278 (3 July 1915), Pennsylvania: *US v Jin Fuey Moy*, 225, Fed Rep 10003 (13 May 1915) and Tennessee: *US v Friedman*, 224 Fed Rep 276 (1 June 1915).

the provisions of the Constitution. It would be unconstitutional were the federal government to attempt to regulate directly the practice of medicine or to assume powers reserved for the states (Musto 1973: 129). In June of 1916 a Supreme Court decision of seven to two in the *US v Jin Feuy Moy* case confirmed the position taken by the lower courts with regard to the legality of directly prosecuting the maintenance physician. It upheld the view that a written prescription by a registered physician absolutely protected the physician from a charge of violating the Act, regardless of the quantities of the drug involved (Musto 1973).

Within the next few years this decision was to be overturned and the sentiments of the judiciary appeared to shift. In 1919 the strict interpretation of the Harrison Act was reinstated by the Supreme Court in two crucial cases. The first, *US v Doremes*, confirmed the constitutionality of the Harrison Act tax on physicians and concomitant control of the manner in which drugs could be dispensed. The second case, *US v Webb*, found, in effect, that legitimate practice of medicine did not include the maintenance of addicts (Musto 1973: 132). In 1922 the findings of *US v Behrman* reaffirmed this position (Musto 1973: 185). However, between 1922 and 1925, the opponents of federal control of narcotics in medical practice won a number of victories. Several Supreme Court decisions (*Linder v US* (1925), and *Starnes v US* (1922) in particular) seemed to reverse the trend towards control of the practitioner's judgment in narcotic use. In January of 1926 the Supreme Court (in *US v Daugherty*) declared that recent decisions 'may necessitate the review of that question [the Act's constitutionality] if here after properly presented' (Musto 1973: 186).

Thus, the Court took the unusual step of inviting a new test of constitutionality of the Harrison Act. The test case was granted and in April of 1928 the Supreme Court, in *Nigro v US*, held by a six to three decision that the Act was indeed constitutional. This judgment was significant because, in effect, it changed the legitimate limits of state intervention. The decision to uphold the more stringent interpretation of the law – which the Courts (District and Supreme) along with the United States Attorney's Office had initially opposed – in effect, established an absolutist response to the regulation of opiates. This repressive interpretation of 'legitimate medical purposes' by the Treasury Department and the Courts effectively usurped the role of the medical professional in the regulation of narcotic drug use.

Musto (1973: 133–4) suggests that this shift in judicial opinion that occurred towards the end of the teens and in the early twenties of last century must be understood in historical context; in particular, in the context of America's entry into World War I, and also in the light of what came to be known as the Red Scare of 1919–1920.[24] Having already been defined by most Americans as immoral, or at least a cause of wasted lives, addiction was, by 1918, perceived as a threat to the national war effort. It was feared that servicemen would become addicted by 'pushers' at the instigation of disloyal elements or spies at home, or through the use of morphine and heroin on the battlefield (1973: 115). Any action that could be interpreted as support for the enemies of the USA was punished severely. Indulgence in narcotics was officially described as leading to anti-social acts and individual degeneracy; it

---

24   Following World War I there was, in America, an enormous fear of Bolsheviks and anarchists; this is referred to as the Red Scare of 1919–1920 (Musto 1973).

weakened the nation and was associated with un-American influences, which would destroy the bonds of society.

The popular conception of the threat posed by narcotics to the war effort, and hence national security, was also expressed in bureaucratic circles. While it did not result in the enactment of special regulations, as was the case in Britain, it did have an effect on the formation of legislative controls. In 1918 the Treasury Department set up a special narcotics committee to study the problem of control and to recommend changes to the law and its administration; more explicitly, it was concerned with addressing the Court decisions finding against the Department's position. In this context, World War I was used as leverage to argue for the restraint of drug use and the regulation of national habits (see *US v Daugherty* in Musto 1973:135). Daniel C. Roper, the Commissioner of Internal Revenue, who had initiated the establishment of the committee, emphasised the need for such action in view of the war emergency. The Public Health Service agreed with this logic, reasoning that 'any work aiming at the reduction of the large number of addicts in this country is intimately connected to the official prosecution of the war' (cited in Musto 1973: 300 note 35). The special committee's report exaggerated the magnitude of the problem, dramatically overstating the estimated number of addicts in the country at that time. In doing so it alluded to the threat that 1,000,000 addicts could pose to national security (Musto 1973: 138–9). Towards the end of 1918 amendments to the Harrison Act to reinforce the Treasury Department's position were proposed and passed quickly through Congress. They came into effect on 24 February 1919. There were no hearings on these changes, and thus no chance for debate. Representative Rainy (who had acted as the Chairman of the Treasury Department's Special Narcotic Committee) feared that hearings would enable industry representatives to argue for changes, which would undermine the law's effectiveness. He defended this absence of due legislative process by arguing that 'there was too much urgent business for such activity in wartime' (Musto 1973: 136). At about the same time the rejection of 8,000 draft-age addicts in New York City prompted a campaign to rid the nation of the 'dope menace' (Musto 1973: 142). In May of 1919 the Mayor of New York established a Committee on Public Safety to review two related problems: the heroin epidemic among young people, and the bombings by revolutionaries (Musto 1973: 134).

The Harrison Act was a controversial piece of legislation, which within a short time of its enactment, was found by the judiciary to be unconstitutional. This decision (again within a relatively short period of time) was reversed, and as a result, federal enforcement bodies gained unprecedented powers that overrode the constitutional reservation of police jurisdiction to the states. In addition, these powers provided for the regulation of medical and pharmaceutical professional practices by Internal Revenue agents who were 'neither lawyers nor physicians'. As was the case in Britain, the process of gaining support for stricter drug control was secured under wartime conditions which provided for the possibility of an appeal to nationalistic concerns in relation to the *preservation* of the state.

The Cold War on Drugs

The perception that narcotics posed a significant threat to the security and sovereignty of the nation did not disappear as the memory of World War I faded, nor was it dispelled in confident belief that the Harrison Act, now sufficiently rigorous, could protect the USA from all manner of dangers posed by drugs. This fear was called into service in the context of later wars, and was to persist well into the twentieth century. In 1951, following World War II, in an emotional atmosphere similar to the years of the Red Scare, the Boggs Bill was passed introducing minimum mandatory sentencing for first drug convictions. This was the beginning of the McCarthy era, characterised by fears of Soviet aggression, concern over the 'betrayal' of China to the Communists, and suspicion of domestic groups and persons who seemed to threaten to overthrow the government. It was not long before narcotics came to be directly associated with the Communist conspiracy (Musto 1973: 231). The Federal Bureau of Narcotics (FBN) linked Red China's attempt to get hard cash, as well as to destroy Western society, to the clandestine sale of large amounts of heroin to drug pushers in the United States.

Throughout the 1950s the Bureau maintained that the main source of heroin available in the USA was Communist China. This view was readily accepted by the administration of the day. A Senate report *The Illicit Narcotic Traffic* (1956) stated that 'subversion through drug addiction is an established aim of Communist China' and that American civilians and military were prime targets (Musto 1973: 331).[25] In 1960 the USA claimed that the principal sources of heroin seized in that country were Hong Kong, Mexico and Communist China. Up until 1964 American representatives continually complained to the United Nations that heroin from the Chinese mainland was being smuggled into the country as part of Red China's 'twenty year plan to finance political activities and spread addiction' (Ashely 1972: 11).[26] The United Nations Commission on Narcotic Drugs, however, noted that there was no evidence that Communist China was exporting opiates, and that the '999' brand of morphine the FBN called 'Red Chinese' was, in fact, delivered by Nationalist Chinese troops from stocks in Burma and Northern Thailand (Ashely 1972: 11–12. To appreciate the complexities of this situation see the discussion below).

The fear of Communism and the Cold War has played a significant role in America's response to the regulation of narcotics. This response, however, has not always been consistent. In the late 1940s, when Soviet troops occupied Eastern Europe and China's Communist revolutionaries seized power, America's post-war leaders were faced with the threat of global Communist expansion. The Truman administration's 'secret' weapon in this global war was the Central Intelligence Agency (CIA). The CIA was established in 1947 by the National Security Act. This

---

25   Senate Report No. 1440, 84th Cong., 2nd Sess., 1956 (cited in Musto, 1973: 331). See also Anslinger and Gregory (1961), *The Protectors*, New York: Farrar, Straus and Co, 223; and Anslinger and Tompkins (1953), *Traffic in Narcotics*, 69–116.

26   United Nations Commission on Narcotic Drugs, Report of the Ninth Session (1954) E/CN 7/283, 22, United Nations Commission on Narcotic Drugs Report of the Fifteenth Session, (1960) E/CN.7/395, 18 (cited in Ashley 1972: 11).

Act contained a single clause allowing the new agency to perform 'other functions and duties' that the President might direct; this clause in effect, provided the legal authority for the CIA's covert operatives to break any law in pursuit of their objects (McCoy 1991). Furthermore, according to McCoy (1991: 18), this vague clause was the foundation for the CIA covert action ethos that repeatedly encouraged alliances with drug lords for over four decades. As the vanguard of America's global anti-Communist campaign, the CIA practised a *radical pragmatism*, with its agents making alliances with any local group, drug merchants included, capable of countering Communist influence. It seems that Communism was perceived as a far greater threat to the nation than heroin or cocaine. A review of the history of post-war traffic reveals a repetitious coincidence between CIA covert action and the activities of major drug dealers. McCoy (1991) describes the CIA's recurring role in the protection and expansion of global drug traffic.[27] A brief outline of his claims demonstrates the multiplicity of ways that reason of state rationalities can be, and have been, mobilised in the context of drug control.

In the 1940s, determined to restrict Soviet influence in Western Europe, American CIA operatives intervened in the internal politics of Italy and France. Between 1948 and 1950 the CIA allied itself with the Corsican underworld in its struggle against the French Communist party for control over the strategic Mediterranean port of Marseilles. With CIA support, the Corsicans overcame their rival, and for the next twenty-five years used their control of the Marseilles waterfront to dominate the export of heroin to the American market. At the same time, the CIA ran a series of secret operations in South East Asia. These were instrumental in the creation of the Golden Triangle. In 1951 it supported the formation of a Nationalist Chinese army for a covert invasion of South-Western China. When the invasion failed in 1951-1952, the CIA installed the Nationalist troops along the Burma-China border; the Nationalist Army transformed Burma's Shan states into the world's largest opium producer (McCoy 1991).[28]

Using the same approach in Laos from 1960 to 1975, the CIA created a secret army of 300,000 Hmong tribesmen to battle Loatian Communists near the border with North Vietnam. The Hmong's main cash crop was opium and the CIA adopted a complicit posture towards the traffic. The Hmong Commander, General Van Pao, used the CIA's Air America[29] to collect opium from his scattered highland villages. In late 1969 the CIA's various covert action allies opened a network of heroin laboratories in the Golden Triangle. In their first years of operation these laboratories exported high-grade heroin to American troops fighting in Vietnam. After their withdrawal the

---

27 McCoy (1991) notes that CIA covert operations in key drug producing areas have repeatedly blocked or restrained Drug Enforcement Agency (DEA) efforts to deal with the problem. As a result America's drug policy has been effectively crippled by this contradiction.

28 These are the same Nationalist Chinese troops that produced the '999' brand of morphine the FBN complained about (p.76 above).

29 Air America was popularly referred to by the Special Forces as 'Air Opium' (Ashley 1972: 15).

laboratories exported directly to the USA capturing one-third of the American heroin market (McCoy 1991).

The involvement of American personnel in the South-East Asian drug trade was no secret. Ashely (1972: 13) explains, for example, that it has been well documented in a number of articles and books. He cites P. D. Scott's article 'Heroin traffic: Some amazing coincidences' published in the March 1972 volume of *Earth*, noting the useful nature of the article's bibliography with regards to the matter. He also refers to a number of pertinent newspaper articles including the *New York Times* report, on 17 May 1972, that:

> United States Special Forces, or Green Berets, and the CIA, were up to here in the traffic – for, to be sure, political reasons. Green Berets were ordered to buy certain supplies of opium in order to make and maintain staunch allies among the growers cum guerrillas (1972: 13).

Ashely also cites an article in the *New York Post*, on 2 June 1972, which explained that the government's involvement resulted from its concern with the war in Indochina, and the related desire to establish loyalty with high officials in Vietnam, Thailand, Laos and Cambodia, and 'if this meant the continued production of opium in these sensitive areas...it was all right with the US' (1972: 14). Indeed the first edition of McCoy's work (cited above) focused on Southeast Asia and was published in 1972.

During the 1980s the CIA's two main covert action operations again became interwoven with the global narcotics trade (McCoy 1991). Nowadays it is common knowledge that the CIA (and the Pakistan intelligence service) played a direct role in funnelling weapons and money to 'freedom fighters' – the Afghan Mujahideen – struggling against the Soviets, as well as at least an indirect role in the local growing trade in narcotics (Chouvy 2004b). The agency's support for Afghan guerrillas through Pakistan coincided with the emergence of Southern Asia as the major heroin supplier for European and American markets. In this context, a substantial force of Drug Enforcement Agency (DEA) operatives posted in Islamabad during the 1980s were restrained by United States national security imperatives. Closer to home, CIA support for the Nicaraguan Contras linked the agency with the Caribbean cocaine trade. Many of the CIA covert agents named in the Contra operations had been associated with the Loatian secret war (Dobinson 1994; McCoy 1991).

More recently in Afghanistan the USA largely condoned opiate production both in areas traditionally controlled by the Northern Alliance and in areas held by local commanders whose support was deemed strategically necessary to fight the Taliban and Al-Qaeda. Pierre-Arnaud Chouvy (2004a; 2004b) explains that before 2003 when opium was denounced as the greatest threat to Afghanistan's stability, peace and forthcoming democracy, the USA was less interested in waging the 'war on drugs' than in using drug trafficking and affiliated warlords as allies to support its short-term Afghan strategy. In doing so, the USA re-enacted a strategy largely used during the Cold war. Had the USA cracked down on opium production and drug traffickers during its new war on terrorism in Afghanistan, it would have alienated intelligence sources and strategic allies in that country. Pursuing and arresting Al-Qaeda and Taliban leaders was of more political and strategic value than dealing with the drug economy. Renewed drug production is now, however, denounced as being a major threat to the fostering of democracy and stability. Indeed, the trade is increasing the wealth and power of local warlords – many of them former allies of the US-led war on terrorism – who are reluctant to submit themselves to the authority of a central government that they do not always recognise as legitimate or independent of foreign influence (Chouvy 2004a).

Representatives of the USA called for and organised the Shanghai Commission and The Hague Opium Convention in order to secure that nation's position as an international power, to prevent it from being closed out of international trade and to establish China as a market for a burgeoning surplus of manufactured goods. It is possible to argue that this action, at the beginning of the twentieth century, was aimed at the *preservation* of America's position within the system of modern states. In this context Bishop Brent's call for an international meeting was indeed timely in relation to America's needs. The realisation of such a meeting required a considerable amount of diplomatic determination. Obtaining binding international agreement in relation to the regulation of opium proved difficult, and, for the convening nation, demonstrating domestic commitment was no easier. The latter involved the enactment of legislation that overturned constitutional proprieties and provided for the unprecedented regulation of medical and pharmaceutical professional practice by federal enforcement agencies. Although the judiciary were quick to declare such legislation unconstitutional, this decision was reversed in the context of wartime conditions and the mobilisation of fears for national security. In later years the same fears – manifest in the alleged link between heroin and the communist conspiracy to destroy America and Western society – provided the rationality for stricter legislative controls.

Paradoxically, the concern for the preservation of the (United) State(s) justified American military involvement in drug traffic that amounted to intervention in the internal affairs of other states. As has been explained, the Westphalian principle of non-intervention remains to this day an important prerequisite for the political order of a state (Hindess 2000b). It involves a set of prudential constraints designed to limit the spread of conflict. States are enjoined to refrain from interference in the affairs of another state of a kind that is likely to provoke retaliation from the state directly, or to threaten the interests of influential third parties. States are also enjoined to refrain from supporting one party in an internal conflict if such support entails sufficient risk that the conflict might spread to other populations. However, a caveat is in order. Whilst it is clear that the maintenance of political order within the territory of a state requires that, as a general rule, there be no significant interference of a disruptive kind by powerful outside agencies (including other states) we do well to remind ourselves that this is a normative condition which few states, if any, have ever been able to guarantee for themselves (Hindess 2000b). William Robinson presents case studies of American programs aimed at influencing the internal affairs of states in various parts of the world – both during and after the Cold War (in Hindess 2000b). While in the later years of this period, many of these programs have been presented in the guise of advancing the cause of democracy, Robinson's discussion shows that they can be seen as part of a more general policy designed to stabilise or promote the formation of regimes of which America, approved and to destabilise regimes, democratic or otherwise, of which it did not approve. The discussion above lends support to Robinson's claims. For example, during the late nineteenth century and early twentieth century the aim was to establish China as a viable trading partner through the suppression of the opium trade, while later military support of opium production and distribution was justified as a means to promote anti-Communist regimes. It also tends to demonstrate that the representatives of the USA have generally perceived the threat to the nation as emanating from external sources: Chinese men in America, opium from China, Bolshevik or Communist conspiracies. With this in mind, intervention in the affairs of other states as well as the participation in the illegal drug trade could be justified in terms of self- or state-preservation.

Contemporary Rationalities of Regulation: The International Treaties

Hindess (2000b) makes another point that bears relevance to the discussion here. He argues that while it is useful to understand the internal as well as the external dynamics involved in the constitution of modern states and the possibility of maintaining internal political order, it is also important not to ignore the relationships between states and the governmental character of the system of states itself. With regard to the regulation of the supply of opium and other drugs, the relationship between the states has been ordered, since the Shanghai Commission, by a series of agreements, treaties and protocols. With the implementation of The Hague Opium Convention as part of the Versailles Peace Settlement, these arrangements came to be managed under the umbrella of more formalised relationships between states described initially by the League of Nations and, after World War II, the United Nations. Today opioids are included in the schedules to the United Nations (UN) international treaties that regulate the manufacture, supply, distribution, possession and use of narcotic drugs – principally the 1961 *Single Convention on Narcotic Drugs* (as amended by the 1972 protocol) and the 1988 *United Nations Convention against Illicit Traffic in Narcotic Drugs and Psychotropic Substances*.

Bruun et al. (1975) argue that the aims of the international drug treaties may be inferred from the preambles of the respective documents. Indeed, an examination of these texts is pertinent in the context of the argument outlined here. In 1961 *The Single Convention on Narcotic Drugs* was adopted to consolidate the considerable number of international treaties, protocols and agreements that had arisen since that first meeting in Shanghai (Bean 1974; Platt 1986). Its preamble identifies the convention's objective as the 'health and welfare of mankind'. While acknowledging the value of narcotic drugs in the medical treatment of 'pain and suffering', it is concerned with the 'duty' of 'preventing and combating' addiction to narcotic drugs which 'constitutes a serious evil for the individual and is fraught with social and economic danger to mankind'. It determines that parties should adopt *any special measures* of control which are necessary having regard to the particularly dangerous properties of narcotic drugs covered by the treaty. Furthermore, 'a party shall, if in its opinion, the prevailing conditions in its country render it the most appropriate means of protecting the public health and welfare, prohibit the production, manufacture, export and import of, trade in, possession or use of any such drug except for amounts which may be necessary for medical and scientific research only' (United Nations 1961 Article 2). Article 4 repeats these aims in describing the general obligations of parties. It requires parties to take such legislative and administrative measures as may be necessary to give effect to and carry out the provisions of the Convention within their own territories, to cooperate with other states in the execution of the provisions of the Convention, and to limit exclusively to medical and scientific purposes the production, manufacture, export, import, distribution of, trade in, use and possession of scheduled drugs.

In 1988 the Single Convention was strengthened by the *United Nations Convention against Illicit Traffic in Narcotic Drugs and Psychotropic Substances*. According to the later treaty's preamble, parties to this agreement express their concern with the 'magnitude of and rising trend in the illicit production of, demand for and traffic in narcotic drugs and psychotropic substances, which pose a serious threat to the health and welfare of human beings and adversely affect the economic, cultural and political foundations of society'. They recognise the 'links between illicit traffic and other related organised criminal activities which undermine the legitimate economies and *threaten the stability, security and sovereignty of States*'. Parties further acknowledge that 'illicit traffic generates large profits and wealth enabling transnational criminal organisations to penetrate, *contaminate and corrupt the structures of government*, legitimate commercial and financial business, and society at all its levels' (United Nations 1988). The Convention highlights the importance of strengthening effective legal means for international cooperation in the matter of suppressing the international criminal activities of illicit trafficking. Its explicit purpose is to promote cooperation among parties enabling them to more effectively address various aspects of illicit traffic in narcotic drugs and psychotropic substances, promoting control from an international dimension. In accordance with this end it obliges parties to adopt measures (in the form of administrative protocols and domestic legislation) criminalising the intentional 'production, manufacture, extraction, preparation, offering, offering for sale, distribution, sale, delivery on any terms whatsoever, brokerage, dispatch, dispatch in transit, transport, importation or export of any narcotic drug or any psychotropic substance contrary to the provisions of the 1961 Convention, and the 1961 Convention as amended or the 1971 Convention', the cultivation of prohibited plants (United Nations 1988 Article 3, paragraph 1); as well as the intentional possession, purchase or cultivation of narcotic drugs or psychotropic substances for personal consumption contrary to the provisions of the 1961 Convention, and the 1961 Convention as amended or the 1971 Convention (United Nations 1988 Article 3, paragraph 2).

The political rationalities expressed in each of these conventions are concerned with protecting the health and wellbeing of populations and the stability, security and sovereignty of states. The 1961 Convention is concerned with combating the danger posed by the problem of addiction to the individual and to 'mankind' (sic), and 'protecting' the public 'health and welfare' from the serious evils and 'particular dangerous properties' of the drugs covered by the treaty. In addition, it determines that parties should adopt any *special measure* for the control of these substances, and provides for their *absolute* prohibition (Article 2, 1961 emphasis added). This provides for the implementation of measures which may override the 'rules of justice or constitutional proprieties' – that is, extra-legal measures – in the interests of state preservation (see p.54 above). The same concerns are sustained in the 1988 treaty which expresses the need to address the 'serious threat' posed by the 'illicit production of, demand for and traffic in narcotic substances' to the health and welfare of human beings, and the 'dangers' to the economic, cultural and political foundations of society. Parties to this treaty acknowledge that such traffic undermines legitimate economies, and 'threatens the stability, security and sovereignty of states'.

The terms of these treaties clearly refer to multiple governmental trajectories that are expressed in the rationalities that found them. Both conventions are concerned with the health and wellbeing of the population and the security and sovereignty of states, in other words, good government of populations and the preservation of states. These treaties are the basis of drug legislation throughout the world; for example, the 1961 Single Convention was originally adopted by more than sixty governments – in 2005 there were 180 (United Nations Office of Drug Control 2007). The specificities of the treaties, along with the nature of the relations that they work to constitute between member states, are the subject of the next chapter. At this point it is sufficient to recognise that they are the product of the complex of material conditions and relationships that came before them.

Conclusion

This chapter has outlined a genealogy of the problematisation of the international supply of opium and its derivatives. Identifying reason of state as a concern expressed in the context of the early regulatory debates and cultural consciousness in Great Britain, it has traced how, over the last two to three hundred years, this rationality had been a recurring theme in the context of various struggles and tensions arising in relation to the trade and supply of opium. The value of such a history of the regulation of opium is that it does not describe, as some might imagine, a teleological march of progress towards tighter control which reduces regulation to the result of disinterested rational or scientific evaluation of the allegedly dangerous properties of the drug – indeed it reveals that at times it was the rhetoric of danger rather than any immanent threat that impelled particular strategic interventions. For example, in Great Britain, police and court reports together with the 1917 report on the use of cocaine in dentistry, indicated that there was little substance to claims made by the proponents of the 1916 DORA 40B regarding the threat that drugs posed for the army or the civilian population. Similarly, the United Nations Commission on Narcotic Drugs found that there was no evidence to support America's claims that during the 1950s and 1960s Communist China was exporting opiates into the country as part of a plot to overthrow 'Western society'. Nevertheless, in England and the USA respectively, such arguments, which hinged on appeals to the preservation of the nation, had been pragmatically mobilised in securing stricter domestic legislation.

The historical analysis above has allowed us to recognise the specific conditions that gave rise to and shaped the contemporary system for the regulation of the supply of opioids. In doing so it worked to highlight the complexity as well as the contingency of the relationships that contributed to eventuality of control. For instance, at the beginning of the twentieth century, the coincidence of a change in British political will, renewed Chinese efforts to suppress the trade and America's acquisition of the Philippines (and the problem of opium smoking in that territory) provided the opportunity for President Roosevelt to instigate an international forum to discuss the problems that the opium trade created for China. Through this initiative, the USA promoted the prohibition of trade in order to reinforce Chinese sovereignty in the interest of securing a useful trade partner – to protect the USA and reinforce the prohibition in the Philippines and to secure a position as an international power (that is, to establish the USA as a particular type of state). The meeting was held in 1909 at Shanghai, and initiated the international system for the control of opium that was to develop over the twentieth century. The Shanghai Commission did not produce a binding international commitment. Yet it achieved a result which was if anything more radical and momentous in it implications. The Commission inaugurated the mutual recognition of the threat posed by the opium trade to the national sovereignty of China, and a commitment in principle to the non-intervention in Chinese affairs by participating states. The governmental effect of this was the constitution of China as a member of the modern state system. While the Shanghai meeting was a commission which gathered facts in relation to the use and trade of the drug, and not a convention which could produce a binding commitment for its participants, it nevertheless led to The Hague Convention – the first of a string of international conventions – which did.

By remaining open to the dispersion of historical transformations, our genealogy is able to accommodate the mutation of events – the invasion and even reversal of historical pathways. In both Britain and America, tension emerged in the wake of the enactment of DORA 40B and the Harrison Act respectively, regarding the distribution of power and authority in relation to the control of opium. In both cases legislation involved strengthening the capacity of the state – through various forms of police – to intervene in the professional practice of medicine. Concerns that subsequently emerged with regard to this shift in authority were addressed by the Rolleston Committee, in Britain, and through a series of Supreme Court test cases in the USA. The divergent outcomes of these two situations were – as we have seen – hotly contested and in no way self-evidently assured by some transcendent rationality. Indeed Delevingne did not anticipate that the Rolleston Committee would fail to provide the style of 'authoritative statement' he desired (see p.69 above). Alternatively, America's seemingly contradictory alliances with opium lords, and apparent participation in the drug trade, become intelligible from a perspective that is able to accommodate a dispersion of historical transformations along with multiple temporalities. Seen from this standpoint (and in relation to the political rationality of reason of state), it is quite possible for the US administration to work to suppress the drug trade in order to protect its citizens from a perceived external enemy or threat – while at the same time supporting and promoting the production of opium in order to strengthen alliances with those who apparently share a common enemy.

In the concluding section of this chapter I described the working out of an amalgam of governmental concerns with the health and wellbeing of the population and reason of state rationality in the international treaties. This brings together the analysis conducted in the first half of the book demonstrating why it was important to begin with an investigation of the conditions of possibility for the regulation of opium and its transformation from an everyday, if sometimes problematic, commodity, to the enemy of nation states. The articulation of this amalgam of governmental concerns in the contemporary instruments of the international regulatory system pays unambiguous testament to the utility of this history of the present and, in particular, to the view that the present reflects a conjunction of elements inherited from the past with current motivations. This is by no means to suggest that the past simply repeats itself, but rather acknowledges that our contemporary problems and practices, while quite distinct from those of the past, were constructed out of materials and situations which existed at earlier points in time.

Chapter 4

An Ungoverned Domain

Rose and Miller propose that the problematics of government can be analysed 'in terms of their political rationalities – the changing discursive fields within which the exercise of power is conceptualised, the moral justifications or particular ways of exercising power by diverse authorities, notions of the appropriate forms, objects and limits of politics and conceptions of the proper distribution of such tasks among secular, spiritual, military and familial sectors' (1992: 175). The first part of this book has described how opium and its derivatives became a problem of government. It traced the expression of this problematisation in terms of the health and wellbeing of populations and subsequently the security and sovereignty of nation states. It concluded that an amalgam of these concerns is expressed in the international treaties that currently regulate the production, manufacture, supply, distribution and use of such drugs throughout the world. In this chapter the international drug control treaties themselves are the subject of analysis. This type of examination is important to bring into focus not only the systems of thought which various authorities have used to pose and specify the problem of opium, but also the systems of action which they have used to give effect to the government of this drug. Rose and Miller go on to suggest that the problematics of government should be analysed not only in terms of their political rationalities but also in terms of their governmental technologies: 'the complex of mundane program calculations, techniques, apparatuses, documents and procedures through which authorities seek to embody and give effect to governmental ambitions' (1992: 175). This idea provides the guiding principle of the discussion below.

The purpose of the work carried out in relation to the treaties is not the discovery of hidden meanings or disguised authoritative intent in the language of the documents. Nor is the objective to describe a field of institutions, of structures or functional arrangements. Rather it is to continue to trace the lines of thought, of will, of invention, of progress and failures of actions and counteractions; it is to see the way in which the language of the treaties functions in connection with other things (cf. Rose 1999). In place of familiar analytical tendencies towards the refinement of explanations and actions that reduce the control of opium and its derivatives to a unifying or singular causal explanation – like social control, class interest or globalisation – this chapter aims instead to draw attention to the heterogeneity of strategies, devices, ends sought, and the conflicts between them, and the ways in which our present – specifically the contemporary control of opium – has been shaped by complex relationships.

Put simply, this chapter examines the mechanisms that give effect to the international system of control. In doing so it describes the programs, technologies and strategies which translate the political rationalities that provide for the regulation of opioids into the realm of everyday life. The analysis begins with a brief historical excursus, which situates contemporary treaties in relation to the control system developed initially by the League of Nations, and then subsumed under the responsibility of the United Nations in 1946. The main objects of analysis are the mechanisms and programs set in place by the 1961 *Single Convention on Narcotic Drugs*. This treaty is the instrument which, to a large extent, regulates the supply of opium (and related drugs) today. It is the outcome of an amalgamation of the technologies of control expressed in nine treaties and protocols that preceded it.[1] As we are concerned primarily with opioids, only passing acknowledgment is made of the 1971 *Convention on the Control of Psychotropic Substances*.[2] However, the discussion does take into account the contribution the more recent 1988 *United Nations Convention on Illicit Trafficking in Narcotic Drugs* makes to the international system of control. This analysis is informed by commentaries concerned with the form of treaties and control published in the *Bulletin on Narcotics*.[3] It also considers resolutions, passed since 1946, by the General Assembly, the Economic and Social Council, and the various drug control bodies – Permanent Central Opium Board (PCOB), Commission on Narcotic Drugs (CND), International Narcotics Control Board (INCB) – of the United Nations. These resolutions are the outcome of extensive deliberation, and while they cannot be read as complete and faithful accounts of all that occurred, they do provide useful background information in relation to the development of the most recent treaties and the programs of control that give them expression.

The System of International Control

The Early Treaties

The 1909 Shanghai Commission, described in Chapter Three, is commonly regarded as the starting point of the international drug control system we have today. International drug control was initiated as a response to a specific problem in a specific area of the world – opium in China. However, as Reverend George Piercy was to unwittingly prophesy with his contribution to the SSOT newsletter *Friend of China* in 1883: 'it begins with the Chinese but it does not end with them' (Milligan 1995: 82, and p. 74 above). The Shanghai Commission led to The Hague Opium Convention which, while still concerned with the problems faced by China, extended the scope of concern to a broader international horizon. Securing ratification for this treaty was difficult and efforts were interrupted by World War I. A large number of countries became parties to the Convention only after the war through their

---

1   Article 44, 1961 *Single Convention on Narcotic Drugs*.

2   A treaty aimed at the regulation of stimulants, antidepressants and hallucinogens modelled on the form of the Single Convention.

3   The *Bulletin on Narcotics* is the official journal of the UN concerned with drug control. Many of the contributors are members of committees and organisations – like the PCOB, DSB or INCB for example – which have been responsible for the application and maintenance of the control system.

ratification of the Versailles Treaty (Renborg 1964: 2). It was also at the Paris Peace Conference that the involvement of the League of Nations in the problem of drug control was established. The League was entrusted with the 'general supervision over agreements with regard to the traffic in opium and other dangerous drugs' (Bruun et al. 1975: 13). At the inaugural assembly of the League, an Advisory Committee on Traffic in Opium and Other Dangerous Drugs was created (Renborg 1964: 2). Its first task was to establish what the world's requirement for opiates, along with some other drugs, might be. After an empirical investigation consisting mainly of the collection of statistics describing identifiable needs in relation to medical and scientific purposes, the Committee concluded that the amount legitimately required was greatly exceeded by the amount produced (Bean 1974).

Between 1924 and 1931 several new drug treaties were drawn up. In 1925 there was an *Agreement Concerning the Manufacture of, International Trade In and Use of Prepared Opium*, followed by the *Second International Opium Convention*. The Convention came into force in 1928. It reiterated the principle embodied in The Hague Convention, that the manufacture of drugs should be limited to legitimate needs, and tightened up the system of voluntary control by transforming it into one of legal obligation: signatories were now required to enact appropriate regulatory legislation. One of the primary objectives of the 1925 agreement was to set in place an administrative framework which would limit the influence of national interests on international control measures by appointing a board of eight experts independent of their respective national governments. This became the Permanent Central Opium Board (PCOB).[4] In the light of the discussion in Chapter 2 (see pp.35–43), centred on the persona of the expert, it should be no surprise that the desire to limit the effects of national interests using such a strategy proved too difficult to achieve. The expression of expertise is not just the functional relay of knowledge and skills. It is shaped by a complex amalgam of ethical modes of comportment that do not necessarily adhere to, or follow, a coherent or consistent set of principles or rationalities. In its early years the PCOB consisted largely of representatives of the producing and manufacturing countries. This should not have been unexpected, as these nations provided the opportunity for the development of such expertise (Bruun et al. 1975). Tied to this state of affairs ought to be the recognition that any expression of the members' 'expertise' is informed by their localised experience derived from a set of circumstances particular to national settings, contexts and interests with which they are most familiar.

The 1925 Convention also introduced statistical control procedures as well as a system of import certificates and export authorisations. These were to facilitate the regulation, and limitation of the licit international trade (Krishnamoorthy 1962; Renborg 1964), and were supervised by the Board. Parties to the treaty were required to provide an annual report of statistics concerning production, manufacture and stocks on hand of opium and other dangerous drugs. Quarterly reports were to be provided in relation to the importation and export of these drugs (Bruun et al. 1975). According to Bean (1974), the annual reports of the Board summarising the

---

4   In time it was known as the Permanent Central Narcotics Board and, with the 1961 Single Convention, the International Narcotics Control Board.

outcomes of its work over the next four or five years were largely responsible for a later convention in 1931.

In 1930 the Advisory Committee produced a plan for estimating the world's legitimate requirements along with a scheme for approximating the amounts to be manufactured and supplied by the various producing countries. The plan was to limit manufacture of each drug to the preceding year's estimates; each country was to decide its own needs and the share to be made on a quota system. No agreement was ever reached on the quotas. The *Convention for Limiting Manufacture and Regulating the Distribution of Narcotic Drugs* was signed in Geneva in 1931. It introduced a compulsory estimates system aimed at limiting the world manufacture of drugs to the amounts needed for any one year (Krishnamoorthy 1962). Advance estimates of national drug requirements, imports and manufacture were to be submitted to the PCOB based on need for medical and scientific purposes. They were, in effect, to be binding. The Convention established the Drug Supervisory Body (DSB), to monitor the operation of the system. The DSB would publish the parties' annual estimates. It was also given power to establish estimates for any countries that failed to furnish them to the Body whether or not they were parties to the Convention. The DSB had the right to point out governments giving excessive estimates, and it could initiate an embargo against countries where imports and exports exceeded their estimates.

These estimates and statistics proved to be essential to the government of opium. In effect they worked to both constitute and represent the domain to be governed; they made it thinkable and amenable to calculation. The use of these figures as a means of inscribing reality (Latour 1986) made the supply of opium stable, mobile, comparable, and combinable; making it susceptible to evaluation, calculation and intervention. The PCOB and the DSB worked as centres of calculation that governed through the accumulation and distribution of information. The League of Nations, through the PCOB and DSB, governed the international arena by exerting a kind of intellectual mastery over it, establishing a network of conduits for the detailed and systematic flow of information from individual locales of production and trade to a centre. In effect this strategy worked to constitute a domain where principal elements could be known and regulated at a distance.

The estimates and statistics and the intellectual technologies described by the 1925 and 1931 Conventions, are key discursive mechanisms that represent the domain to be governed more or less as an 'economy' with specifiable limits and particular characteristics, the component parts of which are linked together in some more or less systematic manner (cf. Rose and Miller 1992). As Rose points out in a more generalised discussion, '[o]nce such an economy had been delineated it can become the object and target of political programmes that would seek to evaluate and increase the power of a nation [in this case the League of Nations] by governing and managing "the economy"' (1999: 213). Such an assessment of the system of estimates and statistics as constituting an economy of opium as a governable domain is convincingly supported by the view of Bertil Renborg (1964), a former Chief of the Drug Control Service of the League of Nations, who described the 1931 Convention as 'one of the cornerstones of the international control system. Through its system of binding government estimates of drug requirements for medical and scientific needs, an effective limitation of manufacture is achieved.' More specifically, he explains that

> From an *economic* point of view, the convention pioneers new territory – *that of a planned economy on a world-wide scale*. It regulates a whole industry throughout the world, from the point at which the raw materials enter the factory to the point at which they finally reach the legitimate consumer. ... The convention not only embodies the principles of a *planned economy* it further creates, as pointed out by the Assembly in 1934, a real international administration. It provides a workable international system clearly defined in a series of precise and binding international obligations, for the quantitative and qualitative limitation of the manufacture of narcotic drugs (Renborg 1964: 7 emphasis added).[5]

The 1925 and 1931 treaties were judged to be effective. There was a decline in the leakage of supplies coming from the legal drug manufactures into the illicit market. However, this was paired with an unintended increase in clandestine factories which, according to Renborg (1964), appeared to fill the demand for illicit supplies of opium and other regulated drugs. The League responded in 1936 with a treaty designed to suppress the illicit traffic. It called for harsher punitive measures against drug traffickers in the system of contracting parties. As Bassiouni[6] explains:

> One of the key provisions of the 1936 Convention was the provision that required the parties to severely punish "particularly by imprisonment or other penalties of deprivation of liberty", the offences of illicit narcotic trafficking, if such offenses are committed intentionally...(1972: 725).

Up until the 1936 Convention the various national legislative systems provided very uneven penalties for illicit trafficking – the spectrum included small fines, imprisonment, hard labour and death (Renborg 1964). The aim of this Convention was to encourage a similar approach to all drug offences in all countries. It sought

---

5   The language of economics is also employed in a commentary on the 1931 Convention, published by the opium traffic section of the League Secretariat (L of N doc C191.M136.1937. XI), which describes the control established in 3 stages:

In the first stage, the international plan incorporating the estimated drug requirements for the ensuing year for every country and territory in the world (for every drug in use) is drawn up by the Supervisory Body. The plan is legally binding on all the contracting parties, both in their relations with each other and with non-parties.

The second stage involves the supervision by national as well as international organs (OAC, PCOB and DSB) of the year's programme of licit manufacture and trade during the year. In general, it may be said that a detailed supervision, with strict *accountancy* to an international authority at each of the principal stages of the year's operations, is exercised over the drugs in their passage through authorised channels from the licensed factory to the consumer.

In the third stage, an international *audit* of the drug *accounts* of each nation takes place. The PCOB reviews the general position of manufacture and trade by comparing the statistics of manufacture and trade with the estimates contained in the year's plan. The Convention prescribes the action which the Central Board may take in the event of this international *audit* revealing serious irregularities (Renborg 1964).

6   Bassiouni was the chief of the UN Drug control body.

to govern through a technique that Rose describes as translation – that is, the 'extent that actors have come to understand their situation according to a similar language and logic, to construe their goals and their fate as in some way inextricable' (1999: 50). Rose suggests that the constitution of shared interests occurs through 'political discourses, persuasions, negotiations and bargains' – these are exactly the processes involved in the formulation of international treaties. Moreover, through these processes, common modes of perception are formed in which certain events like trafficking come to be described according to particular vocabularies, and relations are established between the nature, character and causes of problems facing various individuals and groups 'such that the problem of the one and those of another seem intrinsically linked in their basis and their solution' (Rose and Miller 1992: 184).

By defining the offences and the penalties, and stipulating that they should be included as extradition crimes in any extradition treaty, the 1936 Convention aimed to prevent offenders, especially traffickers, from avoiding prosecution because the law of the country in which they resided did not cover smuggling offences committed elsewhere (Bassiouni 1972; Renborg 1964). It sought to prevent those who were not citizens of a particular state, and thus not subject to its laws, from challenging the sovereignty of that state. The process of setting out those acts relating to dangerous drugs that would be made punishable in all countries in an international agreement amounted to the first steps towards the unification of penal law relating to drug control. As J. C. Starke QC, who was present at the Convention conference in an official capacity, explained at the time:

> Having erected an international system of control and supervision over legitimate activities in relation to dangerous drugs, governments realised that the next logical step was to endeavour to suppress the illicit traffic...

> It was obvious then that there would be a distinct advantage in effecting some unification of penal law by setting out in an international agreement those acts relating to dangerous drugs which would be made punishable without exception in all countries. A certain unification of penal law was desirable for one further reason. *Numbers of cases had proved that it was still possible for persons, by conspiring or otherwise, to break the laws of other countries with impunity.* A certain uniformity in national laws dealing with drug offence committed outside a particular country would prevent illicit traffickers entirely escaping punishment... (Starke 1937: 32).

This treaty proved difficult to implement. It did not achieve the same level of support as the earlier Conventions. In a significant number of countries and territories, illicit traffic did not constitute a serious governmental concern, or else was not considered to exist at all. In such cases the relevant authorities did not consider it feasible to put the Convention into effect (Fox and Matthews 1992; Renborg 1964). Parties also tended to resist determinations relating specifically to the form of domestic legislation. The provisions of this Convention were considered by some to be too much of an infringement on national sovereignty.[7] This could be

---

7   The matter of sovereignty continues to be a key issue in the context of international control. As Musto explained:

considered as somewhat ironic. As we have seen in Chapter 3, the treaty system, that is, the system of international agreements to limit the trade in opium, was inspired by concerns to maintain Chinese sovereignty. Moreover, as Hirst and Thompson (1996 see pp.62–3 above) have pointed out, the conditions of possibility for the formation of nation states were constituted by just this type of international agreement. By September of 1964 there were only twenty-four parties to this agreement (Renborg 1964). While the governmental processes of translation failed to achieve widespread support in relation to the 1936 treaty, the document's formulation, nevertheless, signalled a shift in drug control strategies: previously treaties had been concerned with the health and wellbeing of populations, trade, and diplomatic matters. With this agreement, for the first time, drug trafficking as a crime took its place on the regulation agenda (Fox and Matthews 1992).

After World War II and with the Geneva Protocol of 1946 the United Nations (UN) inherited the functions previously exercised by the League of Nations under various treaties concerned with the control of 'dangerous drugs'. The League of Nations machinery was transferred almost completely into the institutions of the new system. The functions of the League's Advisory Committee were transferred to the UN's Commission on Narcotic Drugs (CND), established in 1946 as a functional commission of the Economic and Social Council (ECOSOC). The CND remains the central policy-making body within the UN's system for dealing with drug control.

In the pre-war period drugs subject to international control were largely limited to those derived from the opium poppy, coca bush and cannabis plant. After World War II there was increasing production of synthetic compounds also having dependence producing effects. These however were not covered by the 1931 Convention. The Paris Protocol of 1948 (which came into effect in 1949) authorised the World Health Organisation (WHO) to place under international control any dependency producing drug (synthetic or natural) (Krishnamoorthy 1962; United Nations International Drug Control Program 1997).

By the middle of the twentieth century – despite the identification of many new 'dangerous drugs' – opium continued to be the focus of concern. After World War II (1950) a Joint Committee of the principal opium producing and drug manufacturing countries was established to investigate the possibility of an international opium monopoly. The Committee was unable to reach agreement on a number of issues.[8]

Foremost among continuing issues is national sovereignty. Because the traffic in drugs is notoriously international, the limits of sovereignty are repeatedly tested by calls for cooperation in the sharing of information and law enforcement activities. The resolution of these real and potential conflicts must rest with each government balancing sovereignty against the danger to institutional integrity posed by drug cartels. It is one of the most persistent concerns when formulating international initiatives, yet the foundation of the United Nations rests on the independence of its Member states (Musto 1997:177).

8   These included the basic price at which the international opium monopoly should conduct opium transactions, the precise form that international inspection of the opium trade should take under the international monopoly, the problem of the competition which would be met by drug manufacturing countries from exports of opium alkaloids by countries producing opium under the interim agreement and the measures required to meet competition from exports made from poppy straw (*Bulletin on Narcotics* 1953).

In the light of earlier experiences with opium monopolies a considerable number of member states were reluctant to commit to such a plan. The project failed. Instead, in 1953, an Opium Protocol was adopted which attempted to restrict production by less comprehensive means. The 1953 Protocol limited the use of opium and the international trade in it to medical and scientific purposes. It sought to eliminate legal over-production through the indirect method of limiting stocks of the drug maintained by individual states. The protocol provided for the *licensing* of poppy farmers in opium producing countries and specified the areas where the crop could be legally cultivated. It empowered the PCOB to employ certain supervisory and enforcement measures – such as requests for information, proposals for remedial measures, and local inquiries. This reinforced the PCOB's position as a centre of calculation. The system of licensing served as another form of inscription which, by mapping the areas where the crop could be cultivated, refined and extended the network of information marking out – or rather making up – the distribution and movement of the supply of opium (*Bulletin on Narcotics* 1951: 5). This geography of supply was reinforced by ongoing attempts to chemically or biologically profile samples of opium, and map their source of origin, in the hope that such a process would facilitate the identification of the source of supplies leaking into the illicit market (Remberg et al. 1994).

With the 1953 Protocol, nine regulatory agreements had been developed. The system had become complex. Bean (1974: 49) describes how participants began to express a desire for codification and simplification of the system as early as the 1930s. By 1950 the Joint Secretarial of the PCOB and the DSB made the following assessment with regard to the workings of the treaty system:

> …the overwhelming disadvantage of the existing international instruments and the system they set up has been their complexity. The texts are involved and contradictory, the administrative machinery which has been set up is too complicated and gives rise to overlapping. If governments have failed to do all their part, this has been due not only to the fact that the Conventions were in advance of public opinion or that governments were too poor or indifferent to set up the necessary administrative machinery, but also partly to the fact that the Conventions were too involved (1950: 83).

A single convention was proposed to consolidate the considerable number of treaties, protocols and agreements which had emerged since Shanghai in 1909. Herbert May,[9] in a commentary published in the *Bulletin on Narcotics*, identified the simplification of the existing controls as one of its general objectives:

---

9   Herbert May, a lawyer by profession, was regarded as a leading statesman in international narcotics control. For over twenty-five years he was associated, in various capacities, with the work of the Opium Advisory Committee of the League of Nations, and subsequently of the Commission on Narcotic Drugs of the United Nations. He took part in many international conferences, including the Limitation Conference of 1931 at Geneva, the Bangkok Conference of the same year, and the United Nations Opium conference in New York in 1953. He was a member both of the Permanent Central Opium Board and of the Drug Supervisory Body, presiding for many years over both bodies (May 1955).

It is the classic objective of consolidation of legal texts to simplify the text and make its use easier. This is particularly necessary in the field of international narcotics law, developed in the nine treaties concluded over a period of more than forty years, at different stages of the evolution of the international society, and under very different economic and social conditions in the States concerned; in these years the various elements of present narcotics control were achieved step by step. It is unavoidable that as a result some provisions are inconsistent, obscure, duplicated and even obsolete. The whole makes for *unnecessary complexity*, as regards both national and international administrations. ... Definitions are sometimes not carried through the treaties, and some provisions are not wholly consistent with one another, so that the business of legislation and administration within the Governments, and of reporting to the international organs, is sometimes unnecessarily complicated. It is this which makes consolidation alone not worthwhile, and even to some extent not feasible. However, all this is not to say that the treaties have not worked well: when it is considered that they represent pioneer international legislation, the response of Governments has been remarkable. But enough experience has accumulated by now to select the essential elements in this legislation and to arrange them in a consistent whole (1955: 2 emphasis added).

The Single Convention on Narcotic Drugs (SCoND), 1961

The United Nations Conference for the Adoption of the Single Convention on Narcotic Drugs met at United Nations Headquarters from 24 January to 25 March 1961. Seventy-three states were represented, Ceylon attended as an observer, and a number of specialised agencies, international bodies and non-government organisations were represented at the conference.[10] By 2005, 180 states had become parties to this agreement (United Nations Office of Drug Control 2007). The drugs subject to the Convention are listed in four schedules (United Nations 1961 Article 2). According to its authors, Schedules I and II include drugs 'liable to abuse or that could produce ill effects'. Schedule I contains those that are subject to the most rigid control (all the controls for the convention) – use of these drugs is limited to medical and scientific purposes. They include heroin, morphine, opium, pethidine, cocaine, cannabis and methadone. Schedule II drugs are subject to slightly less control, while those in Schedule III – preparations of codeine for example – are subject to significantly less control.[11] The final group, Schedule IV, consists of a special class of drugs selected from those in Schedule I. It consists of drugs that are considered to be 'particularly liable to abuse and to produce ill effects, where this liability is not offset by substantial therapeutic advantages not possessed by substances other than drugs in Schedule IV' (Article 3). They are subject to the same measures of

---

10   Specialised agencies included the Food and Agriculture Organisation of the United Nations, the International Civil Aviation Organisation, the International Labour Organisation, and the World Health Organisation. The international bodies represented included the Permanent Central Opium Board and the Drug Supervisory Body. The non-government organisations present included the International Conference of Catholic Charities, the International Criminal Police Organisation and the International Federation of Women Lawyers (UNDCP 1997).

11   Special provisions relating to international trade do not apply and annual estimates are not required.

international control as those in Schedule I, but in addition, each party shall adopt 'special measures of control which in its opinion are necessary, having regard to the particularly *dangerous* properties of the drug' (Article 2). Moreover, if it is the most appropriate means of protecting the public health and welfare, parties shall '*prohibit* the production, manufacture, export and import, trade in, possession, or use of such drugs' (Article 2). In 1973 only four drugs had been listed in Schedule IV – heroin was one of them. By 2007 seventeen other substances, including cannabis but not cocaine, had been listed.

The SCoND provided for the amalgamation, and replacement, of almost all previous conventions, protocols and agreements concerned with the regulation of drugs (Article 44).[12] According to the definitions listed in Article 1 of the document, the use of the term 'drug' throughout the Convention refers to 'any of the substances in Schedules I and II, whether natural or synthetic'. The treaty implicitly acknowledges the definitional ambiguity of this term; the particular quality that designates a substance as a drug is its inclusion in this list rather than some essentially identifiable property. Most fundamentally, the Convention prohibits the possession of drugs except under legal authority (Article 33), and obliges parties to provide for the enactment of specific national legislation which limits the use, cultivation, production, manufacture, distribution and trade in drugs to medical and scientific purposes (Article 4). It describes a cooperative system of regulation that recognises 'the competence of the United Nations with respect to the international control of drugs' (Article 5).

The 1961 Convention continued to provide for the administration of the regulatory system that existed previously, and in doing so it streamlined the control machinery.[13] The role of the CND,[14] which had replaced the original Advisory Committee to the League of Nations in 1946, was maintained, while the International Narcotics Control Board (INCB) was established to take on the roles of the PCOB and the DSB. The INCB maintains the operation of the system of estimates and statistical returns, quarterly and annual reporting, and the distribution of information to member and non-member states – taking on the role of a centre of calculation (Latour 1986).

The provisions describing the form and the function of the INCB reiterate the PCOB's 1925 attempt to limit the influence of national interests by appointing a board of eight *experts* (see p. 87). In the interest of neutrality the contemporary document provides that the Board consists of thirteen expert members, three of whom have medical, pharmacological or pharmaceutical experience, selected from a list of five nominated by the WHO, with ten selected from a list of persons nominated

---

12 The exception being the 1936 Convention, where Article 9, relating to extradition was terminated as between parties to both Conventions, and replaced by a provision in the Single Convention.

13 Articles 35 and 36.

14 Included in the functions of the Commission is the amendment of schedules; calling matters to the attention of the Board; making recommendations for the implementation of aims and provisions of the convention, including programs of scientific research and the exchange of information of a scientific or technical nature; drawing attention of non-parties to decisions and recommendations which it adopts under the convention with a view to their considering taking action (Article 8).

from members or non-members of the UN. In particular subparagraph 2 of Article 9 proposes that:

> Members of the Board shall be persons who, *by their competence, impartiality and disinterestedness, will command general confidence*. During their term of office they shall not hold any position or engage in any activity which would be liable to impair their impartiality in the exercise of their functions. The Council shall, in consultation with the Board, make all arrangements necessary to ensure the full technical independence of the Board in carrying out its functions (United Nations 1961).

Subsequent subparagraphs also provide for equitable geographic representation that includes persons with knowledge of the drug situation in the producing, manufacturing and consuming countries. This contrasts sharply with the earliest formulation of the PCOB which was characterised by membership dominated by representatives originating from the manufacturing states (Bruun et al. 1975).

This ongoing significance of expertise in international governance of opium can be understood if we extend the discussions of Nikolas Rose and Peter Miller on the role of the expert in the governance of individuals as citizens of a polity to consider the role of experts in the governance of individual nation states in an international community of nation states like the United Nations. Rose and Miller (1992) argue that government is intrinsically linked to the activities of expertise. They suggest that the expert's role is not of the type proposed by authors like Illich (1975), Willis (1989) or Cohen (1985), for example, who would describe experts as professionals like medical practitioners, social workers or criminologists weaving regulatory webs of social control. Rather, the expert is engaged in assorted attempts at 'the calculated administration of diverse aspects of conduct through countless, often competing, local tactics of education, persuasion, inducement, management, incitement and encouragement' (Rose 1993: 298). Moreover, the involvement of experts works in the processes of governance because it holds the promise (but, as we saw in Chapter 2, often not the realisation) that the problems of regulation can be removed from the political arena and relocated in some sort of transcendental territory of truth, or simply in a neutral domain of administration. Through such claims to truth and neutrality, self-regulatory techniques can be instilled in citizens or nation states that will align the specific choices of such subjects with the ends of government and various political authorities (as expressed in the United Nations treaties). In this way, the freedom, and continuing sovereignty of subjects (in this case, nation states), becomes an essential ally and not a threat to the orderly government of a polity – the international domain.[15]

Rose and Miller (1992) also propose that the role of the expert works to govern in a specific way – at a distance. This is possible because experts enter into a form of double alliance. They ally themselves with political authorities, focusing upon their problems and problematising new issues translating political concerns (about economic productivity, for example, or, as we shall see, drugs) into the vocabulary of management, administration, agriculture, pharmacy, medicine, law, social science,

---

15   This explains the apparent preoccupation with the protection of national sovereignty expressed in each of the treaties.

architecture, or geography. Alternatively, they seek to form alliances with the individual subjects (specific nation states), translating their daily, localised worries and decisions (over drugs, over how to conduct their own affairs) into a language claiming the power of the truth (which is somehow removed from the forces of politics), and offering to teach them the techniques by which they might manage better (Rose and Miller 1992: 188).

Applying Rose and Miller's account of the significance of expertise in the governmental process, we can see how the INCB, which is defined as 'the independent and quasi juridical control organ for the implementation and monitoring of the United Nations Drug Conventions', has effect in the governmental complex of international drug control. The INCB's role is 'to promote and assist with government compliance with treaties'. This is achieved through the calculated administration of the 'licit manufacture, commerce and sale of drugs', which endeavours to ensure that 'adequate supplies are available for medical and scientific uses, and that leakages from licit sources to illicit traffic do not occur'. To this end the Board administers an estimates system for narcotic drugs and a voluntary assessment system for psychotropic substances and monitors international trade in drugs through the statistical returns system (International Narcotics Control Board 1999).[16] These activities are discussed in greater detail below. Here the Board's role as an 'independent' body concerned with the implementation of the Conventions is of more immediate interest. According to various UN documents, it is the INCB's responsibility to employ its expertise in order to evaluate national efforts in relation to drug control and, on this basis, to make recommendations to the competent UN organs – to specialised agencies and governments – that technical and or financial assistance be provided in support of the governments' efforts to comply with their treaty obligations (International Narcotics Control Board 1999).

In the course of furthering the aims of the treaties the INCB maintains ongoing discussions with governments. As a result of these discussions many countries have become parties to the Conventions and have strengthened their national drug control programs and developed or strengthened relevant legislation (International Narcotics Control Board 1999). In order to enhance the functioning of the respective national drug control administrations, the INCB Secretariat[17] conducts training programs for drug control administrators, particularly those from developing countries.[18] As part

---

16   The Board also monitors government control over chemicals used in the illicit manufacture of drugs, and assists them in preventing diversion of these chemicals into illicit traffic. With respect to illicit manufacture and trafficking of drugs, the Board identifies where weaknesses in the national and international control systems exist and contributes to correcting the situation. Further the Board is responsible for assessing chemicals used to illicitly manufacture drugs, for possible international control in accordance with the provisions of the 1988 treaty that will be discussed below.

17   In accordance with General Assembly resolution 45/179 of 21 December 1990, the Secretariat of INCB was fully integrated into UNDCP (International Narcotics Control Board 1999).

18   These officials receive training in the implementation of treaty obligations, especially those that relate to cooperation between INCB and parties to the treaties. According to the UNDCP such regional training seminars not only helped to improve cooperation from

of this process the United Nations International Drug Control Program (UNDCP) specifically provides training and advice in relation to legislative requirement described by the treaties. 'To this end model laws have been developed for use in countries whose fundamental legal system is substantially based on the common law tradition or the civil law tradition'[19] (United Nations International Drug Control Program 2000). In this context, the INCB enters into the type of double alliance described by Rose and Miller (1992). It is focused on the problem of drug control. Acting as a centre of calculation for the UN, it gathers information on the working of the system and identifies where weaknesses in the national and international control systems exist (United Nations International Drug Control Program 1997), problematising new issues as they arise, and translating political concerns about drug supply regulation into the vocabulary of expertise. At the same time the Board seeks to form alliances with individual nation states bringing them into the treaty system by working with them to translate their localised needs into a language claiming the power of truth and neutrality and offering to teach them the techniques – administrative, legislative, agricultural – by which they might manage better. This type of governmental strategy is mobilised very clearly in the localised adoption of the UN's model legislation to control drugs and meet treaty obligations, which according to a UNDCP document, 'will need to be adjusted to ensure both domestic validity (…in terms of constitutional principles and other basic concepts of its legal system) and domestic operational effectiveness (…in terms of implementation arrangements and infrastructure for optimum impact)' (United Nations International Drug Control Program 1999). In this type of situation the INCB works to govern the supply of opium and other drugs through the freedom and continuing sovereignty of nation states – that is, through their respective constitutional freedom to enact and enforce their own laws and regulations – albeit that they are laws based on the model suggested. Thus, as an allegedly 'independent' control organ the INCB attempts to secure a governmental position between the political authority of the UN (ECOSOC) and the parties (and potential parties) to the treaties.

Following on from this discussion it is relatively simple to establish that the INCB, in accordance with its 'expert' status, is involved in the *calculated administration* of the 'licit manufacture, commerce and sale of drugs', with the objective of ensuring that 'adequate supplies are available for medical and scientific uses, and that leakages

---

participating countries but have also served to enhance collaboration among countries within the regions. These seminars are organised in close cooperation with UNDCP and other competent international organisations, in particular WHO and the International Criminal Police Organization (INTERPOL). National administrations also send officials to the INCB Secretariat for training (UNDCP 2000).

19 Bills for common law system tradition states: Drug Abuse Bill, Extradition Bill, Foreign Evidence Bill, Mutual Assistance in Criminal Matters Bill and Witness Protection Bill. Laws for civil law system tradition states: Model Law on the Classification of Narcotic Drugs, Psychotropic Substances and Precursors and on the Regulation of the Licit Cultivation, Production, Manufacture and Trading of Drugs (with Commentaries); Model Law on Drug Trafficking and Related Offences (with Commentaries); and Model Law on Money Laundering, Confiscation and International Cooperation in Relation to Drugs (United Nations International Drug Control Program 2000).

from licit sources to illicit traffic do not occur' (International Narcotics Control Board 1999). Key features of the Single Convention are the systems of statistical returns and estimates that were introduced by earlier treaties – 1925 and 1931. The INCB administers these systems (Article 13 and Article 12), while it acts as a 'focal point; for international control.[20] By examining and analysing the information it receives from some 190 countries and territories, the INCB 'monitors whether the treaties are being applied throughout the world in as an effective manner as possible' (International Narcotics Control Board 1999).

Over the years that the international system has developed, the collection of numbers has played a particularly important role. A 'Note of the Joint Secretarial of the Permanent Central Opium Board and the Drug Supervisory Body' (1950) which comments on the workings of the 1925 and 1931 Conventions, makes the point that up until the time of that publication (1950) statistical control under Article 22 of the 1925 Convention was the basis of the regulatory system.[21] This provision was the principal instrument at the disposal of the Board to determine whether 'excessive quantities of narcotics are accumulating in any country, or that there is a danger of that country becoming a centre of the illicit traffic' (Article 24). It covers all phases in the movement of narcotics from production, manufacture, imports, stocks, and all kinds of utilisation – consumption, conversion, export. It enables the Board to draw for each country and territory a yearly 'balance sheet' and ascertain whether the amounts utilised and the stock remaining at the end of the year tally with the supply available; or in other words, 'to calculate the balance which should be in hand at the

---

20   Parties are obliged to provide the INCB with statistics describing, for their respective territories: the production or manufacture of drugs; utilisation of drugs for the manufacture of other drugs and preparations; consumption of drugs for medical and scientific purposes; imports and exports of drugs and poppy straw; seizures of drugs and their disposal; stocks held and the ascertainable area of cultivation of the opium poppy (Article 20). They supply estimates of: the quantities of drugs to be consumed for medical and scientific purposes, quantities to be used in the manufacture of other drugs and preparations; quantities of stocks held; quantities of drugs necessary for addition to special stocks; the area in hectares, and the geographical location of land to be used for the cultivation of the opium poppy, and the approximate quantity of opium to be produced; the number of industrial establishments which will manufacture synthetic drugs and the quantities to be manufactured by each establishment (Article 19). The estimates are accompanied by an explanation of how they were calculated and, according to the treaty, they cannot be exceeded. In relation to the maintenance of the estimate system there are provisions for the acquisition of estimates in accordance with the Conventions from non-members (Article 12). The INCB calculates estimates for those parties (non-member or members) which fail to provide the relevant information. This system of estimates and statistical returns is designed to limit the international production and supply of drugs to legitimate needs. The figures calculated are used to determine legitimate quantities for manufacture and importation of drugs (Article 21), limits on the production of opium (Article 21 bis), and supported by Article 29 and 30, make provision for the prevention of the accumulation of stocks.

21   The further control created by the Convention of 1931, under which supply and utilisation are to remain within certain limits, is generally based both on the estimates provided for in that Convention and on the statistics furnished under the Convention of 1925.

end of the year. When this balance does not tally with the stocks declared as actually being in hand, the Board asks the Government concerned for an explanation of this discrepancy' (Joint Secretarial of the Permanent Central Opium Board and the Drug Supervisory Body 1950).

In relation to control instituted under the Convention of 1925, specifically in relation to import and export authorisation, the Joint Secretarial commented:

> Generally speaking the statistics have proven effective; they have made possible the discovery of leakages into the illicit traffic and the exposure of false statements regarding the destination of exports. They have also proved to be the most reliable statistics supplied to the Board. For it is easier to control imports and exports than to control consumption, production, manufacture etc. because they involve import and export authorisations, the verification at customs posts, and ... monetary transfers or barta (sic) (1950: 63 emphasis added).

Moreover,

> the Board is usually informed of one or the other side of these transactions (the export or import), *so that hardly a single transaction escapes its notice.* When it possesses both returns, it is in a position to note any discrepancy between them. Many discrepancies, of course, are noted every quarter, they are the subject of incessant and voluminous correspondence between the Board and Governments. But *the very fact that such questions can be asked*, and that governments are moved to make necessary enquiries speaks in favour of the system; even though it is time consuming (1950: 63 emphasis added).

Clearly the authors and administrators of the international control system valued the use of numbers as a mechanism for the management of supply, around which the system of regulation was built. Considering this, it is no surprise that the systems of statistical returns and estimates were included, and continue to be valued as a technology of control, in the SCoND. This view is evident in a recent UN document that openly acknowledges the value of the estimates in its assessment of the effectiveness of the international control system:

> The international system of controlling the licit movement of narcotics under the 1961 Convention functions in a generally satisfactory manner, and licitly produced or manufactured drugs usually do not constitute a source for illicit traffic. *The fact that the system generally works well is mainly due to the estimates system that covers all countries whether or not parties to the Convention.* Countries are under an obligation not to exceed the amounts of the estimates confirmed or established by the Board. (International Narcotics Control Board 1999: 1 emphasis added).

The figures make visible all phases, from production to consumption, in the movement of narcotics, making possible the 'discovery of leakages into the illicit traffic', 'the exposure of false statements' and the control of imports and exports. Following Rose (1999: 213), the figures included in the statistical returns and estimates work to delineate spaces for the operation of government that are marked out by a grid of standards allowing evaluation and judgment. These figures constitute a calculable domain that is amenable to programming and intervention and in this way, make it possible to 'know' the government of supply as well as its shortfalls. Taking this into account it is apparent that numbers have been intrinsic to the formulation and justification of the program for the regulation of the supply of opium from the outset. The system of statistical returns and estimates make the international regulation of opiates possible because, in describing the supply of the drug, they make up the very object upon which government is required to operate – an economy of supply. As Rose suggests, in relation to the governmental use of numbers more generally, 'they map the boundaries and internal spaces of the domain to be governed' (1999: 197). Moreover, the statistics and estimates work as inscription devices[22] in the constitution of the domain that they appear to represent.

The 1961 Convention is also concerned with the limitation of the production of opium for international trade (Article 24).[23] It controls which states are able to produce opium for export, as well as the quantities that can be produced. When not carried out by a state enterprise, legitimate manufacture, trade and distribution are controlled through structured systems of licensing, accreditations, authorisations and national and international authorities and agencies (Articles 29 and 30).[24] Article 31 establishes, in accordance with the provisions of the 1925 treaty, a system of corresponding import certificates and export authorisations that allow parties (and the INCB) to trace the movement of drugs. Authorisations state the name of the drug, quantity, names and addresses of importer, and exporter, and the period in which the movement is to be effected. Exportation authorisations include the number and date of the import certificate as well as the details of the authority that issued it.[25] I have noted the governmental value of the system of import and export certificates in relation to the constitution and maintenance of the INCB as a centre of calculation capable of governing at a distance through tracing the movement of quantities of opium in relation to the estimated requirements of particular parties (p.94). This aspect of the governmental network is enhanced at the more localised level through provisions for the system of licensure, which provides the material means of regulation, centred not only on persons, but enterprises, establishments and

---

22   Inscription devices according to Bruno Latour (1986) are intellectual technologies that work to provide a means of objectifying, marking, inscribing and preserving phenomena that would otherwise remain ephemeral and subjective. They make it possible to think or know and reason about something. Moreover, they are material techniques of thought that make it possible to extend authority to cover the things that they seem to depict. They are evidence of the ways in which many of the powers that we tend to attribute to cognition and reason actually inhere in little material techniques such as drawing a map, writing a description, making a list or table (see also Hunter 1994, Hacking 1991 as discussed in Chapter two).

23   Where opium poppies are cultivated for purposes other than the production of opium parties must ensure that opium is not produced from such plants, and that the manufacture of drugs from poppy straw is also controlled (Article 25).

24   A discussion of the success of Australian licensing system is available in Murdoch (1983).

25   Parties are not permitted to export drugs to a country or territory where the import of such drugs is against the law (Article 31). This provision responds to the possibility of the type of problem faced by China during the nineteenth century.

premises. It empowers local authorities to regulate more specifically by whom, how, and where the production, manufacture and trade in opiates is carried out.

While the provisions described so far largely address the regulation of the licit trade, three articles are concerned with the illicit supply of drugs: Articles 35, 36 and 37 provide for the suppression of illicit traffic in drugs in accordance with the principles of the 1936 treaty.[26] They require a coordinated universal action against illicit traffic expressed through cooperation and assistance between parties and international regulatory organs. Like other aspects of the treaty these provisions are also monitored by a system of reporting to the Board and the Commission. This includes reporting information[27] regarding any illicit drug activity, be it cultivation, production, manufacture, use, or trafficking (Article 35). In line with the concerns of the 1936 *Convention for the Suppression of the Illicit Traffic in Dangerous Drugs*, Article 36 provides that activities related to the illicit drug traffic are 'liable to adequate punishment, particularly imprisonment or other penalties of deprivation of liberty'. It also makes drug offences extraditable offences in order to prevent evasion of punishment. Article 37 provides for seizure and confiscation of 'any drugs, substances and equipment used in or intended for the commission of any of the offences, referred to in Article 36'.

One final point should be made concerning the SCoND and its relationship to the agreements that preceded it. Unlike earlier treaties, which focused all their attention only on regulating the supply of drugs, this treaty does consider the problem of demand[28] – albeit briefly, and explicitly in the context of the regulation of supply. The 1972 Protocol[29] strengthened the Single Convention provisions relating to the prevention of illicit production, traffic and use of narcotics. It highlighted the need for treatment, rehabilitation and social reintegration – in addition to imprisonment

---

26 See the note at end of Article 44 in relation to 1936 treaty:

Upon coming into force of this Convention, article 9 of the Convention for the Suppression of the Illicit Traffic in Dangerous Drugs, signed at Geneva on 26 June 1936, shall, between the Parties thereto which are also Parties to this Convention be terminated, and shall be replaced by paragraph 2(b) of Article 36 of this Convention, provided that such a Party may by notification to the Secretary General continue to enforce the said Article 9:

(b) (i) Each of the offences enumerated in paragraphs 1 and 2 (a) (ii) of this article shall be deemed to be included as an extraditable offence in any extradition treaty existing between Parties. Parties undertake to include such offences as extraditable offences in every extradition treaty to be concluded between them (United Nations 1961).

27 In addition to information required by Article 18.

28 These articles were the first ever to acknowledge the problem of demand in the context of a treaty as a concern for the international system.

29 The United Nations conference to consider amendments to the Single Convention on Narcotic Drugs, 1961 met at the United Nations office at Geneva from 6 to 24 March of 1972. Ninety-seven states were represented. Cameroon, Dominican Republic, Malaysia, Malta and Romania attended as observers. The World Health Organisation and other interested specialised agencies, the International Narcotics Control Board and the International Criminal Police Organisation were invited to attend. WHO, INCB and ICPO were represented at the conference (UNDCP 1997).

for minor offences.[30] The overall aims of the control measures, nevertheless, remained the provision of adequate supplies for narcotic drugs for medical and scientific purposes and measures to prevent diversion into the illicit market. As the Shafer Commission explained: '[i]n reality,…the Single Convention on Narcotic Drugs, deals most effectively not with illicit traffic but with the lawful production and manufacture of these substances' (1973: 231). In other words, the SCoND was (and still is) chiefly concerned with the consolidation of a system to regulate the licit supply of narcotic drugs. This enduring concern with the supply of drugs is not surprising given that it was the problematisation of the supply of opium entering China that initiated the international system of control.

The SCoND and the Constitution of a Governable Domain

Rose and Miller (1992) argue that the history of government might well be written as a history of problematisations, as it is around these difficulties that programs of government are elaborated. It appears that this assessment holds in relation to the government of opium, as it is around the problem of supply, rather than use, that programs for the regulation of the drug have been most clearly articulated in the treaties (and legislation). According to Rose and Miller, programs lay claim to a certain knowledge of the sphere of problems to be addressed. Knowledge is an essential part of the programs that seek to exercise legitimate and calculated power over them. Governing a sphere requires that it can be represented, or depicted in a way that both grasps its truth and re-presents it in a form in which it can enter the sphere of conscious political calculation. Government depends on this knowledge as a language of representation and calculation (Rose and Miller 1992).

The treaties themselves are a part of this knowledge or language of representation and calculation. At the same time that they work to constitute knowledge of the supply of narcotics, they constitute the domain to be governed by playing a key role in establishing networks that enable rule to be brought about in an indirect manner. This occurs, in part, through the adoption of 'shared vocabularies, theories and explanations' (Rose 1999), which explicitly occurs when any party ratifies or becomes a signatory to a treaty. While each signatory, or party, remains more or less constitutionally distinct[31] and formally independent, the commitment to a convention places each and all in a particular relationship to each other. Even parties who abstain from the treaty processes are drawn into the network. For example, under the terms

---

30   Article 36 paragraph 1 part (b) indicates that parties may, in cases where abusers of drugs have committed offences, provide as an alternative to conviction or punishment or in addition to, treatment, education, aftercare, rehabilitation and social reintegration. Article 38 'Measures against the abuse of drugs' provides that 'Parties shall give special attention to and take all practical measures for the prevention of abuse of drugs and for the early identification, treatment, eduction, after-care, rehabilitation and social reintegration of the persons involved'.

31   The significance of constitutional integrity is emphasised in the treaties, see for example the preamble of both the 1961 and 1988 treaties.

of the SCoND, non-members are also required to supply statistics and estimates. When they fail to do so, the INCB calculates them (Article 12).

Consistent with Rose and Miller's (1992) discussion of technologies of governance, each of the parties to the treaty is enrolled in a governmental network to the extent that it can translate the objectives and the values of others into their own terms. In other words, shared interests are constructed in and through the treaties, and the persuasions, negotiations and bargains that surround them. Through participation in the processes and relationships of the conventions, parties come to understand their situation according to a similar language and logic, to construe their goals and their fate as in some way inextricable, and they are assembled into mobile and loosely affiliated networks. Common modes of perception (truths) are formed in which certain events and entities come to be visualised according to particular rhetorics of image or speech.[32] Relations are established between the nature, character and causes of problems facing various individuals and groups, such that the problems of one and those of another seem intrinsically linked in their basis and their solution.

This describes the very process of becoming a party to a treaty – to the United Nations system of drug control. Most obviously the governmental network is constituted by the obligation expressed by becoming a signatory to a convention or ratifying a treaty when members recognise and make a legally enforceable commitment. For example, the preamble of the SCoND sets out that:

The Parties,

...

Concerned with the health and welfare of mankind,

[Consider] that effective measures against abuse of narcotic drugs require *co-ordinated and universal* action,

[Understand] that such universal action calls for international co-operation guided by the *same principles* and aimed at *common objectives,*

[Acknowledge] the competence of the United Nations in the field of narcotics control and desirous that the international organs concerned should be within the framework of that Organization (United Nations 1961 emphasis added).

The arrangement of relationships and processes described by the treaties works to stabilise the international network of regulation because they act as potent resources in the more localised composition of forces – the enactment of particular forms of legislation, the formulation of particular styles of administrative apparatuses and bureau, and the particular nature of the deployment of resources – 'that are guided

---

32 For example, the demonisation of producer countries in relation to victim countries promoted by the language of UN publications in the mid twentieth century, or the bifurcation of drug problems in terms of styles of speaking which deal separately with issues of supply and demand.

by the same principles and aimed at common objectives'. Thus, the treaties have the effect of codifying particular practices, normalising them, and both transforming them into repeatable instructions as to how to conduct oneself and establishing authoritative means of judgment (cf. Rose 1999).[33] Indeed, the provisions of the treaty set a minimum standard for parties in relation to the regulation of drugs (United Nations 1961 Article 39).

This discussion draws extensively on the work of Latour and Callon which examined the complex mechanisms through which it becomes possible to link calculations at one place with action at another, not through the direct imposition of a form of conduct by force, but through delicate affiliation of a loose assemblage of agents and agencies into a functioning network (Miller and Rose 1990; Rose 1999). The treaties constitute networks, alliances and conduits that in various ways allow action at a distance. According to Latour, a condition of 'action at a distance' is the constitution of a centre(s) of calculation. The formation of a centre of calculation requires the 'accumulation of immutable mobiles, traces that will, when transported to a particular locale represent that which is distant in a single place, making it visible, recognisable, amenable to deliberation and discussion. This requires that events can be inscribed in standardized forms, that these inscriptions be transported from far and wide and accumulated at a central locale where they can be aggregated, compared, compiled and subject to calculation' (Latour 1986; 1987: 219–32). The accumulation of knowledge and its movement and circulation are important factors in the possibility of governance.

From the beginning, the governmental program described by the treaties clearly hinged on the accumulation of knowledge – of particular types of information in particular centres. Bean (1974: 46) draws our attention to an initial desire to solve problems in an empirical way, following the same tradition as the Shanghai Commission. Similarly Renborg (1964) notes that the Opium Advisory Committee of the League of Nations 'understood at an early stage that it could only carry out its task satisfactorily on the basis of *information* regarding the narcotics situation in the various countries'. In a series of resolutions and recommendations it asked governments to furnish the indispensable information. With successive developments in international control the system of reporting was incorporated in the League conventions and agreements, and thus made an *obligation* of the parties. The complete statistical reporting, covering all aspects of the opium (drug) economy, was introduced in the Geneva Convention of 1925. The remainder formed part of the subsequent treaties of 1931 and 1936. By the 1961 Convention provision had been made for the extensive collection of information which included, in addition to the statistics and estimates for member as well as non-member states, reports describing: the texts of all laws and regulations promulgated to give effect to the Conventions and agreements; annual reports on their working; reports on significant cases of seizures and illicit traffic; names and addresses of those authorised to manufacture narcotics; and the names and address of authorities for the issuing of export authorisations and import certificates (Renborg 1964).

---

33   The success of Australian drugs of dependence provisions reported in the *Bulletin on Narcotics* Murdoch (1983) is an example of this.

The SCoND and the agreements which preceded it and contributed to its form, do more than articulate an agreement or a set of obligations between states in relation to narcotic drugs. While they set out in detail how opium and other drugs are to be governed, they do not simply describe the processes involved. The treaties themselves actively engage with the constitution of the very problem that each of them has ultimately sought to address. The government of opium only becomes possible through discursive mechanisms that are able to represent the supply of drugs as an intelligible field, making it possible to conceptualise a set of bounded processes and relations like an economy, which is amenable to management. In a very real sense, the problem of the supply of opium was brought into being, made visible and sayable, by the treaties themselves which defined and individuated a set of characteristics and processes regarding the supply of opium which can be thought of as able to be governed and managed, evaluated and programmed, in order to achieve desirable ends – a balance between legitimate medical and scientific needs and the worldwide supply of the drug.

Unplanned Outcomes and Unintended Consequences: The Illicit Supply as an Ungoverned Domain?

With the complex arrangements, the extensive commitment of resources and the broad reach of the international regulatory bodies (like the INCB) one might optimistically expect that the supply of opium could be effectively controlled. However, things are rarely that clear cut. As Rose and Miller readily admit:

> Government is a congenitally failing operation: the sublime image of a perfect regulatory machine is internal to the mind of the programmers. ... Things, persons or events always appear to escape those bodies of knowledge that inform governmental programs, refusing to respond according to the programmatic logic that seeks to govern them. Technologies produce unexpected problems, are utilised for their own ends by those who are supposed to merely operate them, are hampered by under-funding, professional rivalries, and the impossibility of producing the technical conditions that would make them work – reliable statistics, efficient communication systems, clear lines of command, properly designed buildings, well framed regulations or whatever. Unplanned outcomes emerge from the intersection of one technology with another, or from the unexpected consequence of putting a technique to work (Rose and Miller 1992: 175).

This is no less the case with the treaty system. In 1950, the Joint Secretarial of the PCOB and the DSB, noted just these types of problems in the *Bulletin on Narcotics* (1950). The paper explained that there was considerable variety in the capacity and practices adopted by both parties and non-parties in fulfilling their obligations. Some countries had inefficient administrations due to weakness, indifference or insufficient financial resources. For example, in 'one small country the special control consists of a single official without administrative support, who goes about on a bicycle inspecting Chemist shops and making notes as he can of their stocks. In some countries the legislation is inadequate, in others, the legislation though adequate is not applied. In others again natural conditions make certain forms of control almost impossible to apply' (cited in Joint Secretarial of the Permanent Central Opium Board and the Drug Supervisory Body 1950: 79). At times, the observance of treaties was also affected by political situations and various crises, both internal and external, to the parties concerned. This made it difficult for international bodies to perform their duties. The situation in the years immediately following World War II, for example, was summarised by the PCOB in a 1947 report (document E/OB/2) as follows:

> To sum up, it may be said that the fulfilment by Governments of their obligations to send estimates and statistics has been steadily improving since the end of the war, but that it is still far from satisfactory. It is not sufficiently realised that sending punctual and accurate statistical information to the Board is not an act of grace on the part of Governments, to be abandoned or suspended according to convenience of the moment, a change of Government, or some other domestic event, but a serious contractual obligation undertaken in an international treaty vis-à-vis all other Governments; and if this obligation is not fulfilled, the system of control which Governments intend to institute, and which those governments which carry out the Convention in good faith are trying to 'work' effectively will break down (cited in Joint Secretarial of the Permanent Central Opium Board and the Drug Supervisory Body 1950: 79).

In 1950 the Joint Secretarial concluded that, whatever their cause, deficiencies in the national administrations, show themselves chiefly in connection with inaccurate statistics leading to discrepancies; failure to observe the limits imposed by the Conventions; failure to answer letters; and sending statistics late, or not at all. Taking into account the discussion in this chapter so far, it is clear that the successful governmental effect of the drug (opiate) control system has depended to a large extent on how well the network is maintained, the timely delivery of information to the centres of calculation and how accurate and complete the statistics and other types of information are. A review of more recent reports indicates the timely provision of accurate statistics and other types of information continues to be a limitation in the administration of the system to this day (see for example International Narcotics Control Board 2004, pp.12–17 and International Narcotics Control Board 2003, pp.12–18).

One other hindrance to the regulatory system is also a matter that various authorities and international regulatory bodies have been aware of for some time. With the 1936 treaty (pp.89–91) the participants in the international control system began to acknowledge what can best be described as an unintended consequence of the reasonably successful regulation of the licit supply of drugs (opiates). The 1936 treaty, which received only limited support, sought to address what would have been a relatively unexpected problem. After all, it was only with the regulation of what was defined by the treaties as the licit supply of opiates that it became possible to conceive of a distribution that could be described as illicit. The various regulations introduced by the early treaties, in effect, constituted the licit domain; and anything that fell outside the processes described in the treaties and resultant national legislation and regulatory systems amounts to the illicit supply – cultivation, production, manufacture or trade.

It is with this double move, constituting a regulated licit supply at the same time as an ungoverned illicit supply, that a new set of problems emerged. This assessment is supported by Remberg et al. (1994), who explain how international efforts reduced the number of licit opium producer countries in 1953, from twelve to seven, and ultimately to a single country in the 1970s. This made licit opium production much easier to oversee; however, during the same period two main trends emerged in relation to illicit production and processing. There was an upward trend in both the number of countries, and in global production volumes. The Golden Crescent (part of Afghanistan, Iran and Pakistan) emerged as a major production area in the late 1970s and early 1980s, and opium poppy cultivation began to spread rapidly in Latin America in the 1980s. As a result, trafficking patterns and routes changed frequently, and drug enforcement reports indicated that total worldwide illicit opium production had exploded in the 1980s, 'showing an approximately 152 percent increase between 1985 and 1992'. Second, clandestine opium extraction and heroin manufacturing moved closer to the poppy growing areas, invading practically every major opium production area. Furthermore, innovations in clandestine processing were introduced, including the use of new chemicals resulting in new heroin types and subtypes in the illicit market. Easy availability of heroin, close to the production areas, triggered significant shifts in consumption patterns in various parts of Asia where opium smoking had been the traditional form of consumption.

By the 1980s such changes in the sources and availability of illicit drugs had raised considerable alarm. They were discussed in a number of papers and reports that appeared in the *Bulletin on Narcotics*,[34] which consistently referred to, and highlighted, the risk posed by criminal organisations in relation to illicit drug trafficking. The various authors describe how, throughout the 1970s and 1980s, drug trafficking came to be dominated by organised crime syndicates who intended to secure financial profit and influence society. In conjunction with this trend, criminal organisations enormously increased their mobility and their human and financial resources. Criminal networks crossed over international boundaries and utilised different countries and territories to further their illegal activities. A virtually unlimited flow of money generated by street drug sales moved upwards to high-level international criminals. It is said that these funds helped to perpetuate illicit drug distribution networks, which function without regard for national boundaries and taxation systems, or the regulations applied to legitimate trade and commerce – which as we have seen in relation to the SCoND, are effectively employed in the governance of licit drug trade. The authors respectively went on to explain how, in their view, such criminal organisations, having greater financial resources than many police agencies, conducted illegal business transactions using sophisticated equipment to identify law enforcement intrusion devices and employing counter surveillance methods to protect themselves from detection. They could afford to hire computer, legal and financial experts to assist in the day-to-day operations of their lucrative illegal enterprises. Using sophisticated money-laundering techniques they diverted huge profits to seemingly legitimate business, making it increasingly difficult for law enforcement agencies to disrupt their extremely profitable ventures. The proceeds of drug crimes – illegally acquired profits – were laundered through

---

34   Moynihan (1983); Nagler (1984); Rider (1983); Stamler (1984); Stamler, Fahlman, and Clement (1987).

sophisticated international transactions often covered by legitimate operations (Stamler 1984).

Williams and Florez (1994), discussing the relationship between transnational criminal organisations (TCOs) and drug trafficking, elaborate on the trend just described. These authors note the increasing involvement, between 1974 and 1994, of organised crime in illicit drug trafficking. They further note that it was not simply the involvement of organised crime – however defined[35] – which had traditionally been a domestic phenomenon to be examined and understood at the local and national level, but rather large scale criminal organisations that 'treat national borders as nothing more than minor inconveniences to their criminal enterprise' (Williams and Florez 1994: 10). Much like many transnational corporations – trading in legal commodities – these TCOs had a home base in one state but operated across national borders. Williams and Florez link the emergence of TCOs as key players in the illicit drug trade with changed opportunities; with what Graham Farrell[36] describes as 'many seemingly innocuous factors related to technological, socio-economic and political change and advancement' (1999: 174). They explain how the emergence of TCOs and their involvement in drug trafficking can be understood as a result of a confluence of opportunities: increased interdependence among countries, ease of international travel and communications, permeability of national boundaries, and the globalisation of financial networks which created global markets for both licit and illicit commodities (Williams and Florez 1994). Dramatic growth in global trade has been accompanied by the evolution of global financial networks that have made it enormously difficult for governments to regulate and control monetary transactions across national boundaries. These developments offer new opportunities for TCOs. The scale of global economic activity makes it possible to hide illicit transactions, products and movements, within licit transactions, products and movements. As a result national borders have become highly porous to drug traffic. Moreover, the growth of a global financial system has allowed criminal organisations to move profits from their illegal transactions with speed and relative impunity. The sheer volume of money in the financial system and the ease with which it can be moved electronically have made it possible to obscure, move and clean the profits of illicit activities.

Unlike those organisations involved in the licit supply – cultivation, production, manufacture or trade – of opiates which, as a result of the provisions of the SCoND, conduct their business within bounds of various laws and regulations accessing trade through various regulated domains,[37] illicit traders and operators obtain access through circumvention rather than consent. They systematically seek to evade efforts to detect, monitor, intercept and disrupt their activities. As illicit drug trade (like any other

---

35 Williams and Florez (1994) note the heterogeneity of forms that such organisations can take.

36 Graham Farrell is a UN Officer for Drug Control and Crime Prevention, Centre for International Crime Prevention, and the author of a chapter on 'Drugs and Drug Control' in *Global Report on Crime and Justice* (1999).

37 Licit corporations generally negotiate with governments for permission to conduct operations on sovereign territory.

illicit trade) occurs outside the legitimate economy, regulatory bodies have no way of tracing transactions, keeping accounts or conducting national audits because those involved actively work to conceal the movement of drugs. No statistics describing production, manufacture or consumption, national estimates, import or export, or licensing details are available for national or international regulatory authorities like the INCB. In this regard, various law enforcement agencies constantly highlight the inadequacy of figures relating to illicit drug production and trafficking and its impact on interdiction. In doing so they explicitly acknowledge the difficulties of making visible the illicit supply (Farrell 1999; Wardlaw 1988).

Making the movements of legally produced opiates visible and knowable was the key governmental strategy of the SCoND – this process made visible any leakage from the licit supply. In this way the SCoND consolidated the constitution of the illicit supply of opiates as a new problem of government, as an unknown and thus ungoverned domain. Admittedly, the SCoND did attempt to address illicit supply. In 1977, Alfons Noll, of the United Nations Division of Narcotic Drugs, reported that a resolution of the ECOSOC (E/RES/2002(LX)) urged governments which had not already done so to enact legislation to make financial support provided knowingly, by whatever means, in furtherance of offences enumerated in Article 36, paragraph 1 of the SCoND, a punishable offence, and to cooperate with one another in exchanging information to identify drug traffickers committing such an offence. He explained that the 'importance of this resolution cannot be over emphasized as the ECOSOC adopted it with a view to improving international cooperation by all available means in order to combat more efficiently illicit trafficking in drugs of abuse' (Noll 1977: 42). The changes in illicit distribution during the 1970s and 1980s described above, however, suggest that efforts in this regard were relatively unsuccessful.

The limitations of the SCoND in relation to the growth in illicit production were acknowledged with the introduction of the 1972 Protocol, which strengthened the penal provisions against illicit trafficking in the SCoND, as well as the Convention on Psychotropic Substances.[38] These additional provisions emerged in a context where '[m]any nations [were] experiencing a constantly changing drug sub-culture characterised by an increasing abuse of drugs and psychotropic substances, with all the evil which it entails' (Noll 1975: 37). A report from a congress held by the International Association of Penal Law in 1975 explained that 'judging by the increased rate of drug dependence everywhere in the world, the present system has proved to be ineffective' (Noll 1975: 37). In the late 1970s and early 1980s various international meetings and commentators were reported in the *Bulletin on Narcotics* as coming to a similar conclusion.

---

38 *The Convention on Psychotropic Substances* closely resembles the 1961 Convention; however, it establishes an international control system for psychotropic substances, which are generally produced by the pharmaceutical industry. This was a response to the diversification and expansion of the spectrum of drugs allegedly liable to abuse. It also introduced controls over a number of synthetic drugs (hallucinogens, stimulants, hypnotics, sedatives and anxiolytics) as a result of a growing awareness of an apparently expanding repertoire of 'non-medical' drug use in the 1960s.

These assessments more or less expressed the view which follows. The existing conventions and legislative structures had facilitated the arrest of many drug couriers and low level traffickers who move from one jurisdiction to another, as well as the seizure of illicit drugs. Drug trafficking syndicates, however, receive their profits through a series of transactions made by a number of people over a period of time. Provided the accumulated profits remain intact, drug trafficking syndicates will be able to survive any measure undertaken by a given government to prosecute their members. Highly organised criminals are not likely to become directly involved in the possession, sale or distribution of illicit drugs, thus their identity may not be known when a particular offence is discovered. A sophisticated international trafficker will eventually acquire, possess and use the profits of drug crime which he or she arranges through lower level traffickers or couriers. Existing laws and international systems are inadequate because they are concerned almost exclusively with isolated offences involving the imprisonment of individuals while leaving the profits and resulting power base of the criminal organisation intact. Moreover, most contributions on this matter held that, despite the financial considerations of Article 36 of the SCoND, there are few provisions in the law that can be used to dismantle financial empires run by organised criminal groups, as most national laws and international systems are not designed to provide for or facilitate the freezing and forfeiture of such illegally acquired profits. 'If an international instrument containing provision against such a crime existed it would clearly facilitate the establishment of national laws and procedures for tracing, seizing and securing the forfeiture of the proceeds of drug offences' (Noll 1975: 46).

Recognising that current legislative provisions at both national and international levels were inadequate to support effective action to trace, freeze and secure the forfeiture of the proceeds of crime and to prosecute the individuals who knowingly possess such proceeds, the Division of Narcotic Drugs (DND) of the UN Secretariat convened two expert group meetings – one in 1983 and the other in 1984 – to consider ways and means of dealing with the problem.[39] The second expert group meeting in 1984 concluded that the most appropriate approach would be to negotiate an international instrument that would include a number of clauses addressing problematic issues (Nagler 1984; Stamler 1984).

Taming the Ungoverned Domain: The United Nations Convention on the Prevention of Illicit Traffic in Narcotic Drugs, 1988

The United Nations Conference for the Adoption of a Convention against Illicit Traffic in Narcotic Drugs and Psychotropic Substances was held at the Neue Hofburg at Vienna from 25 November to 20 December 1988. One hundred and six states participated in the conference along with representatives of the Pan Africanist Congress of Azania, the South-West Africa People's Organization and a number of

---

39 *Report of the Expert Group of the Forfeiture of the Proceeds of Drug Crimes*, Vienna, 24–8 October 1983' (DND/WP.1983/23/Rev.1, 20 January 1984); and *Report on the Second Expert Group Meeting on the Forfeiture of the Proceeds of Drug Crimes*, Vienna, 29 October to 2 November 1984 (MNAR/1984/13, 13 December 1984).

specialised agencies,[40] intergovernmental organizations,[41] United Nations organs and related bodies,[42] and observers from a range of non-governmental organizations.[43] By 2005, 170 States had become parties to this agreement (United Nations Office of Drug Control 2007). The UN World Drug Report (1983) succinctly summarised the general provisions of the 1988 treaty, explaining that:

The 1988 Convention complements the other drug control treaties, both of which were primarily directed at the control of licit activities. It was formulated specifically to deal with the growing problem of international trafficking which had only been dealt with marginally by earlier international legal instruments. The Convention includes money laundering and illicit traffic in precursor and essential chemicals within the ambit of drug trafficking activities and calls on parties to introduce these as criminal offences in their national legislation. Its objective is to create and consolidate international cooperation between law enforcement bodies such as customs, police and judicial authorities and to provide them with the legal guidelines: (a) to interdict illicit trafficking effectively; (b) to arrest and try drug traffickers; and (c) to deprive them of their ill-gotten gains. It also intensifies efforts against the illicit production and manufacture of narcotic and psychotropic drugs by calling for strict monitoring of the chemicals often used in illicit production. The INCB is required to supervise implementation of control measures on

---

40   Representatives of specialised agencies included: the International Civil Aviation Organization, International Labour Organization, United Nations Educational, Scientific and Cultural Organization, United Nations Industrial Development Organization and the World Health Organization.

41   Representatives of inter-governmental organisations included: the Arab Security Studies and Training Center, Colombo Plan Bureau, Council of Europe, Customs Co-operation Council, European Economic Community, International Criminal Police Organization, League of Arab States and South American Agreement on Narcotic Drugs and Psychotropic Substances (United Nations International Drug Control Program 1997).

42   Representatives of interested United Nations organs and related bodies included: the Centre for Social Development and Humanitarian Affairs, International Narcotics Control Board, United Nations Asia and Far East Institute for the Prevention of Crime and the Treatment of Offenders and United Nations for Drug Abuse Control (United Nations International Drug Control Program 1997).

43   Representatives of non-governmental organisations included: the Baha'i International Community, Caritas Internationalis, Centro Italiano de Solidarita, Colombia Therapeutic Communities, Co-ordinating Board of Jewish Organisations, Cruz Blanca Panama, Drug Abuse Prevention Programme, European Union of Women, Integrative Drogenhilfe a.d. Fachhochschule Ffm. e.v., International Abolitionist Federation, International Advertising Association, International Air Transport Association, International Association of Democratic Jurists, International Association of Lions Clubs, International Catholic Child Bureau, International Chamber of Commerce, International Confederation of Free Trade Unions, International Council on Women, International Council of Alcohol and Addictions, International Federation of Business and Professional Women, International Federation of Social Workers, International Pharmaceutical Federation, International Schools Associations, Islamic African Relief Agency, Opium De-addiction Treatment, Training and Research Trust, Pace United Kingdom International Affairs, Pax Romana, Soroptimist International, World Association of Girl Guides and Girl Scouts, World Union of Catholic Women's Organizations and Zonta International Committee (United Nations International Drug Control Program 1997).

precursor chemicals. The Convention provides for strengthened mechanisms to ensure the extradition of major drug traffickers, mutual legal assistance between States on drug related investigations and prosecutions and the transfer of criminal proceedings. It also introduces provisions for tracing, freezing and confiscating proceeds and property derived from drug trafficking as well as financial and commercial records.

The Convention requires law enforcement agencies to establish and maintain channels of information exchange concerning the identity and whereabouts of suspected traffickers, and recommends measures aimed at suppressing illicit trafficking by air, land and sea, together with the use of specialised techniques such as controlled deliveries (United Nations International Drug Control Program 1997).

The regulatory measures it describes follow closely, and expand on, the pattern established by existing international drug control treaties. The governmental network described by the SCoND is maintained by promotion and cultivation of cooperation between parties (nation states). Moreover, it is significantly enhanced by the strategy of including a range of other types of organisations (see for example footnotes 40–3), which have various forms of regional and international jurisdiction across extensive membership systems, in the convention process. In addition, Article 15 specifically engages commercial carriers (air carriers and shipping lines), which operate across territories and in an international domain in the regulatory process.

This move, in effect, makes the problem of illicit trafficking into an obligatory concern for organisations not traditionally involved in law enforcement. It requires commercial carriers themselves to take precautions to prevent the use of their means of transport for the commission of offences established by the treaty. These precautions may include training personnel to identify suspicious consignments or persons, promotion of integrity of personnel, submission of cargo manifests in advance, use of tamper resistant seals or containers and reporting all suspicious circumstances that may be related to the commission of an offence. The transnational and regional jurisdictional reach of these organisations – those attending the conference as well as commercial carriers – is able to significantly augment the governmental network without impinging on the sovereignty of states, while at the same time compensating for the governmental limitations of nation states operating in a global domain.

By codifying the means of making the illicit supply knowable, the 1988 treaty reformulated the governmental problem in relation to the supply of opioids. What is more, it succeeded where the SCoND had failed. This process involved the development of technologies and strategies that aim to make transactions involving illicit production and supply of opioids visible and knowable in the same way that the SCoND made the transactions involved in the production and distribution of legally produced opioids visible and knowable through the system of statistics, estimates and import and export certification. The barrier that emerges in relation to illicit drugs, of course, is the desire of criminal organisations involved in the trade to hide their activities. Thus, the focus of the later treaty largely shifted from tracing the distribution of legally produced drugs (in order to prevent leakages from licit to illicit trade), to tracking the flow of money and assets derived from, or other legal commodities and equipment associated with, trade in illegally produced drugs. Attention also shifted from the regulation of nation states like Britain or India, and the trading practices of organisations governed by those states, to the regulation of – or rather attempts to regulate – the activities of transnational criminal organisations.

In order to transform the domain of illicit drug trade from an ungovernable to a governable domain, the 1988 treaty was concerned not only with the regulation of illicit drugs, but also the regulation of money, equipment and precursor chemicals that may be involved in their trade (Article 3, Offences and Sanctions; Article 12, Substances Frequently Used in the Illicit Manufacture of Narcotic Drugs or Psychotropic Substances and Article 13, Materials and Equipment). Tracing such legal commodities, which are more easily monitored, provides a way of making transactions that may be illicit visible and hence governable. It also provides a way of identifying those involved in illicit trafficking.[44] Moynihan (1983), for example, explained that following the movement of money, a necessary part of illegal drug trafficking, assists in the appreciation of the ramifications of the activities of particular groups.[45] In particular it may lead to the identification and ultimately the conviction of those who otherwise remain aloof from criminal activities, but also have a major impact on it – the financiers and organisers. As society is increasingly regulated 'recourse to documentation or other records increasingly and necessarily involved at some stage of large scale transactions involving money, provides opportunities to intercept, assess and follow the flow of money'. Accordingly, 'the absence of records where records might be legitimately expected, or falsification of records to give the appearance of legitimacy, may be an indication of the *true* nature of transactions and the identity of those involved'. Moynihan goes on to argue that 'the financial implications of drug trafficking ought not to receive attention solely in order to deprive traffickers of their ill-gotten gains, however satisfying that may be. The *real* justification is the prospect of providing relatively effective deployment of resources with effective methods of terminating or disrupting criminal activities and identifying those most influential in such activities so that they might be charged and convicted'(Moynihan 1983: 8). Thus, this reformulation also attempts to constitute transnational criminal organisations as governable subjects which, arguably, is a considerably more difficult task.

Unlike nation states, or the various international organisations (see footnotes 40–3 for examples) that support international drug control conventions (and as a result become self-governing subjects in the international polity), transnational criminal organisations seek to avoid regulatory authority. Systematically seeking to evade efforts to detect, monitor, intercept and disrupt their activities, they have been accurately described by Williams and Florez as the 'ultimate example of what James Rosenau refers to as sovereignty free actors' who persistently demonstrate antipathy and disregard for recognised regulatory authorities and boundaries (Williams and

---

44 Such techniques were adopted by both the Australian Royal Commission of Inquiry into Drugs (Canberra, AGPS, 1980) and the New South Wales Royal Commission into Drug Trafficking (Sydney, NSWGPS, 1979).

45 The Honourable Sir Edward Williams, KBE, the Royal Commissioner of the Australian Royal Commission of Inquiry into Drugs, was in 1983 a member of the INCB. Moynihan was one of the Counsels assisting the Australian Royal Commission .

Florez 1994). Indeed, these organisations are constituted in the preamble to the 1988 treaty as the enemy of sovereignty:

> The Parties to this Convention,
>
> …
>
> Recogniz[e] the links between illicit traffic and other related *organised criminal activities* which undermine the legitimate economies and *threaten the stability, security and sovereignty of States*,
>
> Recogniz[e] also that *illicit traffic is an international criminal activity*, the suppression of which demands urgent attention and the highest priority,
>
> [and are]
>
> Aware that illicit traffic generates large financial profits and wealth enabling *transnational criminal organizations* to *penetrate, contaminate and corrupt* the structures of government, legitimate commercial and financial business, and society at all its levels…(United Nations 1988, emphasis added).

Such an assessment is reinforced by research that describes how drug trafficking has flourished where the state has been weak, acquiescent, corrupt or collusive (Williams and Florez 1994), and how governments that are lacking legitimacy and authority, or are not fully in control of territory under their jurisdiction, provide congenial environments for the emergence of these TCOs. Williams and Florez cite the examples of Afghanistan and Myanmar – the two major opium producers – to support this claim (1994). For example, they explain how the writ of the government of Myanmar does not run in the Shan State, which is one of the most important opium producing regions in the world. Myanmar has been characterised by persistent internecine warfare involving ethnic groups, revolutionary movements, the remnants of the Kuomintang armies that fled to Myanmar towards the end of the Chinese civil war, and opium warlords. Not only has much of the country remained outside government control, but opium has been the currency or medium of exchange for ethnic and revolutionary groups, allowing them to create, equip and maintain armies (which as we saw in Chapter 3 (pp.76–9) threaten sovereignty). These authors go on to note how such conditions are exacerbated by a 'global trade system that emphasizes free trade rather than fair trade' – 'continued global inequalities among countries and the biases of international trade systems against developing countries, make illicit roads to economic advancement an attractive alternative to continued poverty and desperation' (Williams and Florez 1994: 23). Chouvy (2003; 2005; 2006) outlines the persistence of this type of situation in Afghanistan.

With the new millennium the threat posed by illicit drug trafficking underwent another transformation which was expressed in the convergence between TCOs and terrorist organisations (Costa 2002; Garrenstein-Ross and Dabruzzi 2007; National Crime Authority 2001; Schmidt 2005). The tendency of terrorist organisations to form alliances with TCOs or to adopt their techniques in the pursuit of money to fund their operations was noted in national and international forums before the attack on the American World Trade Centre on September 11 2001. In Australia, for example, the Financial Action Task Force on Money Laundering warned that some terrorist groups were known to have carried out illicit drug trafficking to raise funds to further their political aims (cited in National Crime Authority 2001: 46). In August 2001, a month before the attack, Resolution 1363 of the United Nations Security Council established an expert group to monitor the implementation of measures against the Taliban imposed by Resolution 1267 (1999) and 1333 (2000) including those concerning

> arms embargoes, counter terrorism and related legislation and, in view of the link to the purchase of arms and financing of terrorism, of measures related to money laundering, financial transactions and drug trafficking (Security Council 2001b).

Following September 11 anxiety expressed in international forums regarding the relationship between terrorism, organised crime and drug trafficking escalated. According to Francisco Aguirre Sacasa (Minister for Foreign Affairs, Nicaragua), for example,

> the gravity of the criminal acts (the September 11 attack) had imposed new and greater challenges on the international community… There had to be a consciousness *that a new common enemy was being faced*, an enemy frequently linked to other international crimes, such as drug trafficking, money laundering and the diverse forms of organised crime that facilitate and finance the commission of such criminal acts (General Assembly 2001a).

While Security Council Resolution 1373 (28 September 2001), which is described as the most important instrument in the fight against terrorism, notes:

> … with concern the close connection between international terrorism and transnational organised crime, illicit drugs, money laundering, illegal arms trafficking and illegal movement of nuclear, chemical, geological and other potentially deadly materials and in this regard emphasises the need to enhance coordination of efforts on national, sub regional, regional and international levels in order to strengthen the global response to this serious challenge and threat to national security (Security Council 2001a).

Other speakers in UN forums regularly highlighted the link between terrorism, organised crime and drugs, frequently expressing the view that illicit drug trafficking constituted one of the largest sources of illegal finance for arms trafficking by terrorist organisations. Alfonso Valdivieso, (Colombia), argued that 'experience had taught that the international community's fight against the global problem of drugs … was a crucial element in the fight against terrorism' (General Assembly 2001b). Similar sentiments were articulated by representatives from other countries including Yugoslavia (General Assembly 2001b) and Algeria (General Assembly 2001a).[46] While Atal Biharhi Vajpayee, then Prime Minister of India, explained how 'terrorist operations are supported by drug trafficking, money laundering and arms smuggling' (General Assembly 2001c: 31). The link between illicit drugs and terrorism has been

---

46   Abdallah Baali: '…the new face of terrorism showed its linkage to drug and arms trafficking'.

reinforced by the resolutions of the UN Security Council and in statements and public addresses made by officials. Antonio Maria Costa, Executive Director, UN Office for Drug Control and Crime Prevention (ODCCP) explained at a Symposium on International Terrorism: 'The UN is involved because narcotics, crime and terrorism pose one and the same threat to civilisation' (Costa 2002, 2005).

While the link continues to feature in debates about the problem of illicit drugs trafficking, terrorism or the reconstruction of Afghanistan, scholarly investigations acknowledge that the relationship between drugs and terrorism is complex (Schmidt 2005; Steinitz 2002). Chouvy (2004c) tracing the political dimensions of the drug trade explains that although there is little doubt that some proceeds of the illicit drug trade contribute partially to the funding of some terrorist groups and their activities, drug trafficking is not the main source of funds when it comes to global terrorism. He argues that terrorists and drug traffickers have differing long term goals which should be considered in the methods used to counter both. Thus, contrary to Costa's view, fighting drug trafficking does not necessarily 'equate to fighting terrorism, even though 'narco-terrorism', depicted as a threat by certain sectional interests, arguably legitimates and reinforces a failed war on drugs' (Chouvy 2004c: 4).

Following on from this discussion, it is arguable that the governmental threat posed by TCOs and now terrorist activity to 'the stability, security and sovereignty' of nation states, and to international efforts to govern the distribution of opioids, reinforces the political rationality of reason of state that provides the basis for the enduring world war on drugs. While this claim – along with whether such a war is winnable or not – warrants further consideration, such a discussion is beyond the scope of this book. The purpose here has been to analyse the treaties, identifying the mechanisms that give effect to the international system of drug control. In doing so I have described the nature of the programs, technologies and strategies which translate the political rationalities that provide the conditions of possibility for the regulation of opioids into the realm of everyday life. The analysis has not been simply concerned with their successes, but has also worked to highlight the significant difficulties faced in operationalising them.

Conclusion

This chapter has analysed the complex of mundane programs, calculations, techniques, apparatuses, documents and procedures that make up the international system of drug regulation. It points out that this program of governance – in accord with the earlier problematisations of opium – is largely concerned with the regulation of supply: the production, manufacture, distribution and trade of opium. It describes how a complex arrangement of diverse forces – legal, expert, and administrative – were designed to shape the decisions and actions of individuals, groups, organisations and 'populations' in relation to 'authoritative' criteria concerned with the regulation of drugs. These 'authoritative' criteria, however, depend on particular styles of knowledge. I argue that the treaties themselves make up this knowledge. For example, the various systems of reporting estimates and statistics described by the SCoND have been essential components of the system. They work to both constitute and represent the domain to be governed; they made it thinkable and amenable to calculation by making all phases visible, from production to consumption, in the movement of drugs. These figures constitute a calculable domain that is amenable to programming and intervention and allows questions to be asked. In short, they make it possible to 'know' the government of supply as well as its shortfalls. At the same time that the treaties work to constitute a knowledge of the supply of narcotics, they make up the domain to be governed by playing a key role in establishing networks that enable rule to be brought about in an indirect manner – at a distance. By becoming a signatory to a treaty, each party is enrolled in the governmental network and comes to understand their problems and their situation according to a similar language and logic – for which the international instruments, and their provisions, become the solutions.

This analysis has not only described how the techniques and strategies for the government of opium work – or are intended to work – it highlighted the difficulties faced by various authorities in operationalising them. Noting, for example, how the successful governmental effect of the drug (opium) control system depends on the maintenance of networks as well as the timely delivery of accurate and complete information to centres of calculation, it describes how the limitations of legislative structures, administrative support, the intrusions of war and other civil unrest, have been seen to impinge on the operation of the system from the outset. This analysis also suggests the very real possibility of unintended effects (cf. Rose and Miller 1992) in particular the constitution of an ungoverned – and difficult to govern – illicit supply. The system described by the 1961 Single Convention was relatively effective in relation to the control of the legitimate supply of drugs for scientific and medical purposes. It provided, however, the conditions of possibility for the emergence of illicit production and supply. After all, it was only with the definition and regulation of the licit supply of opiates that it became possible to conceive of a system of production and distribution that could be described as illicit.

The problem of the growth of illicit production and trade was embodied in the dramatic increase in illicit production during the 1970s and 1980s, innovations in clandestine processing practice resulting in new heroin types and subtypes, clandestine opium extraction and heroin manufacturing moving closer to poppy growing areas, and changes in patterns of consumption in these. It was also linked to the entry of well financed and well-resourced TCOs into the illicit drug production and trafficking industry, and more recently to the worrying convergence between these organisations and terrorist activity. In the late twentieth century the problem of government was transformed from how to regulate the trade activities of nation states, to how to govern these clandestine affairs and organisations. Techniques similar to those of the SCoND, which work through the processes of translation and the constitution of networks, were mobilised by the 1988 *Convention on the Prevention of Illicit Traffic in Narcotic Drugs*. This treaty did not exactly have the effect of making the illicit supply of opium visible. Rather through strategies that traced the movement of certain legal commodities – including money, precursor chemicals and equipment – it aimed to bring the transactions that shadow the illicit supply into view.

In sum, the treaties themselves both describe and make up the governmental domain of drug control. Analysing the governmental techniques and strategies that constitute this system of regulation allows us to identify the mechanisms that give effect to the international drug control treaties and the political rationalities linked to them. It describes not only how this system works, but also the difficulties of putting it into effect. In doing so it exposes the heterogeneous and delicate nature of the multiple networks that connect the lives of individuals, groups, and organisations to the aspirations of various authorities concerned with drug control. The treaties analysed in this chapter describe the conditions of possibility for the operation of programs regulating the supply of opium. These are not the only programs concerned with the government of opium. A review of UN documents reveals more recent concerns expressed in terms of the problematisation of demand. The technologies and strategies that make up these latter programs are the subject of the next chapter.

Chapter 5

Supply in Demand

Up to this point we have generally been concerned with how the supply of opioids has been regulated. Chapter 2 traced the conditions that allowed for the development of various domestic regulations that mainly sought to control the quality and availability of such drugs, while Chapter 3 described the problematisation of international trade in opium which resulted in the growth of an international regulatory system. The last chapter, which analysed the form of the treaties that are the basis of the international regulatory system, established the governmental nature of these documents. The description of the complex of seemingly mundane programs, calculation techniques, apparatuses and procedures provided for by the international treaties, demonstrated how the international drug regulation system, in effect, makes up the domain that its seeks to govern. Recent United Nations Office of Drugs and Crime (UNODC) documents suggest, however, that the control of supply is not the only program concerned with the regulation of illicit drugs. The last quarter of the twentieth century saw another style of program become increasingly evident. It is focused on reducing the demand for these substances (Bull 2002: 313–15).[1] Specific demand reduction methods and techniques are not clearly described in UN documents outlining shared goals along with detailed means that form the basis of international agreements and principles of localised practice: according to the INCB they cannot be 'standardized by legal documents' (International Narcotics Control Board 1998;2). This, according to UN Fact Sheet No. 4, is because they:

> have to cover all areas of prevention from discouraging initial use to reducing the negative health and social consequences of drug abuse…they should be integrated into broader social welfare programs, health promotion policies and preventive education programs to ensure an environment in which healthy *choices* become attractive and accessible. Demand reduction programs should address the needs of the population in general as well as those specific groups more at risk, taking into account differences in gender, culture and education (United Nations General Assembly Special Session on the World Drug Problem 1999: 2).

This chapter examines the types of techniques and strategies that are part of the program for the reduction in demand for illicit drugs. Rather than attempting some sort of inventory and analysis of all the strategies involved in demand reduction, it

---

1   According to the first *World Drug Report*, demand reduction initiatives are 'those undertaken to prevent the onset of drug use, to help and encourage those who have already taken drugs to discontinue use and maintain abstinence, and to provide advice and treatment for problem or dependent users whereby the harm to the users themselves and to society can be limited' (UNDCP 1997).

focuses on a particular group of strategies: those practices associated with treatment and rehabilitation. According to the INCB the treatment and rehabilitation of drug 'abusers' are key elements in any program of demand reduction, because in many countries a relatively small number of users are responsible for a comparatively large proportion of the demand for illicit substances. As a result, interventions focused on this group are likely to have a significant impact in relation to the goal of reducing demand (International Narcotics Control Board 1998).[2] However, according to the INCB, 'no particular program has been effective for all drug abusers, even within a single country, and the transfer of a treatment regime from one culture to another has not always been constructive'. Consequently, treatment and rehabilitation programs must be adapted to local conditions and circumstances (International Narcotics Control Board 1998:3). Treatment programs, like other demand reduction strategies, must be carefully designed by taking into consideration not only the individuals concerned (the target populations) but also the socio-cultural and economic milieux; they must be adapted to the society in question. The apparent need for social and cultural specificity, and the lack of codified international standards, set particular limits with regard to analysis. Instead of analysing how treaties, and the generalised regulatory strategies they describe, are translated across an international domain and reproduced in a range of autonomous states – because there are few, if any, readily available discursive arrangements that would facilitate such analysis in relation to programs regulating demand – this chapter focuses on a specific type of treatment which is delivered in a more bounded social and cultural context. In particular it examines the case of methadone maintenance treatment (MMT)[3] as it is delivered in Australia, a country considered to be a leader in this field.

MMT has been selected as the case study because it is the most widely available and used treatment in Australia (Commonwealth Department of Human Services and Health 1995; Commonwealth of Australia 1993, 1997; 2007). It is not the only pharmaceutical opioid available for the treatment of dependence. Currently buprenorphine and naltrexone are also used for the treatment of opioid dependence. Buprenorphine is a long acting opioid used in a similar way to methadone (see p.11

---

2   This view is reiterated in the 2000 World Drug Report:

Treatment is generally recognised as an essential component of a comprehensive demand reduction strategy, including the Declaration on the Guiding Principles of Drug Demand Reduction. In addition to helping individuals to reduce drug consumption, improve health status, reduce criminality and improve social functioning, treatment reduces drug abuse in an important segment of the population which in most countries, is responsible for the bulk of the consumption of drugs such as heroin or cocaine. …If treatment is readily available and a high percentage of drug abusers receive it, it can have a measurable effect on the overall demand for illicit drugs. With fewer untreated abusers involved in the recruitment of new users, prevalence of drug abuse is likely to decline as well (United Nation Office for Drug Control and Crime Prevention 2000: 117).

3   The *World Drug Reports* (United Nations International Drug Control Program 1997, United Nation Office for Drug Control and Crime Prevention 2000) identify methadone maintenance treatment along with self-help groups, therapeutic communities, and counselling, for example, as key treatment techniques in the reduction of demand for illicit drugs.

above). Along with methadone it is listed as a schedule 8 (S8) drug.[4] It comes in tablet form which is dissolved under the tongue. Its effects are said to be easier to withdraw form, and are longer lasting than those of methadone. Buprenorphine is a partial opioid agonist: while the drug blocks the effects of any other opiate used (such as heroin), it also has some opioid properties and effects. It is less likely than methadone to result in overdose because it blocks other opioids and even itself as the dosage increases (Kosten and George 2002). Naltrexone is an opioid receptor antagonist that works to inhibit the effects of opioids such as heroin. It is used not only to assist with heroin withdrawal but also for the purposes of relapse prevention. A single 50 mg oral dose of naltrexone will block a person's opioid receptors for around 24 to 48 hours, ensuring that any opioid taken during this time will produce no opioid effect. Natlrexone itself has no euphoric effects and as such does not induce either dependence or tolerance in its users. Because, unlike methadone or buprenorphine, naltrexone has no opioid like properties, it is only as good as the motivation of its users (Commonwealth of Australia 2007; Thomas and Buckmaster 2007). These two drugs are relative new comers to the Australian treatment scene. Somewhat ironically they only became available in the context of a controversial proposal to explore the feasibility of diacetylmorphine (heroin) maintenance treatment.

In 1989 the then newly formed Australian Capital Territory (ACT) Legislative Assembly established a Select Committee on HIV, Illegal Drugs and Prostitution. In the face of growing evidence that treatment is the most cost-effective approach to problems resulting from illicit drug use, in 1991 the Committee made a commitment to rigorously review the viability of diacetylmorphine maintenance treatment (Bammer and Douglas 1996: 690). From the moment of its public announcement, the proposal to scientifically study the feasibility of delivering heroin maintenance treatment in Australia was politically controversial, and often seemed destined to fail (Bull 2002: 9–22). In 1997 after more than five years of lobbying the national governing body, the Ministerial Council on Drug Strategy (MCDS),[5] finally gave approval for the trial to proceed as part of an evaluation of a range of new treatments. A critical factor in the decisions was the Council's approval for plans to trial other opioid pharmacotherapies in other States. These alternative treatments also involved the use of the opioid class of narcotic drugs. As Peter McKay, Tasmania's Health Minister, who had strongly opposed the trial in the previous year, explained: 'the fact is if you go down the path of trying all these other treatment options, and don't include heroin, you haven't covered all the bases' (in Lyall 1997: 25). Then Prime Minister John Howard, however, was of a different view and personally intervened to block the trial. He overturned the decision of the MCDS, and in doing so a majority of state, territory and federal health and law enforcement ministers. The government moved

---

4   Schedule 8 (S8) substances are consistently defined across Australian jurisdictions by the Standard for the Uniform Schedule of Drugs and Poisons (SUSDP) (Therapeutic Goods Administration 2007). S8 substances are included Schedule 1 to the SCoND, are described as having a 'very high risk of dependence and abuse' and are subject to the strictest regulatory protocols.

5   MCDS is comprised of two Ministers, one each from health and law enforcement, from each jurisdiction (the Commonwealth and each Australian State and Territory).

to rescind approval for the trial; the evaluation of the alternative pharmacotherapies was nevertheless to proceed. In 1998 the Commonwealth Government commissioned the *National Evaluation of Pharmacotherapies for Opioid Dependence* (NEPOD). It was a three-year project, which concluded that methadone, buprenorphine and levo-alpha-acetylmethadol (LAAM) produced substantial benefits for drug dependent individuals and reduced the use of illicit drugs and criminal activity (Mattick et al. 2004).

While buprenorphine was registered for use in the management of opioid dependence at the conclusion of the trial in 2001 (Australian Institute of Health and Welfare 2007) (and LAAM continued to be unavailable) methadone maintenance has been used as a treatment in Australia for many years. Since 1969 there has been a continuous growth in the number of people enrolling in methadone maintenance treatment.[6] This has been accompanied by the development of a seemingly diverse range of treatment settings.[7] Although such diversity conceivably poses a problem for analysis, a national review of methadone services in 1995 found that:

> a comparison of methadone treatment services throughout Australia indicates that there are many areas of commonality between the States and Territories in regard to their philosophy of treatment. The principles of methadone maintenance treatment described in the National Methadone Policy underpin all services. The various State Guidelines for treatment are similar in their content, and provide for comparable treatment regimens across State boundaries (Commonwealth Department of Human Services and Health 1995: 46).

In short, while the means by which services are delivered may vary, similar principles for methadone maintenance treatment are embodied in all programs throughout Australia (Commonwealth Department of Human Services and Health

---

6   Between 1969 and the early 1980s the use of methadone treatment grew gradually to approximately 3,000 clients nationwide (2,000 in 1985). Through the second half of the 1980s and up to the present time there has been a steady and substantial growth in the number of individuals receiving methadone treatment in most jurisdictions of Australia. At June 1995 there were around 17,000 clients in methadone treatment throughout the country – an average annual growth rate of approximately 15 per cent per annum since 1985–1986 (Commonwealth Department of Human Services and Health 1995; Commonwealth of Australia 1997). In June 2001 there were approximately 32,000 clients in methadone treatment in Australia (Mattick et al. 2004), and the latest pharmacotherapy statistics suggest that by June 2006 it involved some 38,569 clients; 27,588 (71 per cent) of whom were receiving methadone (Australian Institute of Health and Welfare 2007). Since 2002 growing numbers of opioid dependent persons have been treated with buprenorphine. There is some movement between these types of pharmacotherapy; in June of 2006 8,950 people were registered to receive the newer option (Australian Institute of Health and Welfare 2007).

7   This has largely been an effect of the various histories of delivery in the respective States as well as the mechanisms by which services have been provided, for example, the extent of centralised, decentralised or localised control, the different roles of the public and private sectors, or the extent to which methadone services are provided by larger specialist clinics compared to private practitioners as part of their general practice (Commonwealth Department of Human Services and Health 1995).

1995: 2). Moreover, these principles have been documented over the last the twenty years in National Methadone Guidelines (Commonwealth of Australia 1985, 1987, 1988), National Policy on Methadone (Commonwealth of Australia 1993, 1997), State and Territory guidelines (for example Queensland Health 1994; Victorian Department of Health and Community Services 1995) and following the expansion of the treatment domain to include buprenorphine and naltrexone the more broadly framed *National Pharmacotherapy Policy for People Dependent on Opioids* (Commonwealth of Australia 2007; seev also Drugs and Poisons Regulation Group 2006; New South Wales Health Department 2006). The new national clinical guidelines are more specifically focused on naltrexone, methadone or burprenorphine respectively (Bell et al. 2003; Henry-Edwards et al. 2003; Lintzeris et al. 2006). While the maintenance spectrum has been expanded the delivery of new treatments follows the procedures developed for the delivery of Methadone. As the New South Wales manual for the accreditation of pharmaoctherapy prescribers explains:

> There is limited experience with buprenorphine treatment. All that has been said about assessment and factors influencing methadone maintenance is presumed to apply to buprenorphine. Issues about review of treatment and the importance of the therapeutic relationship are all assumed to pertain to buprenorphine as they do to methadone maintenance treatment… (New South Wales Health Department 2001: 96).

The apparent popularity and widespread and enduring availability of methadone maintenance treatment, along with its relatively consistent codification in national, State and Territory policy documents, and the recent policy transfer of this codification to newer pharmacotherapies for opioid dependence make it a compelling or, at the very least, viable case study.

It should be noted at the outset of this chapter that it is not my intention to engage with the debate regarding whether methadone is a cure for addiction/drug dependence or not. This has been extensively explored. As is often noted, MMT is the most evaluated treatment there is (Commonwealth Department of Human Services and Health 1995; Ward et al. 1992). The point here is to understand how methadone maintenance treatment, along with the more recent addition of buprenorphine maintenance treatment (BMT), works to govern the use of illicit opioids and heroin in particular. Put simply, this chapter examines the mechanisms that give effect to – and make possible – this localised system of regulation. In doing so it demonstrates how the political rationalities that provide for the regulation of opioids work. It describes the programs, technologies and strategies which translate these rationalities into the realm of everyday life. This analysis begins with a brief historical review of the emergence of methadone in response to dependent opiate use; it then situates the Australian example of MMT in relation to broader systems of international drug control. This provides a backdrop for the analysis of national, State and Territory policy documents that is concerned with how MMT (and BMT) works to govern the demand for opioids.

Making up Methadone Maintenance Treatment

Methadone maintenance treatment as a form of therapy for intravenous heroin users has been popular, mainly in medical circles, for about forty years. Most simply, it is a drug substitution program that replaces illegal heroin with legally available methadone. It involves making a pure drug available to opioid depended people, under supervision, at a minimal cost. The use of methadone as a substitute opioid is considered to be appealing for a number of reasons: it allows the supply of an opioid to be legal and controlled; compared to heroin, which may satisfy the user for 6–12 hours, methadone only needs to be taken once a day due to its longer duration of action; a daily dose can eliminate opiate withdrawal symptoms for twenty-four to thirty-six hours; methadone can be administered orally;[8] and finally, it can allow the opioid user to separate from the drug subculture in order to improve his or her health and social functioning (Hall et al. 1991). Despite much support for this treatment, its role in the therapeutic spectrum concerned with opioid dependence remains contentious (New South Wales Health Department 2001: 35–6), and the relative virtues of abstinence and maintenance therapies continue to be hotly debated in the Australian context (Thomas and Buckmaster 2007). To understand why controversy persists – even in the light of this drug's apparent utility – it is helpful to explore the history of the experiments and the theoretical foundations and assumptions underlying the development of this mode of maintenance treatment for people who are opioid dependent. A brief review of the literature explaining the medical theoretical footing of methadone maintenance follows.

Methadone as a Treatment for Addiction

The earliest documented work using methadone as a treatment option in response to opiate addiction, is that of Isbell and Vogell (Isbell et al. 1947; 1949). These authors reported the successful daily substitution of the 'synthetic opiate methadone' in the attempt to 'wean an addict off heroin'. In the course of this treatment the addict entered an inpatient facility and received progressively larger doses of methadone until no heroin withdrawal symptoms were evident; the patient was then expected to take this dose of methadone daily and indefinitely. Intensive support therapy was included in the treatment in order to 'reestablish ego interaction and normal social functioning especially a steady paying job' (Isbell and Vogell 1949: 909). Once this was achieved the patient was seen on an ambulatory basis. During the 1950s further experimental work with the drug was conducted at the Public Health Hospital in Lexington, Kentucky (Eddy et al. 1957).

Publicly available treatment for opiate dependence with methadone maintenance was first introduced as a result of growing concern regarding problems related to 'addiction'[9] which, in 1959, inspired the New York City Mayor to provide funds on

---

8   Indeed, it is said that it works best when administered orally, because of the slower uptake.

9   The problem that inspired such a response was most notably the escalating incidence of property crime (Davies 1986; Newman 1977).

the basis of advice from a joint committee of the American Medical Association and the American Bar Association, to the New York Medical Centre for research into treatment for addiction (Joint Committee of the American Bar Association and the American Medical Association on Narcotic Drugs 1958). The funds were explicitly provided for the development of '... a pharmaceutical substitute for heroin which would enable addicts to function' (Newman 1977: 3). Vincent Dole (a biochemist), and Marie Nyswander (a psychiatrist), began this particular search for such a substitute drug. Dole was to later explain that the '...object at the onset was simply to find a medication that would keep addicts content without causing medical harm and that would be safe and effective for use over long periods in relatively stable doses. The goal of social rehabilitation of addicts was not part of the original plan. Merely satisfying addicts, although not an ideal result, seemed better than the existing policy that forced incurable addicts into criminal activity' (Dole 1988: 3025).

The initial investigation began with a series of opiate-like drugs, including morphine, heroin, hydromorphone, codeine, oxycodone, and meperidine. In the view of the researchers, none of these was able to provide the kind of outcome they were looking for. The experiments with methadone were the first to show positive results. Their favourable findings inspired Dole and Nyswander to launch a Methadone Maintenance Research Program in 1963. Although only six patients were treated in the first year of the project, the researchers felt that their results were sufficiently impressive to justify a trial of maintenance treatment in heroin addicts admitted to open medical wards of general hospitals (Dole et al. 1966). In 1965 a group of twenty-two patients, previously addicted to heroin, were stabilised with oral methadone hydrochloride (Dole and Nyswander 1965).

Dole and Nyswander explained that the patients included in this experiment 'ceased to behave as addicts'. They reliably reported illegal drug use; patients on high doses of methadone found their experiments with heroin unrewarding, and they discontinued use without the imposition of negative sanctions. The researchers also noted that an 'interesting phenomenon, was the production of symptoms typical of drug deficiency by acute emotional stress' (Dole and Nyswander 1965: 84). Anxiety in some susceptible patients caused malaise, nausea, yawning, and sweating, indistinguishable from the effects of abstinence, even though the patients were being maintained on large doses of medication. The researchers concluded, 'these observations suggest that the effectiveness of methadone can vary with changes in psychological and metabolic state' (Dole and Nyswander 1965: 84).

This early work identified the relief of 'narcotic hunger' and what Dole and Nyswander called the pharmacological 'blockade' of the euphoric effect of an average illegal dose of diacetylmorphine (heroin), as the two most useful effects of methadone in the treatment of 'addiction'. It indicated that these effects, together with a comprehensive program of rehabilitation, could facilitate the social reintegration of 'addict patients' (Dole and Nyswander 1965). Dole and Nyswander's subsequent work provided evidence which supported these findings (Dole et al. 1966; Dole and Nyswander 1967; 1968; Dole and Joseph 1978). It should be emphasised here that, although the authors felt that methadone had contributed in an essential way to the favourable results of the maintenance experiment, they acknowledged that it was quite clear that the giving of methadone was only part of the program.

Addiction as a Metabolic Disease?

Following this early work, Dole and Nyswander persistently reported dramatic improvements in social status of patients on the treatment programs (Dole and Nyswander 1965; Dole et al. 1966; Dole and Nyswander 1967, 1980; Dole 1988). These improvements exceeded all expectations. The researchers explained that the '[i]nitial hope was only that heroin seeking behaviour would be stopped by a narcotic blockade, it was not expected that we would be able to retain more than 90 per cent of patients and that almost 75 per cent of these would be socially productive[10] and living as *normal citizens* in the community after only six months of treatment' (Dole et al. 1966: 309). This unexpectedly favourable response of addicts to a maintenance program inspired Dole and Nyswander to reassess the traditional psychogenic theory of addiction which generally focused on individual deficits. They suggested, on the basis of their own research, that addiction is the expression of some sort of metabolic disorder (Dole et al. 1966).[11]

In a number of different papers, these authors explain that historically the psychogenic theory had been based upon the study of established addicts, and not upon data obtained in the pre- or post-addicted state; in consequence the so-called addictive personality could be interpreted either as a cause or an effect of addiction (Dole et al. 1966; Dole and Nyswander 1967, 1980). In reviewing the literature, Dole and Nyswander (1965; 1967) concluded that two key factors were put forward as support for the psychogenic, or character defect, theory. The first was the sociopathic behaviour and attitude of addicts; and the second was the inability of addicts to control their drug using impulse. The researchers' commentary on the first factor argues that the decisive proof for the psychogenic theory would be a demonstration that potential addicts could be identified by psychiatric examination before drug usage had distorted behaviour and metabolic functions. Dole and Nyswander claimed that their search failed to disclose any study in which a characteristic psychopathology, or addictive personality, had been recognised in a number of individuals prior to addiction (1967: 21). With regard to the second argument, Dole and Nyswander, like other commentators (Gossop 1987; Krivanek 1988; Ward et al. 1992), criticised the normative nature of any concept of self-control. Furthermore, they argue, as does more recent research, that addicts do control their drug use to some degree (Gossop 1987).

Concluding their critique of the psychogenic perspective Dole and Nyswander asserted that psychotherapy is ineffective in the treatment of addiction. The search of the literature, referred to above, failed to disclose a single report in which

---

10   Social productivity was indicated by participation in employment and school, improvements in family relations, and reductions in criminal behaviour.

11   Dole (1988) compared addiction to diabetes and other chronic diseases; this metaphor maintains resonance in the contemporary treatment field. The current Victorian policy document explains that 'maintenance pharmacotherapies can be compared to other drugs that are effective in treating serious, chronic, relapsing conditions such as hypertension and diabetes. These conditions, like opioid dependence, are chronic, require daily treatment and have a high risk of adverse effects if treatment compliance is poor' (Drugs and Poisons Regulation Group 2006:7, see also Wodak 2007).

'withdrawal of drug and psychotherapy has enabled a significant fraction of the patients to return to the community and live as *normal* individuals' (Dole et al. 1966: 204). Nevertheless, at this relatively early point in their research, they admitted that it is conceivable that a basic character defect might lead to initial drug use and this in turn to an irreversible addiction in which the subsequent behaviour of the subject is determined by conditioned reflexes (Wikler 1965: 85), or by metabolic changes in neurons following repeated exposure to narcotic drugs. Thus, like the inebriety specialists of the late nineteenth century (see p.33 above), they conceded that answers may lie in a 'hybrid' of theories, in which psychological and metabolic factors are combined in various ways, or alternatively, that addicts are heterogeneous, some psychological and others metabolic (Dole and Nyswander 1967: 23).

In support of their own metabolic position, Dole and Nyswander asserted that most street addicts engage in property crime to support their addiction and, therefore, it (property crime) is nearly an inevitable consequence of addiction (1967; 1980). Moreover, these authors claim that crime statistics show both the force of drug hunger and its specificity: almost all of the crimes committed by addicts related to the procurement of drugs.[12] They argued that rapid disappearance of theft and antisocial behaviour in patients on the methadone maintenance program, strongly supported the hypothesis that the crimes they had previously committed as addicts were a consequence of drug hunger, not the expression of some more basic psychopathology.

In short, these authors supported their own work by claiming that drug-seeking behaviour, like theft, is observed only after 'addiction' is established and the narcotic drug has become euphorigenic, and that it is possible to judge whether this abnormality stems from character weakness, or whether it is a consequence of drug usage, when drug hunger is relieved. As evidence for this claim they explained that the patients on methadone maintenance programs, 'blockaded against the euphorigenic action of heroin, turn their energies to school work and jobs. ...Their struggles to become self-supporting members of the community should impress the critics who had considered them self-indulgent when drug-hungry addicts. When drug hunger is blocked without production of narcotic effects the drug-seeking behaviour ends' (Dole and Nyswander 1967: 22).

Furthermore, Dole and Nyswander argued that one of the reasons why methadone maintenance is effective at reducing illicit opioid use, is because when high doses (greater than 80 mg) are used, the substantial level of tolerance to methadone that develops induces sufficient cross-tolerance to heroin, preventing it from producing its desired effects should a patient relapse. They referred to this high level of cross-tolerance as 'narcotic blockade' (Dole et al. 1966). Dole and Nyswander believed that opioid dependence was a metabolic disease and insisted that high, blockading maintenance doses of methadone for long periods of time were a necessary component of successful methadone maintenance (Dole and Nyswander 1967). The most refined account of the metabolic theory was presented by Dole in a paper titled *Implications of Methadone Maintenance for Theories of Narcotic Addiction*, published in 1988.

---

12 From the state of current research it is apparent that this is an oversimplification of the relationship between heroin use and crime (Makkai 1999).

Of all the work in this area it most clearly articulates what Dole and Nyswander's metabolic theory of addiction might be.[13]

Dole's 1988 paper explains that analysis of the clinical results of methadone maintenance treatment during the preceding twenty-five years, coupled with advances in the understanding of narcotic receptors and their ligands, suggests that compulsive use of narcotics stems from receptor dysfunction. Thus, methadone maintenance treatment is corrective: it normalises neurological and endocrinologic processes in patients whose endogenous ligand-receptor functions have been deranged by long-term use of powerful narcotic drugs (Dole 1988: 3025). In this paper, however, it still remains unclear why only some individuals who are exposed to narcotics are more susceptible to 'addiction' than others, and whether long-term dependent users can recover normal function without maintenance therapy. Nevertheless, Dole maintains 'that there seems to be a specific neurological basis for the compulsive use of heroin by addicts and that methadone taken in optimal doses can correct the disorder', moreover, '[w]hen somatic function has been normalised the ex-addict, supported by counseling and social services, can begin the long process of social rehabilitation' (Dole 1988: 3026).

In this paper Dole also contends that the seventy-year history of attempts to maintain opiate addicts prior to the use of methadone failed primarily because 'the physicians were using the wrong drugs' (Dole 1988: 3028). Methadone proved to be more suitable for substitution treatment because its long action facilitated a more stable state of neuroadaptation, and this is important for the development of a steady and stable state in the patient.[14] The concentration of methadone in the blood is stabilised by reversible absorption into the tissues, mainly the liver (Dole 1970; Dole and Kreek 1973). The key factor is the reversibility of this absorption. Immediately after ingestion of the daily dose, 99 per cent of the medication is bound to tissues in equilibrium with the concentration in blood. It is gradually released as the blood concentration falls, thus buffering the medication level in the blood. With a relatively steady concentration in blood, the narcotic receptors in critical cells remain continuously occupied, and the patient becomes functionally normal.[15]

---

13   This paper summarises the work which won Dole the Albert Lasker Clinical Medicine Research Award.

14   The significance of the drug's longer action seems to be confirmed by the positive results obtained by recent research in relation to maintenance with buprenorphine and LAAM which have longer actions than methadone (Mattick et al. 2004).

15   Zweben and Payte (1990) generally agree with Dole's conclusions. They explain that methadone hydrochloride is a synthetic opioid-agonist drug that acts primarily at the u-opioid receptor sites. Taken orally its absorption from the gastrointestinal tract is essentially complete. There is extensive initial hepatic uptake of around 90 per cent. Methadone is then gradually released from hepatic binding (storage) sites in an unchanged form into the blood (Zweben and Payte 1990). In accordance with Dole and Kreek (1973: 10) these authors believe that the liver probably plays a major role by maintaining a large reservoir of methadone. They suggested that this reservoir of methadone, nonspecifically bound in tissues and in equilibrium with methadone in plasma, would be necessary to explain the relatively low peak plasma levels and relatively high steady-state levels in patients 24 hours after a dose (Zweben and Payte 1990).

The essential feature in the treatment is the stability of receptor occupation, which permits interacting systems in the body to function normally. Dole suggests that the physiological and behavioural disturbances in heroin addiction – the unpleasant conditions and erratic behaviours commonly associated with heroin use – are consequences of the rapid changes in the status of the endogenous narcotic receptor-ligand system. When the addict takes short acting narcotics, the system cycles between abstinence and narcosis several times a day. A stable state of adaptation is impossible (Dole 1988: 3026).[16]

Dole suggests that, 'ideally', methadone could be used as a stabilising medication to provide immediate intervention, stopping the use of illicit narcotics and normalising general metabolism. Later, after medical and social rehabilitation, the maintenance medicine would be withdrawn slowly and the patient would be totally 'cured' (Dole 1988: 3029). This is somewhat of an oversimplification: while some patients do well after therapeutic intervention, or 'rehabilitation', coordinated with the termination of methadone maintenance, the majority, although equally motivated, describe dysphoria, restlessness, irritability and recurrent urges to use heroin (Rosenbaum and Murphy 1984). Researchers have reported that measurable physiological disturbances persist after detoxification from heroin or any other narcotic that has been used for a long time. Those interested in the nature of the abstinence syndrome have observed signs of dependence (sympathetic nervous system hyperactivity) up to two years after the initiation of abstinence. As a result, the danger of relapse, after the withdrawal of methadone, is great (Dole 1988; Lynskey 1998; Mattick et al. 2004; New South Wales Health Department 2001; Rosenbaum and Murphy 1984).

Methadone Maintenance in Australia

In the late 1960s a few clinicians in Sydney began using single daily oral dosages of methadone in the long-term treatment of patients who had become dependent on daily intravenous doses of illicit heroin. Methadone was initially used to prevent,

---

16 Other researchers have also identified methadone's long action – when taken orally – as a significant phenomenon in the maintenance of opiate addicts with methadone. Kreek explains that constant availability of drugs to specific receptors is essential for steady-state maintenance of the tolerant and dependent state, and it is the constant availability of the drug to specific receptors, resulting in a steady state, which is essential for the pharmacological, physiological, and thus clinical efficacy of methadone maintenance treatment (Kreek 1973). Zweben and Payte also agree that 'a steady concentration of methadone in the blood is essential to the normalisation of endocrine and neuroendocrine functions that occurs with the long-term administration of methadone' (Zweben and Payte 1990). The success of buprenorphine maintenance is similarly linked to its high affinity to u-opioid receptor sites and its ability to displace other opioids including methadone and heroin (Mattick et al. 2004, Lintzeris et al. 2006, NSW Health Department 2006). This characteristic means that its action can (and is) more accurately, than that of methadone, be described as 'blockade' (Lintzeris et al. 2006, NSW Health Department 2006, Commonwealth of Australia 2007). Buprenorphine works by aggressively occupying u-opioid receptors, displacing other opioids and hence blocking their effects. Methadone works through the process of cross-tolerance. This important difference also means that buprenorphine use is less likely to result in overdose.

or at least minimise, the effects of heroin withdrawal for the dependent individual; it also facilitated this person's diversion from drug-using subcultures and the associated temptations. Despite Dole and Nyswander's conclusions regarding the metabolic foundation of opioid addiction, many of these early Australian endeavours were abstinence oriented; daily doses were gradually reduced until an opiate free state was reached. As a result there was a high rate of relapse. While some doctors perceived this as therapeutic 'failure', and expelled patients from further methadone treatment, others were more tolerant believing that the continued offer of daily methadone dosages at least encouraged patients to keep in touch with medical and other health service providers (Bull 1991). A few of the early prescribers did apply the research findings published by Dole and Nyswander. Stella Dalton was the most renowned of these. She implemented a pilot program using methadone blockade at Wisteria House (located in the Blue Mountains, NSW) in 1970. Her program did, however, deviate from Dole and Nyswander's model; its aim was to achieve total abstinence from all drugs within a three- to four-year period. Dalton's early efforts were considered to be successful and as a result methadone programs in Australia expanded. Her efforts were reproduced in other states, particularly Western Australia and Queensland (CEIDA 1989).

Towards the end of the 1970s methadone blockade fell into disrepute. Critics claimed that methadone was taken for granted by those who were responsible for its administration, and that it was given liberally by both clinics and doctors who had come to believe that the drug itself would constitute a cure. Maintenance therapy, using smaller doses, became popular – and as an unintended consequence, patients were inclined to supplement their therapy with street heroin. Lax controls over the dispensing of methadone facilitated the diversion of substantial quantities of the drug to the illicit market (Murdoch 1983). At the same time a growing range of therapeutic alternatives, which were ideologically opposed to the use of methadone, emerged. These included, for example, detoxification facilities, self-help groups, outpatient counselling and drug free therapeutic communities. In this milieu methadone maintenance treatment came to be considered just one – relatively extreme – option in the therapeutic spectrum (CEIDA 1986; Wells and McKay 1989).

Around this time the National Health and Medical Research Council issued the first guidelines for the use of methadone in treatment programs for opiate dependence (Commonwealth of Australia 1987; Wells and McKay 1989). The acknowledged focus of these guidelines was improving the health and social function of individuals who had been long-term habitual users of heroin and who had become physically and psychologically dependent on the drug. These guidelines had strong therapeutic objectives, emphasising the need for very thorough medical assessment and psychological counselling of drug users before they were accepted for treatment – and careful monitoring thereafter by urinalysis to detect any continuing use of heroin or other psychotropic drugs, with intensive medical and social follow up until hopefully complete rehabilitation (that is, abstinence) from dependence on methadone and other drugs was achieved. The providers of methadone treatment in Australia were generally satisfied with these guidelines; however, those receiving treatment or wanting admission to programs were not so pleased. Many people who had become dependent on heroin and wanted treatment were refused admission to programs because they could not meet the very strict entry criteria. A significant number of those who achieved admission were later rejected as a consequence of urinalysis indicating that they were still using heroin – sometimes only occasionally. The complete rehabilitation, that is, withdrawal from methadone and other drugs by these means was more difficult to achieve than many of the responsible authorities had initially hoped. It became clear that many participants required long-term and possibly indefinite treatment (Wells and McKay 1989).

During the early 1980s a reduction in services was met with an apparent increase in demand for methadone. It was beyond the resources of existing programs to accommodate the high number of requests from eligible drug users, many of whom had attempted several previous treatments. The launch of the National Campaign Against Drug Abuse (NCADA) in 1985 acknowledged that methadone treatment should be expanded; national policy was introduced to increase the number of places available on programs though, generally, access remained limited. The Campaign also acknowledged that there should be some relaxation of the admission criteria (Wells and McKay 1989). Consultations with service providers regarding the appropriate amendment of the national guidelines revealed that there was still considerable disagreement about the role of methadone and the way it should be used. All agreed that regular daily oral doses of methadone could prevent most of the effects of withdrawal from intravenous heroin use. Further, the majority felt that methadone was only an adjunct, not without value, to other medical and psychosocial management, and that methadone should be administered in the lower dosage ranges with the clear objective of eventual withdrawal. These few points of consensus formed the basis for the National Methadone Guidelines (NMG), which were endorsed by the Australian Health Ministers' Conference of May 1985 (Wells and McKay 1989), and subsequently reviewed in 1987 and 1991.[17]

These guidelines explain that they were to be used as a framework for jurisdictions throughout Australia in their more localised formulation of policies and procedures for methadone treatment. In 1993 the Commonwealth, State and Territory governments agreed that the guidelines should take the form of a national policy that would assist in establishing a common set of standards for providing methadone treatment in Australia (Commonwealth of Australia 1993). The first major revision of that policy was published in 1997 – with a subsequent reprint in 1998 incorporating a number of further amendments (Commonwealth of Australia 1998. 1). The *National Policy on Methadone* (NPM), in its various editions, reflected a

---

17   The Dole and Nyswander methadone 'blockade' philosophy, that is, the provision of doses substantial enough to discourage additional heroin use, was not addressed in the 1985 guidelines, nor was it included in the revision of these guidelines in November 1987. The 1988 guidelines indicated that 'doses above 80 mg per day are usually not required' (Commonwealth of Australia 1988). The Victorian application of these guidelines indicated that doses above 50 mg per day are usually not required (Alcohol and Dug Services Unit 1990), while the Queensland guidelines in 1990 indicated a recommended upper limited of 130 mg per day (Queensland Department of Health 1990). Most clinicians with experience in methadone treatment agree that doses below 80 mg per day usually do not prevent clients from obtaining a pleasurable 'high' if they continue to use heroin (Prescott 1987; Ward et al. 1992).

national position on the role of methadone and provided core operational procedures to guide the provision of services. It was the foundation of State and Territory guidelines discussed in more detail below. It defined the goal for MMT as reducing 'the health, social and economic harms to individuals and the community associated with illegal opioid use', and proposed that the key objectives to achieve this goal were: the reduction of unsanctioned drug use; improving the health of 'clients'; helping to reduce the spread of infectious diseases associated with illegal opioid use – especially HIV/AIDS and hepatitis B and C; reducing deaths and crimes associated with illegal opioid use; and facilitating the improvement in social functioning of those in treatment. The recently released *National Pharmacotherapy Policy for People Dependent on Opioids* (Commonwealth of Australia 2007; see also Henry-Edwards et al. 2003) continues to provide a broad context and framework for State and Territory policies and guidelines. It retains the same broad goal of treatment; but shifts the focus of treatment objectives which are now listed as: bringing to an end to or significantly reducing an individual's illicit opioid use; reducing the risk of overdose; reducing the transmission of blood born disease; and improving general health and social functioning, including a reduction in crime (Commonwealth of Australia 2007: 7; Henry-Edwards et al. 2003). The renewed prioritisation of the desirability of abstinence seems to be a qualification of the earlier interpretations of harm minimisation and normalisation. Demonstrating international influences on drug policy some recent State policy documents now explicitly acknowledged the United Nations rhetoric of supply and demand reduction (Drugs and Poisons Regulation Group 2006; New South Wales Health Department 2006).

Governing Methadone

Supply in Demand

Methadone is a controlled substance. It is listed in Schedule I of the SCoND. Accordingly, it is 'subject to all measures of control applicable to drugs under [that] convention'.[18] Unlike heroin, however, it is not included in Schedule IV, which is reserved for a 'special class' of drugs described as being 'particularly liable to abuse and to produce ill effects, where this liability is not offset by substantial therapeutic advantages not possessed by substances other than drugs in schedule IV'. As a result of its inclusion in Schedule I of the SCoND, it is also subject to the control of the 1988 UN treaty which provides that parties shall adopt measures necessary to establish 'the production, manufacture, extraction, preparation, offering, offering for sale, distribution, sale delivery on any terms whatsoever, brokerage, dispatch, dispatch in transit, transport, importation or exportation of any narcotic drug or any psychotropic substance contrary to the provisions of the 1961 Convention, the 1961 Convention as amended or the 1971 Convention', as criminal offences under its domestic law (United Nations 1961). In Australia these two international drug conventions are

---

18   It is subject in particular to those measures described in Articles 4 (c), 19, 20, 21, 29, 30, 31, 32, 33, 34 and 37. Buprenorphine is not currently listed in the Schedules and as such is not subject to the same level of international control.

explicitly given expression in the 1967 *Narcotic Drugs Act,* the *Crimes (Traffic in Narcotic Drugs and Psychotropic Substances) Act 1990* and most recently the *Law and Justice Legislation Amendment (Serious Drug Offences and Other Measures) Act 2005,*[19] State and Territory legislation further reflects the form of the Commonwealth statutes and in so doing the intent of the treaties. These respective Acts describe in detail the administrative apparatuses concerned with licensing, wholesale and retail practices, professional practices, systems of documentation and statistical reporting, relating to the manufacture, sale, possession and use of opiates by the population.

The Australian Capital Territory *Drugs of Dependence Act 1989*, for example, makes provision for the licensing of manufacture and wholesale supply of a drug of dependence (as defined in the *Criminal Code Regulation 2005*, Schedule 1 (Controlled Drugs) part 1.1, including methadone and buprenorphine). Every seven days from the date of issue of the licence until its expiry, the licensee – whether involved in manufacture or wholesale supply – must provide a detailed report of all transactions in the drug of dependence covered by the licence to the chief health officer (Part 2 and Part 3, *Drugs of Dependence Act (ACT) 1989*). The Act also regulates professional practices. Section 58 prohibits the prescription of a drug of dependence, except if the drug is methadone (or buprenorphine) for treatment in accordance with Section 59 of Act, or in any case for the treatment of a person's mental or physical condition (which does not include drug dependence). If there is reasonable evidence that a person is dependent on any drug of dependence or prohibited substance, or a person has used any such drug for two months or more, the treating practitioner must obtain approval from the chief health officer before prescribing a drug of dependence for that person. Only with such approval can the medical practitioner prescribe methadone for the treatment of the person's drug dependence. As a final example, Part 8 of the Act, subtitled 'Records, Safe Keeping and Disposal', provides for a complex system of record keeping in relation to the general supply and administration of such drugs (opioids). It provides for the keeping of drug registers and ward registers, and describes a system of accounting for supplies using a method of double entry book-keeping (Hopwood and Miller 1994). Drug legislation in other states makes similar provisions (See for example, Victoria's *Drugs Poisons and Controlled Substances Act 1981*, and the Queensland's *Health (Drugs and Poison) Regulation 1996*). In Australia, the availability of methadone is strictly controlled by legislation,[20] and as

---

19   Each Act refers specifically to respective treaties.

20   See for example, Victoria's *Drugs Poisons and Controlled Substances Act 1981*, and the Queensland *Health (Drugs and Poison) Regulation 1996,* Tasmania's *Alcohol and Drug Dependency Act 1968,* NSW *Poisons and Therapeutic Goods Act 1966,* South Australia's *Controlled Substances Act 1984*, Northern Territory, *Poisons and Dangerous Drugs Act 1993* and Western Australia's *Drugs of Addiction Notification Regulation 1980*. The policy and procedure manuals along with prescriber training manuals for the respective States and Territories all make – at least implicit and often explicit – reference to relevant State or Territory legislation (statutory provisions) regulating the supply of opioids, in particular, the supply of these substances to drug dependent persons. (Victorian Department of Health and Community Services 1995; Western Australian Alcohol and Drug Authority 1994; Department of Community and Health Services 1995; Bell and O'Connor 1993; Directorate of the Drug Offensive New South Wales Department of Health undated; Drug and Alcohol Services

a result is in effect governed explicitly through the codified regulatory mechanisms described in the international treaties. Taking this into account, it is not surprising that the various national and State and Territory policy and procedure documents all include a range of apparently mundane techniques which work to regulate the supply of a controlled substance. Indeed they exhibit many of the governmental characteristics described in the context of the last chapter; admittedly they are designed to operate on a much smaller and more localised scale. Drug laws like the Australian Capital Territory (ACT) *Drugs of Dependence Act (1989)* described above, provide an example of how a regime of licensure or accreditation empowers particular bodies to regulate those who seek to act in a certain professional capacity, both legitimating and regulating at the same time. In the way that Rose and Miller (1992) describe, the enactment of legislation creates centres of calculation, and these laws translate aspects of a governmental program into mechanisms that establish, constrain or empower certain agents or entities and set some of the key terms of their deliberations. While embedding principles in law may not determine the decisions made by doctors who prescribe methadone, it does set – as we shall see – the terms under which those decisions must be calculated and justified.

Prescribing Methadone

The most obvious effect of this network of legal governance is that, throughout Australia, only authorised medical practitioners who are accredited and registered through specialised professional training are able to prescribe methadone as a maintenance treatment for individuals (Commonwealth of Australia 2007). Authorisation is given through centralised State and Territory bodies – the respective health departments or commissions, and it is often the responsibility of the most senior officer (the Minister or permanent head, under advice from a specialist unit), and subject to codified ongoing annual or biannual review. Authorised prescribers must: adhere to specific conditions of practice in the delivery of MMT and recognise the centralised supervisory authority of the respective State or Territory regulatory bodies which monitor the compliance of authorised prescribers with regular reviews; notify the authority of any changes in service delivery; accept legal responsibility for treatment of a participant until treatment is formally terminated or transferred and keep accurate records (Drug and Alcohol Services South Australia 2006: 57; Drugs and Poisons Regulation Group 2006; New South Wales Health Department 2006; Northern Territory Department of Health and Community Services 2006). Authorisation alone does not meet the statutory requirements for the prescription of methadone; an individualised application must be made with respect to each prospective patient/client, and an individualised authority granted by the jurisdictional authority, before treatment can commence. This is regularly reviewed (every six months in New South Wales, and every one or two years in other States). Centralised jurisdictional records of these individual authorisations are maintained. This system

Council 1992, 1994, 1994a; Miflin et al. 1995; Queensland Health, 1994; Drug and Alcohol services South Australia 2006; Drugs and Poisons Regulation Group 2006; Department of Health and Community Services 2002, New South Wales Health Department 2006).

is used to ensure that the patient or 'applicant' is not currently receiving methadone form another prescriber – that is, to prevent double dosing.

The delivery of methadone to those registered in treatment is closely monitored. The National Pharmacotherapies Policy (NPP) advises that 'in general, methadone…should be consumed under direct supervision at a location[21] approved by the responsible jurisdictional authority' (Commonwealth of Australia 2007: 18). Daily supervised dosing is a key strategy for preventing the diversion of the drug by insuring that it is consumed by the person it is prescribed for. A number of the State policy and procedure documents go on to provide very specific directions to dispensers regarding the delivery of a dose and the regulation of their supply. The South Australian documents in particular provide instructions to pharmacists explaining that they should 'make sure the client speaks before leaving the dosing area…to ensure that the dose is not held in the mouth and then transferred to a hidden container' (Drug and Alcohol Services South Australia 2006: 57; Drugs and Poisons Regulation Group 2006). They also outline specific guidelines with regard to the filling of prescriptions, ordering and storage of stock, and dispensing. The proper methods of measurement, labelling and recording transactions are described in some detail in order to facilitate 'full accountability of methadone transactions' (Drug and Alcohol Services South Australia 2006; Drugs and Alcohol Services Council 1994a: 19; Drugs and Poisons Regulation Group 2006).

Where participants are considered to be stable,[22] prescribers may authorise and arrange for takeaway doses of methadone that can be consumed at their own convenience – without supervision. Any judgment about a patient's suitability to receive such doses – and take responsibility for their own consumption of methadone

---

21 A review of the State and Territory documents indicates that these locations can be a public or private clinic, the rooms of an accredited private prescriber (psychiatrist or general practitioner), a specialist methadone dispensing pharmacy, a community retail pharmacy or (often in regional areas) a hospital.

22 Various jurisdictional guidelines indications of stability include:

Duration in treatment (more than two/three months, depending on jurisdiction)

Compromised parenting skills or Department of Community Services (or equivalent) involvement with child/children

Ongoing legal issues or criminal activity

No significant destabilising life events

High doses (limiting takeaway availability)

Chaotic or self harming behaviour

Stable accommodation and access to secure storage

Employment or educational activity

Medical and psychiatric stability

Evidence that the client is not engaging in continuing hazardous use of opioids, benzodiazepines, alcohol and/or psycho-stimulants;

Regular, reliable contact with clinic or pharmacy and compliance with program philosophy; and

Prior history of responsible takeaway doses (NSW Health Department 2006, Drugs and Poisons Regulation Group 2006, see also earlier documents Commonwealth of Australia 1997).

– is tempered by an assessment of the risks involved. The NPP identifies the risks associated with takeaway doses as:

- methadone diversion and involvement in drug dealing;
- self-administration by injection, potentially resulting in sorbitol toxicity, bacterial infection and the spread, or potential spread, of blood-borne viruses; and
- overdose or death of the individual or of a third person (particularly a child) (Commonwealth of Australia 2007: 19).

The provision of takeaway doses must be approved by and arranged by the designated prescriber in advance, and the delivery of each dose must be specifically recorded according to jurisdictional requirements.[23] There are limits with regard to the frequency with which takeaway doses can be prescribed. In Victoria, for example, three levels of supervised dosing are available. High intensity supervision involves no takeaway doses. Medium intensity supervision allows patients who have demonstrated stability in treatment and regularity of dosing for at least two continuous months to access one or two takeaway doses per week, and low intensity supervision allows patients who have demonstrated stability and regularity of dosing for at least six continuous months, and who are assessed as a low risk for misuse up to five takeaway doses per week, but with no single supply exceeding three doses (Drugs and Poisons Regulation Group 2006; see also Northern Territory Department of Health and Community Services 2006 for a similar protocol).

Under *special* circumstances – in the case of illness, travel or employment, for example – prescribers may authorise more takeaway doses in a week (Commonwealth of Australia 2007). In general no more than three or four consecutive doses are supplied as takeaways without special approval of the senior medical officer of the jurisdiction (Drug and Alcohol Services South Australia 2006; New South Wales Health Department 2006; Northern Territory Department of Health and Community Services 2006). These most recent guidelines are a considerable relaxation on previous requirements (Bull 2002). Before the implementation of a generalised review of policy documents conducted across States and Territories in the mid-1990s,

---

23   In NSW, legislation requires that all takeaway doses should be recorded in the drug register – either the Methadone Syrup Record, or a separate takeaway doses register – which records: date, person's name, date of birth (or identification number), dose, reasons for takeaway dose, dates for which takeaway doses are supplied, the prescriber's name and the signature of the person who made the entry. All registers are to be subject to random audits by the Pharmaceutical Services Board of the New South Wales Health Department. The prescribing doctor is to provide the clinic or pharmacy with written authorisation (which should be in the prescriber's own handwriting and signed) for takeaway doses. This must be attached to, or incorporated in the, the current prescription and must specify the date or (when regular takeaway doses are provided) the days of the week on which the patient is to receive takeaway doses. In South Australia and Victoria regular takeaway doses must be recorded on each prescription, others in case notes, and the decision communicated in writing to the pharmacist. Authorisation should be attached to the prescription and specify the date or, where regular takeaway doses are provided, the days of the week for which the client is to receive them.

patients on doses considered to be high – greater than 50 mg in Victoria, greater than 80 mg in New South Wales and greater than 100 mg in Queensland – were to be given permission to takeaway only in extenuating circumstances (Queensland Department of Health 1990; Select Committee on HIV/AIDS Illegal Drugs and Prostitution 1991). Victorian and New South Wales guidelines explained that this might encourage individuals to reduce their dose from the higher levels (Bull 1991). Moreover, in some States and Territories, access to takeaway doses was considered to be a privilege that was used to gain compliance with program expectations and requirements (Commonwealth of Australia 2007). Some current documents continue to identify takeaway doses as a 'privilege' or 'reward' for compliant behaviour (Drugs and Poisons Regulation Group 2006; Northern Territory Department of Health and Community Services 2006).

Dispensing to clients who wish to move or travel (for longer than four days) within Australia is centrally coordinated by the jurisdictional authorities with the designated role of monitoring the supply of methadone. The NPP (Commonwealth of Australia 2007) advises that it can take up to four weeks, most States and Territories follow the recommendation that at least two weeks written notice be provided of intention to transfer, and a letter establishing the participant's identity, including a certified photograph, dose, exact dates of transfer, and relevant clinical information (duration of treatment and general progress), should arrive at the new transfer destination prior to arrival at their dosing destination. Several States have additional requirements. The policy and procedures manuals of New South Wales, Victoria and South Australia require permanent address and address at the place of stay at transfer destination to be included. The Victorian document also includes the reason for transfer.[24] Those wishing to travel overseas must provide at least thirty working days written notice in order to organise a transfer. They need to secure the permission to travel with methadone from the relevant authorities in this country – from their respective jurisdictional authority, and the Treaties and Export Section of The Therapeutic Goods Administration – as well as from those in their country of destination (Commonwealth of Australia 2007). Jurisdictional authorities responsible for controlling the supply of methadone are also notified when the treatment of any specific individual is terminated.

In the day-to-day delivery of MMT it is the responsibility of the prescriber and dispenser to monitor the consumption and regulate the supply of methadone to those registered to programs. Current monitoring options used widely in Australia include urine testing, self-reporting and clinical observation. Urine testing has long held a controversial role in treatment (Commonwealth Department of Human Services and Health 1995; Ward et al. 1992).[25] In recent years there has been a tendency to shift away from such intrusive monitoring techniques; self-report techniques are

---

24 The 1990 Victorian and past NSW guidelines required information on mode of travel (bus, train or air) and indicated that copies of tickets were also required. Moreover, in Victoria those on doses higher than 50 mg were not considered eligible for temporary transfer (Alcohol and Drug Services Unit 1990).

25 The observation of clients urinating – which is considered to be an essential component of testing because it prevents substitution – has been described as demeaning and degrading

more often preferred. The NPP advises that urine testing should only be undertaken 'with good reason, such as in the initial clinical assessment of individual clients or as part of program evaluation. Urine testing can also be useful when clients are unstable... and when there is some uncertainty about their drug use' (Commonwealth of Australia 2007: 9). A New South Wales training and accreditation document identifies urinalysis as a 'method of monitoring the performance of patients during treatment and detecting extraneous drug use or methadone diversion' (New South Wales Health Department 2001: 78; 2006: 35). In the past the value of this procedure in verifying the presence of methadone in order to assist in the 'detection and prevention of methadone diversion by clients not ingesting their methadone' was widely acknowledged in most of the State and Territory guidelines (Commonwealth Department of Human Services and Health 1995; Commonwealth of Australia 1993: 16-17; Drug and Alcohol Services Council 1992; New South Wales Department of Health undated; Queensland Health 1994; Western Australian Alcohol and Drug Authority 1994). In more recent clinical guidelines specific consideration of the merits of urinalysis has all but disappeared, even though the New South Wales manual referred to above recognises that it 'continues to be some what of a ritual in methadone maintenance programs' (2001: 79). This is confirmed by the instruction in that state's clinical guidelines that '[a]ccess to takeaway doses should be granted conditionally and gradually increased if and when the patient demonstrates continuing stability and negative urine screens for opioids'(2006: 52).

The delivery of methadone is clearly in accordance with the intent of the 1961 SCoND. The policy and procedures documents (in the context of legislation) describe the nature of legitimate transactions along with techniques for tracing the movement of the drug in and beyond the legitimate system of supply. As a result, treatment is regulated in such a way as to prevent leakages from the legal system to the illegal one. This coordinated system of delivery of MMT, consisting of processes that trace the movement of methadone stocks from the moment of manufacture to consumption, in effect, constitutes a localised economy of supply that can be mapped and monitored in ways that are very similar to the generalised processes governing the supply of drugs described in the international treaties.[26] This system of mundane practices has other important governmental effects which impact more directly on those involved in the delivery of treatment. In short, not only does it work to constitute the supply of methadone as a governable domain, it is also involved in the constitution of governable subjects: prescribers, dispensers and clients. The arrangements involved are discussed in more detail below.

---

by both clinic staff and clients. Moreover, it is said to promote distrust and resentment that is counter productive to clinical relationships.

26   In relation to travel the delivery of methadone is specifically articulated to the treaties as described above.

Governing through Methadone

Methadone and the Panopticon

A number of aspects of the daily application of treatment bear a striking resemblance to the practices of standardisation and individualisation which Foucault (1977) called normalising discipline. Methadone maintenance could be a contemporary analogue of the panopticon; regulating individuals enrolled in the programs through techniques of surveillance, examination and the normalising judgment. The daily dose of methadone is consumed under direct supervision at a dispensing unit approved by a centralised jurisdictional authority responsible for the control of narcotic drugs. Special application to prescribe methadone must be made to and approved by this authority for each individual accepted onto the program. Once signed up for treatment the participant must routinely attend his or her designated dispensing unit at a predetermined time. Supervised dosing prevents diversion and provides an opportunity to monitor the wellbeing of the participant – their use of other drugs and possible intoxication. Generally speaking, dispensing is organised so that doses are delivered from the same location and at roughly the same time each day (Drug and Alcohol Services South Australia 2006; Drugs and Poisons Regulation Group 2006).[27]

As we have seen, processes of authorisation are concerned with ensuring that a participant is not receiving methadone from more than one prescriber. This system serves to individualise the patient-prescriber relationship, ensuring through a centralised administrative authority that only specific prescribers are authorised to prescribe methadone for specific patients, under specific conditions. Prescribers must make provision in advance for any absence from their practice, as only specifically approved locums can provide temporary substitute care. These arrangements amount to a far more formalised and rigid set of relationships between the doctor and patient (and doctor and state authorities for that matter) than are characteristic of other areas of medicine. Moreover, the specificity of these relationships is governed by law. While this may not determine the decisions made by doctors, it does set the terms in which those decisions must be made.

The processes of authorisation also provide for an almost national system of notification with regard to opioid dependence. Particularly as (in some States at least) those who merely seek access, and may not end up in a treatment program, are included on a centralised register of the drug dependent. According to Western Australia's *Drug of Addiction Notification Regulation 1980* it is a statutory requirement that doctors 'notify the Health Department of any person *suspected* of being a drug addict... [c]lients requesting treatment with methadone are notified to the Health Department as addicts' (Western Australian Alcohol and Drug Authority 1994: 6). In Tasmania when a general practitioner, who is not an accredited methadone

---

27   There are therapeutic arguments for delivering the dose at the same time each day: keeping the level of methadone available for absorption stable. There are the also organisational ones: the prevention of overlap in the paths of clients (Dole 1988, Drugs and Poisons Regulation Group 2006).

prescriber, is approached by a patient seeking access to a methadone program, the patient should be directed to Alcohol and Drug Services (in the Department of Community and Health Services) or an accredited methadone prescriber, and the general practitioner is obliged to complete a *Notice of Drug Dependence* and forward it to the Pharmaceutical Services Branch in accordance with the *Alcohol and Drug Dependence Act 1968* (Tasmanian Department of Community and Health Services 1995).

An application for authority to prescribe to a particular client must be renewed regularly. The process of initial application must establish a person's identity through accredited sources similar to those used by banks for people wanting to open an account. An individualised profile records the applicant's name, any pseudonyms, date of birth, sex, address, indigenous status, medicare and healthcare card numbers, income source, country of birth, primary opioid drug of dependence, other drug use, treatment history, HIV status and (for women) pregnancy status (New South Wales Health Department 2006; Northern Territory Department of Health and Community Services 2006). In the past such details as mother's maiden name, occupation, height, build, eyes, hair, marital status, weight, distinguishing marks and tattoos where also included (Commonwealth of Australia 1993; Queensland Health 1994). Once accepted into treatment patients are regularly reviewed in relation to their stability. It is a legal requirement that whenever a prescription for methadone is provided or renewed the prescriber personally assesses the patient. Prescribers must routinely review each patient at regular intervals[28] or when three or more consecutive doses have been missed. At these reviews information is recorded in relation to: patient requests, issues or concerns; treatment mechanics such as dosing location or takeaway doses; adequacy of dose and any pharmacological issues (side effects, or interactions with other medicines/drugs); recent drug use – prescribed and other (including alcohol and tobacco); physical and psychological health; social functioning; behaviour with a risk of HIV, hepatitis B and hepatitis C infection and plans for the patients treatment program, including strategies to enhance the patient's capacity to withdraw from the opioid treatment program (New South Wales Health Department 2006). Through this process of examination, individuals are classified and judged, and located in a field of visibility. The information collected and maintained on each client – or case – from admission to termination, is differentially encoded in written reports and files which are organised into a jurisdictional data system, which monitors the operations

---

28   NSW clinical guidelines indicate that all patients should be reviewed regularly – at least four times a year for those who appear to be progressing well (NSW Department of Health 2006). In contrast Victorian Guidelines provide for much more frequent review: once or twice in the first week of treatment, then at least every two weeks during the initial phase of treatment (or until the patient has reach a stable dose). Throughout the first two years of treatment, the minimum frequency of medical review should be monthly. Those not progressing well should be reviewed more frequently (Drugs and Poisons Group 2006). The Victorian review process records information in relation to: attendance at reviews, provision of urine drug screens, opioid use; benzodiazaphine use; alcohol use, stimulant use, evidence of recent injecting sites, stable accommodation, intoxicated presentations at dispensing point or clinic, overdoses, diversion of takeaway doses, missed doses, mental state assessment and medical co-morbidity.

of methadone programs as well as those enrolled in them. A further collation adds this information to a national data collection[29] (Commonwealth of Australia 1997, 2007; Miflin et al. 1995). These techniques and methods of documentation facilitate the description and analysis of specific individuals as well as (at risk) groups – they are, thus, individualising and totalising strategies. That is, they allow the identification and classification of commonly occurring attributes and differences between individual subjects in the treatment population at the same time that they set all of those enrolled in MMT apart from the general population.

Like all population management strategies, MMT is dependent on a well articulated and comprehensive system of communication and record keeping. Detailed information about both participants and prescribers is held on a centralised database. Participants can be monitored almost instantaneously regarding their address, health, criminal and social (family and socio-economic) status. They are tied to a particular dispensing unit and are unable to change their conditions of treatment, without, or before, receiving formal written approval through the centralised State or Territory bureaucratic channels. Clinic timetables and transfer procedures guarantee that any participant's movements can be fairly well monitored. These arrangements ensure that they remain potentially visible at all times, regulating their paths of circulation by organising an arranged space to facilitate observation, and by rendering participants knowable, making it possible to govern them. In contrast to this assessment, Pat O'Malley (1999) makes a compelling argument that in the closing decades of the twentieth century disciplinary rationalities in the field of drug control were replaced by what amount to more liberal arrangements.[30] In the following section I explore O'Malley's argument and its connections to wider discussions of liberal governmentality.

Liberating Addiction

O'Malley, in framing this alternate position, is not referring to liberalism as a normative political doctrine or theory that treats the maintenance of individual liberty as an end in itself. Instead he draws on a formulation of liberalism derived from Foucault's work on governmentality (Barry et al. 1996; Burchell et al. 1991; Dean and Hindess 1998; Rose 1999). In these accounts, liberalism is seen as giving rise to a prudential concern that one might be governing too much, and the view that, rather than pursuing governmental objectives through the detailed regulation of conduct in the manner of police or disciplinary power of the nature described in *Discipline and Punish* (Foucault 1977), it might be more effective for government to

---

29   The data fields are sector of treatment: public/private/prison; age, gender, employment status, treatment history, duration of treatment, number of clients in programs, average dose, and deaths from methadone.

30   Elsewhere O'Malley reminds us that with respect to the nature and impact of actuarial techniques we need to 'think out their relationships with sovereign and disciplinary forms, in terms of articulations and alliances, colonisations and translations, resistances and complicities between them, rather than in terms of their unilinear development' (O'Malley 1996) or, as Dean (1999a) puts it, we need to be aware of political polyvalence.

work through the maintenance and promotion of certain forms of individual liberty. According to this latter account, liberal political reason sees individual liberty as a limit, not simply to the legitimate reach of government, but also to its effectiveness.

In short, O'Malley proposes that drugs – including heroin and methadone – have come to be regulated through strategies that govern through 'freedom'; in particular through strategies that rely on the autonomous choices of individuals, and that are careful not to govern too much. This shift is expressed through the introduction of risk management modes of governance that focus on governing through the calculation of risks and the distribution of norms. They are more concerned with the effects of problematic actions, and the mitigation, containment or prevention of such effects, than with more overtly disciplinary techniques that attempt to eliminate problems through locating and eliminating causes. They are less concerned with the individual – whether with correcting them or understanding why they create problems – and more focused on the patterns and characteristics of aggregates and distributions. Where individuals are concerned it is almost always in terms of their membership of risk categories, their relationship to risk factors and their performance of risk bearing behaviours, rather than the familiar disciplinary sense of a biographical individual in need of correctional intervention (Castel 1991; Cohen 1985). This is particularly evident, he suggests, in the emergence of the governmental program of harm minimisation; that is, the array of discourses and strategies concerned with minimising the harms that arise for individuals and societies as a result of the problem of illicit drugs.

O'Malley argues that discourses associated with the program of harm minimisation have shaped the nature of emergent governmental categories of drug use or user by pointing to a number of examples under the headings: 'excessive use and poly drug use'; 'responsible users; choice and self government'; and most pertinently, in this context, 'dependent use, choice and responsibility' (1999: 204). Under this last heading he asserts that methadone maintenance programs (MMPs)[31], informed by harm minimisation regimes in this new governmental environment, have as their primary target the governance of risks generated by drug dependency, rather than the governance of drug users themselves. He describes how these risks – the transmission of contagious blood borne diseases, adulteration, crime and economic hardship – and the ways in which MMPs manage them, are identified quite clearly in the literature made available to dependent users. He notes that such benefits are presented openly to users along with the costs of being on an MMP – while the user remains opiate dependent, program requirements have the effect of regularising their lifestyle by requiring daily attendance at a clinic or a pharmacy and limiting the possibility of spontaneous travel (O'Brien 2004a, 2004b; Rural and Regional Health and Aged Care Services 2006) – and argues that these are matters for rational choice making. Moreover, he positions this choice making as 'voluntarisation' that emerges out of the recognition that compulsory programs failed to deliver results because of the fear, stigmatisation and hostility that compulsory treatment created among users:

---

31   MMP and MMT are used synonymously.

Voluntary programs working through the rational choice users' preference and based therefore on their recognition of the risk reductions associated with enlistment in such programs, are held to deliver better results. Governing through choice thus displaces government through coercion not on the basis of 'humanity' (although such ideas are certainly present) but primarily on the basis of optimising effective rule. Through their participation in the program, methadone consumers are normalised, and as rational, calculating risk takers they enter the sphere of responsible drug use (O'Malley 1999: 205 emphasis added).

O'Malley has a point about the responsibilisation of program participants and users, and their constitution as choice makers. This is clearly evident in recent trends in the structure of available treatment. In policy documents written in the mid 1990s and more recently in the 2000s, systematised streaming of treatment to meet individual needs with regard to levels of intervention replaced more rigid approaches which tended to arbitrarily limit dose levels and restrict the availability of takeaway doses and dosing outlets. High intervention treatment is recommended for clients who are endeavouring to change many aspects of their lives, low intervention for stable clients and high supervision strategies are outlined for those who demonstrate little stability in treatment (Commonwealth of Australia 1993, 1997; Drugs and Poisons Regulation Group 2006; Northern Territory Department of Health and Community Services 2006). According to South Australian policy documents – which provide the most detailed guidelines in relation to streaming – 'tailoring programs in this way enables clients to take more *responsibility* in determining the goals and structure of their individual programs'; it also acknowledges that they will have 'different, and individually fluctuating, levels of commitment to change – change in their lives and changes in their patterns of unsanctioned drug use' (Drug and Alcohol Services Council 1992: 20–2; Drugs and Alcohol Services Council 1994b: 13–14).

Australian methadone maintenance programs operate through the promotion of users as responsible choice makers. A national review of methadone services (Commonwealth Department of Human Services and Health 1995) identifies a number of relatively successful ancillary services – or treatment techniques – commonly linked to MMPs. Prominent among these is a behavioural therapy referred to as relapse prevention (Henry-Edwards et al. 2003; New South Wales Health Department 2006; Ward et al. 1992). This is described by Sweet (1994), and Daley (1991), as a practical method for people to help themselves prevent a return to addictive behaviours – that is, [uncontrolled] illegal heroin use. It is based on the principle that relapse is a process, and it is possible for individuals to learn to recognise the onset and components of this process, and implement their own strategies to avert it.[32] In the context of drug treatment, relapse is regarded as a chain of events that can trigger a return to the dependent drug using behaviour; it is characterised by changes in attitude, thinking, behaviour and moods. Relapse prevention involves the development of practices of the self (Foucault 1988) that allow the individual to identify risk factors that contribute to relapse. These include: reconstructing biographical accounts surrounding relapse; interrogating the relapse

---

32 See Miflin (1995) for an example of the application of this concept in treatment delivery.

process with self-reflexive questions concerning the physical, emotional, social, behavioural, geographical, and historical circumstances of relapse (Daley 1991; Sweet 1994). These therapeutic practices of the self have the effect of transforming what seems to be a series of 'apparently irrelevant decisions' and unconnected experiences into an orderly process that facilitates self-regulation.

This therapeutic regime has much in common with stoic practices for the care of the self (Foucault 1988), and in particular the stoic philosophical tradition of *askesis*. According to Foucault's work on technologies of the self, the principal features of *askesis* include exercises where the subject puts her or himself into a situation where she/he can verify whether she/he can control events and use the discourses with which she/he is armed. *Askesis* is characterised by exercises of *melete* and *gymnasia*. It is the former – *melete* – that is most relevant here. *Melete* is a type of meditation. It is work undertaken in order to prepare a discourse, or an improvisation, by thinking over useful terms and arguments – it is concerned with the anticipation of a real situation through dialogue in thought. The philosophical meditation is composed of memorising responses and reactivating those memories by placing oneself in a situation where one can imagine how one would react (Foucault 1988).[33] In a similar, way relapse prevention focuses on the relationship between thought and behaviour. Negative thought patterns are associated with destructive or self-defeating 'addictive' behaviours. By making such an association, this form of intervention invokes a range of activities and techniques for identifying and challenging self-defeating thoughts: 'ways of "changing" your thinking'. These include: keeping a written journal; carrying practice cards – index cards with a negative thought on one side, and several counterstatements on the other (these are used to review and practise – that is, memorise – positive rather than negative thoughts); repeating the slogans of the self-help programs, practising (negative) thought interruption; as well as methods for development of consequential thinking (Daley 1991; Sweet 1994).

Hence, relapse prevention is a technique which works to help users develop an awareness of risk situations and skills to avoid such situations and manage them when they arise. In doing so it seeks to enable users to isolate themselves from pressures that may lead in directions other than those sought by harm minimisation. By rendering behaviour more calculable it allows users to choose to avoid 'negative' drug taking behaviour (admittedly they may also choose not to). It is worth noting that this intervention is based on exercises whereby the user puts her or himself into a situation where she/he can verify whether she/he can *control* events using the discourses with which she/he is armed. Overcoming drug use, or even the effects of drug use, continues to involve – much as it did in the late nineteenth century – the reinstatement of control; that is, it relies on the *will* of the user to make healthy choices.

O'Malley (1999) links the emergence of responsibilisation as a strategy concerned with governing drug use and drug users to a shift in the political rationalities underpinning the governance of drug use, and proposes that this exemplifies the new ways of thinking the problem of drug control described by the discourse of harm

---

33 *Gymnasia* is concerned with 'training in the real situation, even if it has been artificially induced' (Foucault 1988).

minimisation. As I have noted, he proposes that this is evidence of the replacement of disciplinary rationalities with more liberal rationalities in the field of drug control; in particular the replacement of practices promoting abstinence with those framed in terms of harm minimisation, which are less concerned with the person using drugs than with (the effects of the) drug use practices themselves. Virginia Berridge (1990), on the other hand, suggests that harm reduction or harm minimisation is nothing new; it has always coexisted with the abstinence-oriented approaches. She explains, for example, that in some countries – the United Kingdom rather than the USA[34] – drug replacement therapies, like methadone maintenance, have long been considered safer, and prescribed drug use considered the less harmful alternative to illicit drug use. Nevertheless, it would be a mistake to simply assume that the relationship between treatment practices shaped by ideas of harm minimisation and those shaped by practices associated with abstinence has been a harmonious one (Thomas and Buckmaster 2007). Tension between the goal of abstinence and harm minimisation appears to have been an enduring theme in the delivery of methadone maintenance treatment from the outset (Bull 2002).

Thus, in the context of MMT, there is some indication that tends to suggest that O'Malley could be oversimplifying the case in relation to the replacement of disciplinary modes of governance with more liberal modes. This point becomes even more evident when we take a closer look at his description of MMPs as voluntary programs working through the rational choice users' preference and based on the recognition 'of the risk reductions associated with the enlistment in such programs'. A review of such claims in relation to governing through choice and freedom in the light of an ethnographic study of methadone clients, service providers and case managers, conducted in Brisbane, Australia, suggests that the processes of governance are a little more complex (Christie and Hil 2000). With this is mind, some of the findings from this study are discussed below.

Freedom and Constraint

Reframing the responses reported in Christie and Hil's (2000) study in the context of the analysis developed here highlights the importance of the relationship between freedom and control. Most clients claimed to have joined the program in order to gain control over various aspects of their lives that had been affected by heroin and involvement in the illicit drug culture. Methadone provided an opportunity to avoid the difficulties associated with detoxification and the 'merry-go-round' of illicit drug use. It helped provide the necessary 'space' for reflection and to gain some control over heroin use. At the same time, however, a number of clients stated that they 'hated' methadone despite acknowledging that the drug had helped them to gain control over various difficulties associated with heroin use. Almost from the point of registration, most clients felt that methadone brought with it a range of complications

---

34 The reappearance of opioid maintenance as a form of treatment in the USA during the 1960s was a radical shift away from it being regarded solely as a criminal matter.

and difficulties. They referred to it as 'liquid handcuffs' because they were now dependent on another opioid, which had a set of institutional strings attached.

Christie and Hil (2000) concluded that clients felt that the program's insistence on the daily pickup was tantamount to a form of regulation whereby users were monitored in terms of their compliance with the program rules and regulations. The negative consequences of methadone treatment – identified by O'Malley (1999) as the routinisation of clients' lives and ongoing dependence on an opioid – were associated with feelings of entrapment and negative side effects on health, for example, depression and reduced sex drive. These authors explain that clients enter the program with feelings of confusion, antipathy and despair. Moreover, a number of clients were resentful of the MMP because of the lack of drug substitution options available to them.[35] They were also critical of many of the policies, rules and regulations associated with the program, describing them as 'inflexible and restrictive'. This sense is unmistakably echoed in the following quotations from clients:

> Well it stinks, because what they are doing is dictating to people's lives. I'm sick at the moment right. I've got to go every day from my place into town. Right, walk into town every day... They're saying it's a medical problem, well okay, if someone's got terminal cancer, you don't make them get out of bed every day and then crawl down the road and get their medicine (Christie and Hil 2000: 49).

Or another:

> It's a bloody nuisance because I spend over half of my day, just getting my dose. I've never, ever had a day at home, you know where you have a lazy day. Or you might want to do your housework for the day and not go out. Well it just never ever happens. I've got to get up, have a shower, come down here, rah rah and walk out. To them, *I'm just an addict* and they're doing me a favour! So, I suppose in general, and then you've got to add your travel costs. And it costs, and it takes time and it's costing me a lot of money (Christie and Hil 2000: 51 emphasis added). [36]

---

35 The NPM explained that at that time:

Methadone is the only pharmacological treatment intervention currently available in Australia for opioid dependence. However, there are a number of alternatives to methadone as a substitute for heroin, including buprenorphine, LAAM and naltrexone (Commonwealth of Australia 1997).

These other drugs were trialled as part of NEPOD (Mattick et al. 2004), and buprenorphine joined methadone as a maintenance treatment option in 2001 – depending on the geographic location and jurisdiction. It is still not as widely available as methadone. While buprenorphine is longer acting it usually involves dosing daily or on every second day. Dispensing restrictions very similar to those used in MMT apply (Commonwealth of Australia 2007).

36 In the data reported clients alluded to a number of other negative concerns besides the daily regulatory chore of pickup. Prominent among these were the stigma associated with clinic attendance and the continued presence of heroin users in and around the clinic. National registration as a drug user was experienced as a potential problem, especially where disclosure of information may be required. In terms of dispensing practices clients called for more leniency towards takeaway doses and for longer dispensing hours (Christie and Hil 2000).

Service providers (case managers) similarly described the regulatory effects of the MMP – in particular, the need to attend the pharmacy or the clinic each day – on the clients' freedom.

Restricting. Very restricting. Yes controlling. It's addictive, but I don't think that enters into it all that much. I think it's controlled and very restrictive – you can't move away, you can't make arrangements without first of all, you have to think, where am I going to pick up my methadone dose. So it's controlled.

I don't know what impact it has on their life. I know it controls their lives. And this is long-term. Long-term most clients complain that it is what they call liquid handcuffs. They are always tied to this program. Even if they do well on the program they are linked to it by picking up everyday, by being *called in to account for their health every so many weeks*, they are always linked to this clinic…

I also tell them that it's incredibly controlling in that you have to pick it up every single day of your life. If you miss a dose, we need to know before we can restart you. If you want to go down to the Sunshine Coast or up to, down to the Gold Coast, we need to know about that the day before so we can arrange a pharmacy for you to be dosed. If you want to go interstate, then the same thing applies. We need three weeks notice. So it is incredibly controlling and it's not something that you enter into lightly. And I think it is that, it's the lack of autonomy, I feel, that people say that they refer to methadone as liquid handcuffs. And I think it is that it does control their life and they can't do what they want to…

Well they have to go to the chemist every day. At least at first they have to. So they're tied to one place fairly much. They can organise to go away but that's more organisation that *normal people* have to do. I mean, if they are restricted from getting to that chemist each day, they have constant fear that they might miss their dose and be really sick and so they're probably living in fear half the time that something might prevent them from getting to that next dose (Christie and Hil 2000: 82–3 emphasis added).

Taking into account the nature of the views cited above, from both the clients and staff of the program, it seems that the opportunity for choice making, in relation to what O'Malley (1999) refers to as the benefits and the costs of methadone, along with the significance of what he refers to as voluntarism, should not be glossed over too quickly or easily. Indeed a number of staff members go on to explain that those people who present seeking admission to methadone treatment are 'at the end of the line', '[t]hey see no other way out' because 'there's not a lot of alternatives', or because there are 'no other choices'. In sum, the view expressed was that generally clients seeking admission to methadone maintenance treatment are at a crisis point with drug use. In many cases, they may have already tried other ways of gaining control over the 'addiction' but without success. A number of case managers indicated that for the majority of their clients, methadone is the last, or alternatively the only, available option in an attempt to better manage their drug use:

Many because I think methadone is the only option that is left. They've either been using heroin, which has become problematic in that they're getting in trouble with the law or they've had to resort to thieving or they realise if they go on like that they will certainly end up in jail. So many, many times, it is a last resort

...

Because methadone really *hasn't got a good reputation* out on the street, you know in the street culture, it's seen as being poor, a poor option for them and they come onto it only because they believe no other option is left for them (Christie and Hil 2000: 65 emphasis added).

On the matter of the lack of choice in relation to participation in the program the problem is twofold. Firstly, methadone is often the only treatment available as an intervention for opioid dependence. Second, once engaged in a program and stabilised on methadone the choice of whether to take the drug, or not, is effectively curtailed by the shadow of the unpleasant effects of withdrawal.

One consequence for them is the *lack of choice* ... Because one of the down sides of methadone is that it's a long acting drug so that if you decide no this is bigger than I expected I don't want to be this committed. I don't want to be tied into fronting up to a pharmacy every day and having to present at the clinic regularly. Jumping off methadone is pretty tough. The withdrawals are as severe as stopping taking heroin but because the drug is a more active drug, they're so lengthy that it's almost intolerable. A couple of people have told us that they've jumped off but in general most people will tell us that it's more than they can bear because it may last for three to four weeks because sort of week 2 being really quite intensive, whereas heroin withdrawals are uncomfortable but would last a week to ten days, with day 3, 4, 5 being pretty rugged to get into that week 2, they would be feeling intenser, sick and uncomfortable and know that it's going to last for quite a long time. It's pretty hard to deal with. I guess that's an unexpected consequence for some people (Christie and Hil 2000: 86 emphasis added).

Christie and Hil (2000) summarise the service providers' point of view by suggesting that they tend to agree that the main reason why clients choose methadone is desperation. This sense of desperation is related to their dependence on narcotics and the chaos that this dependence has visited on their personal and social lives. The picture that emerges of the presenting clients is generally one in which they are afraid, confused and with few or even no remaining options:

... the image of client desperation serves to illustrate why it is sometimes difficult for clients to deal with the negative aspects of methadone the drug. This is because in the clients' experience, they can conceive of nothing worse than where they are. Consequently it is only after stabilisation and a period free from heroin that the negative impact of methadone becomes apparent (Christie and Hil 2000: 63–4).

The program is very much clearly explained when they first present. But (especially new) clients are so preoccupied with themselves that they do not hear the explanation.... Christie and Hil 2000: 84).

While Christie and Hil (2000) seem to dwell on the controlling effects of treatment in relation to the clients' lives, it would be a mistake to suggest that they failed to draw out some of the enabling or liberating dimensions of the program. For example, they report that for some clients the experience of methadone has been perceived as beneficial in terms of facilitating the development of a greater sense of stability and control over various aspects of their lives. This, in particular, included control over finances and a greater degree of security in relation to housing. Indeed, a number of quotations from both clinic staff and clients clearly articulated such 'stabilisation' as a valuable dimension of treatment. This view is expressed, for example, in the following assessments made by a number of clients in relation to their initial experience of the program.

> ... I was relieved ... because my choice was either be very, very sick withdrawing and have my life fall apart, or get a government sanctioned alternative. So yeah, I was happy to go on the program (Christie and Hil 2000: 33).

> [methadone] is better for me because I don't have to find more money everyday and I don't have to do anything wrong, do I?

> ...when I first went on it, the relief was amazing. No pressure to score everyday and come up with the money (Christie and Hil 2000: 34).

The enabling dimension is also evident in some clients' responses to questions relating to their expectations of the program:

> the main purpose of the program would be to allow people with addiction to have a *normal life*, be able to pay their rent, be able to hold down a job and still be *an active member* within society, without having the need to use heroin constantly. So I think the methadone program allows that for people (Christie and Hil 2000: 37).

> It keeps me off the heroin and it keeps me feeling *normal*. It just keeps me feeling like I can keep my house clean and do whatever I want to do. You know what I mean? Like, I've had such a restricted life in the last ten years, you know what I mean (Christie and Hil 2000: 54 emphasis added).

> Well I think it's good for drug users. I mean I really do believe that it does help you get a lifestyle, and helps you maintain a *normal life*, by going back to work. You know, just the whole, it brings stabilisation into you life. That's what I believe. But then it, it all depends on the individual, I find. If you're, I mean I believe the methadone program is better to get off the drugs, and then you get off the methadone. But, how many people still use when they're on the methadone. Even though you have random urines and blood tests and all that. You know, I mean, you sit in the waiting room and you listen, you know what I mean yeah. But I'm a believer that methadone is to bring stabilisation in one's life, and to *bring you back to normal* (Christie and Hil 2000: 55 emphasis added).

Clinic staff similarly acknowledged the positive aspects of treatment – and in doing so point to the seemingly paradoxical controlling and liberating aspects of the treatment. On the positive side, staff saw being on methadone as giving the clients freedom to choose whether to use heroin or not, giving them time to do other things because life does not have to be centred on the acquisition of and recovery from heroin. They noted that methadone maintenance treatment also enabled some clients to pursue employment. Christie and Hil (2000) explain, however, that options in this regard were limited by the constraints associated with daily dosing as well as regular clinical reviews. As a result, the authors concluded part-time work was perhaps the only real opportunity of entering the workforce. Indeed, the unlikelihood of clients holding down full-time work is implicitly acknowledged in the State guidelines which indicate that 'under special circumstances', which specifically included employment, prescribers may be more generous with the authorisation of takeaway doses (see p. 136 above).

In sum, methadone maintenance treatment is described as liberating by both the clients and staff (service providers and case managers) of the clinic studied by Christie and Hil (2000). The freedom it offers, however, is a very circumscribed style of freedom. Clients are free to choose not to use heroin (although they may also choose to use the drug), and without the need to acquire and recover from heroin they are freed from the routines of illicit drug use and are able to choose other lifestyle activities – for example, tia chi, swimming or employment (Christie and Hil 2000). The expression of this freedom is confined, nevertheless, within certain bounds. These bounds are shaped by a number of factors. Firstly, the rules and regulations of the program that are the result of legal requirements in relation to the supply of a S8 drug (see p.201 above). Staff members explained, for example:

> Some of the prescribing guidelines around methadone prevent us from being more flexible. We have some flexibility, but we also do have many criteria that we must meet and so we're not able to universally accommodate people's preferences and needs, even in situations where we feel that we would like to. So that's an area where some decisions are made for us (Christie and Hil 2000: 85).

> So there's a *lot of regimentation* and *checking* and *security* because methadone is an *S8* restricted drug. They *can only ever collect at one venue* so if you go to your mate's place on the other side of town and stay the night and would really prefer to stay again tonight, it isn't just a *matter of well can I get my dose over here. They can't go to a pharmacy that they're not known at and before they can go to any pharmacy, you have to cancel your authority at pharmacy A and you know, it's often a matter of a couple of phone calls and maybe even a trip into the clinic to get a letter with your photo on it, because there's no pharmacy that can safely identify you. It takes away a lot of your freedom to make spontaneous plans. If you want to go to the coast for the weekend you need a pharmacy down there and that might need a trip to the clinic first to get an authority and if you want to go interstate, it's even more complicated because our scripts are state bound so we can't even script you to pick up in northern New South Wales. We have to cancel the authority here and find you a prescriber if we can, and we can't always, to take over your prescribing and that might be for people who only want to go away for a week. So there's lots of limitations on the sorts of things, in lots of ways you'd like to encourage for people visiting family, rebuilding your networks and also for people who work. They have that tie of needing to be able to fit into their work day a trip to a pharmacy (Christie and Hil 2000: 81 emphasis in the original).*

As I have explained – even in the medical context – constraints like those just described are the consequence of the provisions of the international treaties to which Australia is currently a party.

Linked to the legal requirements governing the supply of a S8 drug is another form of regulation that is exercised by clinic staff. It arises in the context of provisions for regular periodic reviews, which are described in various jurisdictional guidelines (see p.134 above), and the authority staff members or case managers have to stop the client's prescription for methadone against the client's wishes. As a result, the staff in Christie and Hil's (2000) study explained, clients feel that they are always accountable to someone else while they are on the program.

> … I think that people feel very tied down when they're on a program. But I think some of the consequences are largely that they feel a bit trapped into having to be compliant to a certain extent with the recommendations or requirements. They don't understand often that they need to be seen reasonably regularly depending on how they're travelling with/at various timeframes where the clients are reviewed. Initially they need to be seen daily when they first come in to stabilise. So, there's that. They've got to actually be *compliant* and they've got to come in and they've got to understand that being on methadone is a *schedule 8* drug and with that comes some responsibility in our prescribing (Christie and Hil 2000: 85 emphasis added).

Finally, there is the tie that emerges as a result of the client's physical dependency on methadone – a longer acting opioid than heroin with an attendant increased duration (and some argue severity) of withdrawal. As one staff member noted with regard to clients:

> They'll often comment on the difficulty of getting off the stuff. If I'd known how hard it was going to be to get off it I'd never gone on to it. I didn't know I'd get hooked to this stuff (Christie and Hil 2000: 85).

Clearly the legal provisions governing the supply of methadone – as an S8 drug – impact on the responsibilising and normalising capacity of MMPs. For those engaged in a MMP, choice making in relation to drug use is clearly quite circumscribed and at times, it is simply determined by others. While there is certainly a capacity for normalising dependent drug users – by enabling them to routinise their lives and participate in conventional lifestyle activities – MMPs in many respects serve to constitute them as other and abnormal. This effect becomes increasingly apparent when you consider the number of times that both the staff and clients interviewed by Christie and Hil draw the distinction between the capacities of clients and of 'normal' people. For example, a staff member explained:

> Well they have to go to the chemist everyday. At least at first they have to. So they're tied to one place fairly much. They can organise to go away, but that's more organisation than *normal* people have to do (Christie and Hil 2000: 82 emphasis added).

This assessment was echoed by one of the clients who said:

> I think if I didn't have to pick up everyday I could feel *more normal* (Christie and Hil 2000: 56 emphasis added).

That the delivery of methadone works to distinguish those enrolled in treatment programs from 'normal' people, was reinforced by the view that clients need to hide, and lie about, their methadone intake in order to engage in social interactions involving relationships and work. One client, for example, described how this caused her to leave her job:

> I had to hide the fact that I picked up my daily dose... The boss wanted to know about my teeth falling out and why I couldn't gain weight. He was sympathetic and seemed concerned but eventually, I just couldn't take it any more. I knew if he knew the truth he would have the same attitude as everyone else which is prejudiced. So I gave up working (Christie and Hil 2000: 46).

Another explained how it prevented him from having a 'normal' relationship:

> I've probably had a dozen relationships in the last few years and it just naturally goes, you more or less need to find a girl that uses drugs as well. Because straight chicks look down their nose, of course, at people who use drugs etc. So, being on the methadone you can sort of hide it, you know. You have to go to the clinic every day, you've got to be honest in your relationship, you've got to find the right lady that's going to accept the fact that you're taking this medicine every day, because you're a junkie. So, can't hide it in a relationship, so more or less, nine times out of ten, you're going to end up with a girl that's got the same problem as you (Christie and Hil 2000: 48).

From Bad Habits to Better Habits

To analyse MMT in relation to neo-liberal techniques of governance brings into focus significant changes that doubtlessly have occurred in the treatment domain over the last twenty years. Nevertheless, while it is clear that strategies which cultivate the capacity for choice making in relation to illicit drug use are available in the context of streaming, relapse prevention, and the addition of longer acting buprenorphine to the treatment spectrum, disciplinary techniques that continue to take account of the biographical individual in need of correctional intervention have not been replaced altogether. Indeed, relapse prevention continues to rely on the *will* of the user to 'just say no' and abstain from heroin. This involves – much as treatment did in the late nineteenth century – the reinstatement of self-control. Taking this into account, the rising significance of risk in the government of drug use might be better understood if – as Mitchell Dean suggests – governing through risk is not limited to its liberal formulation. Dean (1999a) identifies, for example, a number of different forms of risk rationality in order to highlight the diversity of understandings of risk, how risk can be linked to quite different programs and technologies, and the way the vocabulary of risk can cross and bind together quite disparate sets of practices. The category that he refers to as case management risk might usefully be considered here. He explains that this kind of risk has a long history and is linked to a clinical practice in which certain symptoms lead to the imputation of dangerousness. Here, risk concerns the qualitative assessment of individuals and groups as falling within 'at risk' categories. Risk techniques are closely allied to the use of case management; those judged 'at risk' of being a danger to the wider community are subject to a range of therapeutic (for example, counselling, self-help groups, support groups), sovereign (prison, detention centres) and disciplinary (training and retraining) practices in an effort to eliminate them completely from communal spaces (for example, by various forms of confinement) or to lower the dangers posed by their risk of alcoholism, drug dependency, sexual diseases, criminal behaviour, long-term unemployment and welfare dependency.[37] Case management risk draws upon techniques of the interview, the exercise of bureaucratic or clinical judgment, the case note, and the file. These techniques might be supplemented by other, less observational modes that might employ techniques derived from quantitative analysis – jobseeker classifications index, or the addiction classification index – a checklist of questions regarding particular characteristics (cf. Dean 1999a).

Clearly there is some parallel here with the analysis of the delivery of methadone maintenance treatment above. This raises the question of how it is possible that these quite disciplinary techniques and the liberal techniques – of the type highlighted by O'Malley – can coexist in the treatment domain? Moreover, what is the relationship between these rationalities that start from apparently contradictory premises: that those enrolled in methadone are dependent drug users/addicts characterised by an impaired will who therefore cannot be trusted to, or are unable to, control their own drug use, and alternatively that those enrolled in methadone are autonomous choice makers capable of responsible drug use? How can MMT work to govern demand using these apparently conflicting approaches?

A review of the Foucaultian governmentality literature tends to suggest, in accord with the position taken by O'Malley, that authoritarian forms of government are not a significant dimension of liberal rule that relies on the governmental uses of liberty (Burchell et al. 1991; Ewald 1991; Gordon 1991). Hindess (2000a) argues, instead, that there is more to the relationship between the liberal commitment to liberty and what he calls the 'liberal government of unfreedom' than seems to be suggested by the Foucaultian account of liberal political reason (or mainstream political theory for that matter). Far from being a simple matter of liberal hypocrisy, of denying its commitment to liberty, the resort to authoritarian rule in certain cases is a necessary consequence of the liberal understanding of that commitment. He suggests, that liberty and domination are joined in liberal thought like two sides of a single coin, reminding us that in the past liberal political reason has been as much concerned with paternalistic rule over minors and adults judged to be incompetent as it has with the government of autonomous individuals – with the subject peoples of imperial possessions as much as with the free inhabitants of Western states.

Marianna Valverde (1996b), in a paper concerned with the complex connections and disjunctions between liberal governance (as a set of rationalities and technologies) and the concrete combinations of liberal and non-liberal practices of government that persistently shape our lives, makes a similar point. She argues, however, that Foucault-inspired work on ethical governing has thus far seriously underestimated

---

37   Rather than being replaced by new risk technologies we have witnessed something of a proliferation of case-management approaches beyond the older delineation of social work and clinical medicine (Dean 1999a).

the ability of quite despotic forms of rule to coexist alongside refined liberal practices. She explains in support of her claim that historically liberal rule was only for those who passed the tests of cultural cognitive and moral fitness – pointing to liberalisms strong tendency to marginalise subjects judged unfit to be free. She cites Mill's argument that:

> It is perhaps hardly necessary to say that this doctrine (liberalism) is meant to apply only to human beings in the maturity of their faculties. We are not speaking of young persons below the age at which the law [note – law, not nature] may fix as that of manhood or womanhood. Those who are still in a state to require being taken care of by others, must be protected against their actions as against external injury. For the same reasons we may leave out of consideration those backward states of society in which the race itself may be considered as in its nonage … a ruler full of the spirit of improvement is warranted in the use of any expedients that will attain an end, perhaps otherwise unattainable. Despotism is a legitimate mode of government in dealing with barbarians, provided the end be their improvement (Mill (1859) 1975, 15–16 cited in Valverde 1996b: 360).

Valverde argues that this principle remains today – that authoritarian rule, or the 'good despots', can be justified by reference to a *defect of the will*.[38] Moreover, it can be reasonably mobilised in the pursuit of the 'remoralisation of those whose "habits" and whose very souls are perceived as requiring some combination of liberal therapeutic, disciplinary and morally coercive techniques to bring them up to the level of liberal subjects' (Cruikshank 1993, 1994 in Valverde 1996b: 361).

What both Hindess (2000a) and Valverde (1996b), seem to be getting at is that while liberalism has been concerned with the practical implications for government of the belief that members of the population to be governed are naturally endowed with a capacity for autonomous, self-directed activity, the Foucaultian account of liberal and neo-liberal government has been somewhat preoccupied with the implication in relation to this belief, that government should make use of this capacity, and it must, as a result, focus exclusively on the governmental deployment of individual liberty. According to Hindess (2000a), the issues are a little more complex; while individuals may be naturally endowed with a capacity for autonomous action, this does not mean that the capacity will always be fully realised in practice. Modern political thought has tended to take the opposite view. While there may be contexts in which suitable 'habits' of self-government are able to form, there are many more in which they are unable to do so. Liberalism has usually seen the realisation of this capacity for autonomous action in historical and developmental terms, suggesting that an extended period of education and training is required before it can be realised in an individual and that it will be well established amongst adult populations only in relatively civilised commercial societies. Having made this point, Hindess considers how liberal political reason has dealt with the problem of governing the remainder of the population – those it identifies as being less than fully autonomous. He argues that it is possible to distinguish three broad types of response:

---

38 Note that weakness of the will was the defining characteristic of inebriety in the nineteenth century (55–8), and it continues to be central in the diagnosis of drug dependence today (Bull 2002).

1. That some people – the hopeless cases – are so far from acquiring the relevant capacities that they should simply be cleared out of the way (genocide).

2. The view that the capacities for autonomous conduct can be developed in a population only through compulsion, through the imposition of more or less extended periods of discipline. In this view the treatment of deviant members of civilised populations is founded on the belief that the problem arises from the relaxation of discipline and the corruption of manners. The only remedy is to *break the bad habits and establish better ones* in their place.

3. The view that at least in relatively civilised populations many of those who lack capacities required for autonomous action do so largely for what might be considered external reasons – reasons to do with ill health, poverty or inadequate education – and that the role of government should be to facilitate the development of their capacities by establishing a benign and supportive social environment. The implication here is that the improvement of many individuals within an already improved population can and should be brought about with only limited resort to authoritarian means (Hindess 2000a: 10–13).

Hindess (2000a) warns that while we might be tempted to conclude that this last category has little to do with the liberal government of unfreedom, this would be a serious mistake. First, the allocation of individuals to one or other of these categories is itself an act of government; and second, liberal government performs its allocation on the basis of various kinds of expertise. He concludes that in the late twentieth century little has been done to undermine the characteristic liberal demarcations between settings inhabited largely by those who can safely be treated as autonomous agents and settings that are not of this kind, and the problem of what to do about people who inhabit these latter settings remains.

Applying this frame to the analysis of MMT outlined above allows us to answer the question of how it works to govern demand. While there are those who argue that dependent drug users should simply be cleared out of the way – with little concern for, or account of, how that might be done – MMT can usefully be understood in terms of Hindess' second and third categories. For some of those engaged in this form of treatment, MMT is concerned with the imposition of more or less extended periods of discipline, and for others it seeks to facilitate the capacities required for autonomous action – the self-government of their own drug use – by establishing a benign and supportive environment. The clinical guidelines which appeared in the 1990s introduced a differentiation between participants requiring extended periods of discipline and those whose capacities for self-regulation might be enhanced by a more benign but supportive environment. The Western Australian policy and procedures document (Western Australian Alcohol and Drug Authority 1994), for example, identified two streams for clients as did the NPM (Commonwealth of Australia 1993, 1997): a high intervention stream, for those being stabilised on methadone, characterised by more prominent disciplinary aspects – frequent clinical review, daily supervised dosing at a specialised dispensary, no takeaway doses and regular urinalysis; and a low intervention stream, for well stabilised clients, intended to promote the responsibilisation of clients with infrequent clinical review, access to community pharmacy dispensing, takeaway doses and less frequent urinalysis. The Tasmanian, South Australian and Queensland State guidelines explicitly described the provision of a benign and supportive environment for stable clients, which included more flexible attendance times and access to ancillary services, including welfare advice and support, social skills training, vocational advice and training and aftercare (following the completion of MMT – that is, a return to abstinence).[39] This last category reflects the liberal ethos of welfare, which Hindess explains 'focuses on the condition of those members of an already improved population whose condition has been set back by accidents of ill health, poverty, incomplete education and the like' (Hindess 2000a: 12). He argues that this ethos finds its clearest expression in J. S. Mill's case for allowing those who exhibit a relatively high degree of improvement to improve themselves further by participating in government, and in T. H. Marshall's (1978) argument for the importance of social policy in the full development of citizenship (Hindess 2000a: 12).

Taking this into account, perhaps the 'potential' for the substitution of methadone for heroin[40] to transform individuals (clients of MMP) from 'criminal' to law abiding citizens has been too frequently overlooked, or at least undervalued. Indeed, Dole and Nyswander (1965) were impressed by patients, included in their early experiments, who 'ceased to behave as addicts', and 'that almost 75% of these would be socially productive and living as *normal citizens* in the community' (Dole et al. 1966: 309). Various dimensions of the treatment regime easily fit with what Cruikshank (1994; 1996) describes as 'technologies of citizenship' – the 'multiple techniques of self-esteem, empowerment, consultation and negotiation used in community action and development programs, social and environmental impact studies, health promotion, community policing and the combating of various kinds of dependency' (Dean 1999b: 147). As David Burchell (1995) argues, the category of citizen is not natural, and the modern figure of the disciplined citizen, with its affiliation to stoic and Christian techniques of self-formation, is a key figure in the modern persona of the 'passive citizen'. Moreover, the citizen is a creation of techniques of social discipline and derives his or her capacities as a product of the activity of government. According to commentators on civic conduct and manners of the late sixteenth and seventeenth centuries (during the rise of the modern state), self-discipline and restraint of the 'errant passions' are the chief hallmarks of good citizenship. Taking this into account, MMT can easily be framed as a governmental technology concerned with self-discipline and restraint of errant passions (like drug use), that is, the cultivation of personal attributes and capacities that are consistent with citizenship. Moreover, the application of treatment constantly negotiates the governmental problem of the one and the many. It is bound to what Foucault (1991) describes as the difficult relationship between individualising and totalising elements that construct human beings as both self-governing individuals within a

---

39   Currently in some states (NSW, for example) the distribution of participants between public clinics (that cater for more difficult cases), specialist private clinics and complete integration through the delivery of services in general practice settings provides an opportunity for this type of differential streaming.

40   Remember the simple use of heroin is a criminal offence.

self-governing political community, and clients to be administered, governed and normalised with respect to governmental objectives (Dean 1994).

Conclusion

The delivery of MMT is clearly in accordance with the 1961 SCoND as well as the 1988 *United Nations Convention on Illicit Trafficking in Narcotic Drugs*. The policy and procedure documents describe the nature of legitimate transactions along with techniques for tracing the movement of the drug in and beyond the legitimate system of supply. Treatment is regulated in such a way as to (ideally) prevent leakages from the legal system to the illegal one. The coordinated system for the delivery of MMT, consisting of processes that trace the movement of methadone stocks from the moment of manufacture to consumption, in effect, constitutes a localised economy of supply that can be mapped out and monitored in ways that are very similar to the generalised processes governing the supply of drugs described by the international treaties. At the same time, however, they have another governmental effect that impacts on all those involved in treatment. Not only do they have the effect of constituting the supply of methadone as a governable domain, they are also involved in the constitution of governable subjects: prescribers, dispensers and patients/clients. MMT, for example, could be described as a type of panopticon, where participants are tied to a particular dispensing unit, and clinic timetables and transfer procedures ensure that they remain potentially visible at all times, regulating their paths of circulation. From this standpoint, the mundane techniques for the delivery of treatment work to organise an arranged space that facilitates observation and by rendering clients (more) knowable, makes it possible to govern them (better). Alternatively, it is possible to argue that MMT regulates users through liberal strategies that govern through freedom and that position users as autonomous and responsible choice makers enhancing their capacity for (law abiding) self governing citizenship. This does not mean that there has been a replacement of disciplinary rationalities with more liberal ones in the field of drug control: the replacement of practices promoting abstinence with those founded on harm minimisation. An analysis of the data described in Christie and Hil (2000), from a governmental perspective highlights the tensions that constantly emerge as a result of the coexistence of strategies governing through freedom with those governing through constraint. These tensions are often linked to the S8 status of methadone, described by drug legislation, and hence, the provisions of the international treaties. Moreover, it is clear that these legal provisions governing the supply of the drug impacted in limiting ways on the responsibilising and normalising aspects of the MMP.

To analyse MMT in relation to neo-liberal techniques of governance that rely on the rational choices of autonomous individuals (freedom) highlights significant changes that have occurred in the delivery of treatment in Australia over the last twenty years or so. The discussion above demonstrates, however, that such an analysis is at best partial. Disciplinary techniques have not disappeared; indeed they continue to make up a significant dimension of the treatment regime. This conclusion alerts us to the danger of too readily accepting the view expressed in much of the

Foucaultian literature: that authoritarian forms of government are not a significant dimension of advanced liberal (or neo-liberal) rule. It suggests that we should remain attentive to the accounts of liberalism – like those described by Hindess (2000a) and Valverde (1996b) – based on the principle that while individuals may be naturally endowed with a capacity for autonomous action, this does not mean that the capacity will be fully realised in practice. Furthermore, certain standards must be met, and cultivated where absent, for subjects to be judged fit for freedom – that is, fit to govern themselves.

How does methadone govern the demand for illicit opioids or heroin? The answer, it seems, depends on how it is positioned in relation to particular problems of government. The positionings that have been described here include: the regulation of the supply of opioids, the health and wellbeing of the population (the promotion of 'life'), the prevention of the spread of disease ('addiction' and blood borne diseases like HIV/AIDS and hepatitis C) and juridical concerns with the prevention of crime (the use and traffic of illicit heroin and crimes related to the acquisition of heroin). MMT is a technology that is clearly linked to a range of governmental programs and political rationalities concerned with sovereignty, discipline and government (cf. Foucault 1979: 19), and as Mariana Valverde reminds us, technologies always stand in problematic relation to political rationalities. 'Particular technologies can be used for different purposes and can have quite different meanings depending on their articulation with different rationalities. Although technologies are either logically, or as a matter of historical practise, associated with certain rationalities there is no one-to-one relationship between the two' (1996b: 358).

Chapter 6

Security and Freedom: Rethinking Drug Control

This book has mapped the development of the international system of drug control. It investigated how opium and its derivatives became a problem of government and the subsequent prohibition of heroin and related drugs became the solution. In describing the conditions that have given rise to this contemporary problematisation of opioid use, I draw attention to the complexity and contingency of the relationships that have contributed to the seemingly paradoxical possibilities in the system of control. I consider, for example, how American interests have at times been able to condone or even support illicit production, while maintaining a 'war on drugs'; or how maintenance prescribing with methadone, an opioid with properties very similar to heroin, is incorporated into the system of control. In asking what are the chief political and governmental rationalities that shaped the conditions of possibility for the problemisation and regulation of opioids, this book examined the ways in which it has been possible to think about the problem of opioids, the knowledges and practices that have made this possible, and the tactics and strategies that have emerged from these various configurations.

In sum, we have seen how during the nineteenth century opium was transformed from a legitimate commodity found in every home into a dangerous substance and an enemy of the state. This problematisation occurred in the context of the crystallisation of the complex of technologies, knowledge, actors, powers, institutions and social arrangements around the phenomena of life (Foucault 1980). For example, it was through the technology of life insurance that English society was first forced to confront the social issues of opium use. A series of court cases following an insurance company's refusal to pay out on the policy of a confirmed opium eater the Earl of Mar, served to initiate medical debate on the matter, and identify the use of the drug as an unacceptable risk.

In this process of transformation the role played by various forms of expertise (statistical, actuarial and medical) was not straightforward, involving some sort of functional transfer of knowledge. Chapter 2 described how the hybrid formulation of the disease of addiction characterised in terms of both degenerative constitution as well as moral failing should not be interpreted as the respective success or failure of medical science (Berridge 1979; Berridge and Edwards 1987) or the moral crusades of the Quaker-influenced SSOT (Harding 1986; Johnson 1975). Employing the multiplex and discontinuous characterisation of personhood implied by Foucault's (1984b) concept of *pluralite'd'ego* it is possible to recognise that the same individual can, in some circumstances, acquire the habits of thinking and capacities for being affected which are appropriate to apparently conflicting ways of comporting oneself.

This means that it is not necessary to privilege the moral or the scientific, as it allows us to acknowledge that such apparently conflicting values can coexist in the persona of the doctor, as well as the expression of medical expertise relating to opiate use. Similarly, the medical dimension of the nineteenth century anti-opium movement does not represent a conspiracy to colonise a previously moral domain, as a medicalisation or professionalisation thesis might have it, but rather is an example of doctors self-consciously constructing themselves as ethical subjects. A consequence of the hybrid conceptualisation of the disease of addiction was that the weakening of the will was not seen as total and irrevocable. Doctors presupposed the existence of at least some residual rationality, autonomy and self-control thus, free will – a key technical requirement of liberal government – was not wholly lost in the addict (Valverde 1998). This way of thinking 'addiction' allowed a formation of government reflecting the inseparability of discipline and freedom, which became an enduring feature of treatments associated with opioid dependence.

The initial problematisation of opium, its subsequent regulation, and the identification of the addict in the nineteenth century, were bound to rationalities concerned with the government and preservation of life: the life of the population and the life of individuals. By the end the century such rationalities had become well entrenched where opium was concerned. Not only were they expressed in the knowledges that represented medical expertise but, as Milligan's (1995) work demonstrates, they had come to permeate popular culture. Concerns regarding the health and wellbeing of the population were rehearsed in a widely consumed literary genre, which abounded with medical metaphors of infection and contagion relating to the evil of opium smoking. Here the concern with the moral fortitude of individuals (particularly women) was clearly evident. The distinction between the practice of smoking opium and Chinamen – who smoked it – was blurred, confounding the source of threat and danger. Employing what was to become a familiar formula, the narrative described how Chinese men used the seductiveness and will-usurping quality of opium to gain sexual power over white women. By the end of the nineteenth century, this expression of fears relating to racial purity was a significant consideration in relation to the strength and wellbeing of the population. It was construed in terms of an attack on the family as the backbone of English society, and an attempt to dissipate the British national identity and undermine England's control of the Empire. Similar views were expressed in examples of popular culture from the USA and Australia. By the beginning of the twentieth century, opium smoking, in popular discourses at least, came to represent the threat of an alien invasion and conquest. Hence, opium was constituted not only as a problem for the health and wellbeing of the population but for national stability and security as well. Importantly, this signalled the emergence of a new rationality – expressed in terms of reason of state – that was to become a more powerful motivation for regulation throughout the twentieth century.

The alleged threat posed by Chinese men to European women was both important and ironic. It is important because it signals the emergence of a novel rationality concerned with the control and regulation of opium. It is somewhat ironic because, from the late eighteenth century, opium had increasing come to represent foreign dominion of the Chinese by the British, and was blamed for the degeneration of the once powerful Manchu Dynasty and Chinese empire (Fay 1975). I have argued that reason of state is a political rationality that is repeatedly expressed in the context of early regulatory debates. Moreover, it is possible to trace how, over the last two- or three-hundred years, this rationality has been a recurring element in the context of various struggles and tensions arising in relation to the trade and supply of opium. This is not, however, part of a teleological march of progress towards tighter control, as in accounts which reduce regulation to the results of disinterested rational or scientific evaluations of the allegedly dangerous properties of the drug. Rather, it is often the mobilisation of the rhetoric of danger rather than any immanent threat that has resulted in the implementation of particular strategic and allegedly pragmatic regulatory interventions.

The analysis in Chapter 3 highlighted the complexity, as well as the contingency, of the relationships that contributed to the eventuality of control, accommodating various mutations of events, as well as what seem to be invasions or even reversals of historical trajectories. For example, at the beginning of the twentieth century the coincidence of a change in British political will, renewed Chinese efforts to suppress the opium trade and Roosevelt's desire to establish America's position in the world trade system (previously dominated by Britain and the opium trade), articulated with colonial acquisition of the Philippines, provided the conditions of possibility for the Shanghai meeting. The Shanghai meeting did not have the status of an international convention; nevertheless, it initiated the international system for the control of opium (and other drugs) that was to develop over the twentieth century. It recognised the threat posed by the opium trade to the national sovereignty of China and instigated a commitment, in principle, to the non-intervention by participating states in Chinese affairs. This had the governmental effect of 'bringing China in', or constituting China as a member of the twentieth-century system of modern states. In addition, America's seemingly contradictory alliances with opium producers [warlords] and apparent participation in the drug trade, later in the twentieth and into the twenty-first century, becomes intelligible from a perspective that is able to accommodate a dispersion of historical transformations along with multiple temporalities. Seen from this standpoint, and in relation to the political rationality of reason of state, it is quite possible for the US administration to work to suppress the drug trade in order to protect its citizens from a perceived external enemy or threat while, at the same time, supporting and promoting the production of opium so as to strengthen alliances with those who apparently share a common enemy.

The international treaties, the 1961 *Single Convention on Narcotic Drugs* and the 1988 *United Nations Convention Against Illicit Traffic in Narcotic Drugs and Psychotropic Substances*, form the basis of the current international drug control system. They grew out of the Shanghai meeting, and consist of an amalgam of not necessarily consistent governmental concerns with the health and wellbeing of the population and issues of sovereignty – the preservation and security – of states. The formulation of these international treaties highlights how our contemporary problems and practices, while quite distinct from those of the past, are constructed out of materials and situations which existed at earlier points in time. The analysis of treaties, in Chapter 4, brought into focus not only the systems of thought which various authorities have used to pose and specify the problem of opium, but also systems of action through which they have sought to give effect to the government of the drug.

Following Rose and Miller (1992) in Chapter 4, I examined both the political rationalities and the technologies – the complex of mundane programs, calculations, techniques, apparatuses, and procedures – through which authorities seek to embody and give effect to governmental ambitions. This analysis demonstrated how the international treaties work to both constitute and represent the domain to be governed; they make it thinkable and amenable to calculation by making visible all phases, from production to consumption, in the movement of drugs. This occurs largely through the collection of statistics and estimates – by the INCB – at a central point. These figures constituted a calculable domain that is amenable to programming and intervention. They make it possible to 'know' the government of supply as well as its shortfalls. At the same time that the treaties work to constitute a knowledge of the supply of narcotics, they make up the domain to be governed by playing a key role in establishing networks that enable rule to be brought about in an indirect manner – 'at a distance' as Latour (1986) argues. By becoming a signatory to a treaty each party is enrolled in the governmental network and comes to understand their particular problems and situations according to a similar language of logic – for which the international instruments and their provisions become the solution.

The successful governmental effect of the drug control system has depended, to a large extent, on how well the international network is maintained, the timely delivery of information to the centres of calculation and how accurate and complete the statistics and other types of information are. The 1961 SCoND worked to constitute a governable domain and governable subjects, that is, nation states, in the context of the licit supply of drugs. At the same time, by largely excluding heroin from the legitimate drug economy, it had the unintended consequence of constituting the ungoverned domain of illicit production and supply, along with TCOs as ungovernable subjects. TCOs conduct their trade outside the legitimate economy, or they hide it within the avalanche of legitimate transactions associated with the technological enhancement of global financial networks that occurred at the end of the twentieth century. In doing so they made the movement of drugs, along with any associated transactions, very difficult to trace. As a result, TCOs, and terrorist organisations adopting similar *modus operandi*, are able to accumulate large profits and, according to both the treaties and recent commentators (see pp.114–6 above), they have the capacity to undermine the stability, security and sovereignty of states.

The treaties themselves both describe and make up the governmental domain of drug control. Analysing the governmental techniques and strategies that constitute this system of regulation allows us to identify the mechanisms that give effect to the international drug control treaties and the political rationalities linked to them. This book has described not only how the system works but also the difficulties of putting it into effect. In doing so the discussion foregrounds the heterogeneous and delicate nature of the multiple networks that connect the lives of individuals, groups and organisations to the aspirations of various authorities concerned with drug control (Rose and Miller 1992). The treaties describe and constitute the conditions of possiblity for the operation of programs regulating the supply of opium. I argue that this is because, throughout the twentieth century, opium has been problematised largely in terms of supply. However, at the beginning of the twenty-first century these are not the only programs concerned with the government of opium. UN debate toward the end of the twentieth century expressed anxieties about heroin and other illicit drugs in terms of the problematisation of demand.

In the international control system, MMT – and other forms of pharmacotherapy for opioid dependent people – is located explicitly in relation to programs that aim to reduce the demand for illicit drugs. It is listed amongst the recognised methods for the treatment and rehabilitation of drug 'abusers' (sic) (United Nations International Drug Control Program 1997; United Nations Office for Drug Control and Crime Prevention 2000). I argue that things are however, a little more complex. A brief survey of the provisions that allow for MMT in Australia – the policy and procedures documents and legislation – reveals that the form of delivery of this treatment has much in common with the mechanisms described in the international treaties that regulate the supply of opioids. The techniques and strategies, which allow the possibility of treatment, work to constitute a localised economy of supply that can be mapped out and monitored. Moreover, they are also effective in rendering those involved in treatment more knowable and governable.

As a population management technique, MMT illustrates explicitly those practices and processes that Foucault (1977) describes as normalising discipline. MMT regulates those enrolled in programs through techniques of surveillance, examination and normalising judgment. The daily dose of methadone is consumed under direct supervision at a dispensing unit approved by a centralised jurisdictional authority responsible for the control of narcotic drugs. Special application to prescribe methadone must be made to and approved by this authority, for each individual accepted onto the program. Once signed up for treatment the client must routinely attend his or her designated dispensing unit daily at a predetermined time. Nevertheless, as O'Malley (1999) suggests, changes to the Australian treatment domain in the 1990s – largely in relation to HIV/AIDS and hepatitis C and framed in terms of discourses of harm minimisation – have introduced more liberal techniques of government that work through a kind of regulated freedom and position users as autonomous choice makers. If we look a little more closely, however, at the experiences of those enrolled in MMT it becomes clear that any such freedom is clearly circumscribed.

The legal provisions governing the supply of methadone – which are shaped by the international treaties – impact in significant ways on the delivery of treatment. They limit the responsiblising and normalising capacities that MMPs promise clients by preventing them (clients) from making certain types of decisions about their daily lives, even when such decisions are considered to be of positive therapeutic value – such as working, or visiting family. Moreover, they work to differentiate those involved in treatment from the 'normal' population. The apparently conflicting authoritarian and liberal dimensions of MMT can arguably be accounted for in terms of Hindess' (2000a; Valverde 1996b) discussion of liberal governmentalities. For example, the streaming that is characteristic of the operation of MMT in Australia can be understood as a type of continuum of treatment that is able to accommodate a range of clients, in more or less authoritarian ways, depending on their readiness to participate in their own governance. How, then, do we account for limits to this liberal mode of governance, which is concerned with the cultivation of self governance, imposed by the elements of treatment that are shaped by techniques concerned with regulating the supply of opioids and linked to reason of state rationalities? That is, the techniques that work against the responsibilising and normalising capacities of treatment, by marking drug using behaviour as abnormal and subject to authoritarian or punitive modes of regulation, offering no space or possibility for the development of self rule.

Not one but a range of governmental rationalities, programs, technologies and strategies, makes up the form of methadone maintenance treatment in Australia. The technologies that constitute it are concerned with the government of both the supply and demand for opioids. They are linked with rationalities of sovereignty, discipline and government, that is with reason of state and the health and wellbeing of the population (generally and that of individual users more specifically). They stand in problematic relation to these rationalities (Valverde 1996b). They should not be thought of simply as a two-pronged approach for the control of supply on the one hand and demand on the other. They operate on quite contradictory assumptions about the nature of dependent drug use and the possibilities for its regulation (Garland 1996). The rhetoric, perceptions and emotions invoked by the punitive and disciplinary strategies that govern supply have the effect of undermining the responsiblising and normalising strategies that might work to cultivate self-governing subjectivities that are compatible with citizenship.

Changing Horizons of the Problem of Heroin

Rose and Miller (1992) argue that the history of government might well be written as a history of problematisations, as it is around these difficulties that programs of government are elaborated. It appears that this assessment holds in relation to the government of opium. Heroin is currently being reproblematised, and these same rationalities – the health and wellbeing of the population and reason of state (the preservation of the (nation) state) are being effectively remobilised to turn the arguments which have supported prohibition on their head. In Australia, the Australian Capital Territory (ACT) Legislative Assembly Select Committee on HIV/AIDS, Illegal Drugs and Prostitution 1991 recommendation that research be undertaken in to the feasibility of conducting a carefully controlled trial of heroin as a therapeutic agent was driven by a pragmatic concern with the health and wellbeing of the population (see p. 121 above). The delivery of heroin was seen as a way of increasing the number of drug users in treatment and in contact with medical authorities. This would reduce illicit drug use and associated deaths, limit unsafe injecting practices and the transmission of blood born diseases between intravenous drug users and the broader population, reduce drug related crime and improve the social functioning of dependent drug users (Select Committee on HIV/AIDS Illegal Drugs and Prostitution 1991).

In August of 2001, approximately ten years after the initial proposal for the ACT heroin trial was launched, a National Crime Authority (NCA) report on organised crime, resurrected the heroin debate. Gary Crook, Chairman of the NCA called on the Federal Government to consider options 'previously deemed unpalatable', such as treating the supply of addictive drugs as a medical and treatment matter, 'subject to the supervision of a treating doctor and supplied from a repository that is government controlled' (Banham and Doherty 2001: 1). He admitted that the drug trial approach was 'pretty radical', however, in his view: 'Everything should be considered, nothing should be rejected, we've got a terrible problem here on our hands and the essence of that approach is to attack the profit motive...If something can be done to combat this enormous opportunity to make profit and to control price, perhaps that is one of the many matters worthy of consideration'. He also said that drug trafficking had 'grown exponentially' and the profits had 'almost gown beyond comprehension', and it should be given the same priority and attention as threats to national security (Banham and Doherty 2001: 1; Sydney Morning Herald 2001: 36). According to the NCA report, illicit drug trafficking, money-laundering and numerous other criminal ramifications seriously impact on the national economy, moreover 'drug trafficking should be accorded the priority and attention of threats to national security' (Sydney Morning Herald 2001: 36).

On this occasion – three months before a federal election[1] – then Prime Minister John Howard was less 'ambivalent' than in 1996. He was quick to repeatedly reject even the possibility of a trial:

> I take this opportunity of totally rejecting the suggestion raised by the chairman of the National Crime Authority that consideration be given to a heroin trial...It remains the policy of this government to totally oppose heroin trials in this country. We will give no aid or comfort, or any encouragement, to any State or Territory (cited in Banham and Doherty 2001: 1)...

> While I'm Prime Minister, while this Government is in power, we will not give any aid or comfort to heroin trials (cited in Banham and Doherty 2001: 2).

And

> While ever this Government is in office and while ever I am Prime Minister of this country, there will be no heroin trial (cited in Sydney Morning Herald 2001: 36).

While Australia did not go ahead with the trial, posing the question of heroin prescribing ultimately had the effect of usefully expanding the treatment domain (to include buprenorphine and naltrexone) in that country. Elsewhere in the world, however, similar arguments have been made to much greater effect.

A growing number of voices have advocated the prescription of heroin for the treatment of opiate dependence. They echo the Select Committee's concerns for health and social functioning. They propose that current treatments are insufficiently attractive or effective for some heroin dependent users. Prescribing their drug of choice would attract more people into treatment and retain them in treatment for longer (one of the best indicators of recovery). More heroin users would get help and there would be fewer untreated heroin users in the community. Heroin prescription

---

1 The liberal Party's November 2001 victory gave John Howard a third term in power, making him one of Australia's longest serving prime ministers.

would help some people to stop or reduce their illicit heroin use; this would undercut the black market in illicit heroin and ensure that heroin users can use a drug of known quality and strength which would reduce drug related deaths. It would help people avoid health problems such as overdose and unsafe injecting practices that can lead to the transmission of HIV and hepatitis B and C (HBV, HCV) (Fischer et al. 2002; Gerlach 2002; Small and Drucker 2007; Strang 1994). It may lead to less acquisitive crime to support a drug habit and to improved social functioning (work, housing and family life) (Fischer et al. 2002; Ribeaud 2004). It would provide an opportunity for a gradual change away from heroin use to methadone and from injecting to oral use. 'Individual heroin users would benefit and so would society – by having less drug related crime lower criminal justice and prison costs, fewer or less visible drug markets, lower aggregate health care costs and lower social welfare costs' (Stimson and Metrebian 2003: 2).

Beyond Australia a number of countries have trialled the prescription of heroin. In the UK it has been available since the 1920s, when the Rolleston Committee report effectively limited intervention by the Home Office and reinforced the autonomy of medical responses to drug dependence (p.69 above). From time to time, in that country, heroin's place in the treatment spectrum has been re-evaluated and maintained according to pragmatic criteria. In the mid 1960s it was used to control the black market, in the 1970s and 1980s health concerns were paramount when HIV/AIDS was a major issue, and in the 1990s reducing crime became the official reasoning for allowing heroin to be available legally to some users (Stimson and Metrebian 2003). Trials have taken, or are taking, place in Switzerland, the Netherlands, Germany, France, Belgium, Spain and Canada. The therapeutic delivery of heroin is generally located within a wider range of treatment options and positive results have been achieved (Bammer et al. 2003; M. Farrell and Hall 1998; M. Farrell et al. 2001).

Alex Wodak (2007) argues that the evidence in favour of prescription heroin treatment is now much stronger than it was ten years ago. The Dutch trial involved 430 severely dependent heroin users who had not benefited despite multiple other treatments (Blanken et al. 2005). The majority (52 per cent) of those treated with prescription heroin improved according to an index reflecting physical health, mental health and social function. Just over a quarter (28 per cent) of those who had received prescription heroin treatment were transferred to standard methadone maintenance treatment, 82 per cent of this group, who had previously improved, then substantially deteriorated. The Swiss (Rehm et al. 2001), Spanish (March et al. 2006) and German (Michels et al. 2007) studies found similar benefits. According to Wodak (2007) the heroin trials have gone ahead have demonstrated unambiguous and worthwhile health and social improvements. Though more expensive than standard methadone treatment, prescription heroin treatment has proven more cost effective. Concerns about possible risks have not been borne out. Prescription heroin has not been diverted to the black market. More permissive community attitudes to illicit drug use did not develop. Clinics were not inundated by large numbers of inappropriate drug users from neighbouring areas. In Switzerland the delivery of prescription heroin was the subject of a national referendum in September 1997, 71 per cent of Swiss voters supported retaining the treatment. The United Kingdom,

Switzerland and the Netherlands now provide heroin-assisted treatment but only as last resort.

Beyond this mobilisation which is strongly linked to the domain of health and specifically treatment, others have in their critique of the current UN approaches echoed the concerns expressed by Gary Crook. New research consortiums and research clusters have formed to provide a reasoned and evidence based argument in relation to the problems of international trade. The Transnational Institute explains '[t]he wisdom of the UN Drug Conventions is increasingly being questioned'[2]; in some countries non-government organisations and parliamentary commissions have held inquiries on the reform of national drug policies that also touch on reform of the UN Drug Conventions. It cites for example the International Drug Policy Consortium's *The United Nation's Review of Global Policy on Illegal Drugs –An Advocacy Guide for Civil Society* (2007), along with the Senlis Council Drug Policy Forum critique of current regulatory controls which argues that:

> …the use of licit and illicit drugs is a harmful societal reality with potential negative impact on individuals and communities and needs to be tackled in a more realistic, dynamic way. Policies based solely on criminal sanctions have failed to demonstrate effectiveness: economic corruption increases, organized crime prospers and developing economies are hard hit by military and environmental (crop eradication) interventions. At the same time the marginalisation of drug-users is compounded. It is now widely recognized that an effective international drugs policy should be based on the minimization of harm both to individuals and to the community at large.

The Beckley Foundation Drug Policy Programme (BFDPP) is governed by a number of principles, key amongst these are the view that: the current global drug control mechanism, (as enshrined in the three United Nations Conventions of 1961, 1971 and 1988), is not achieving the core objective of significantly reducing the scale of the market for controlled substances, such as heroin (cocaine, methamphetamine and cannabis); and the negative side effects of the implementation of this system may themselves be creating significant social problems[3]. A number of reports produced by the program have highlighted the problems with the international system of control (Bewley-Taylor and Trace 2006) and its relationship to organised crime and terrorist activity. Roberts, Bewley-Taylor and Trace cite an independent assessment which identifies narcotic trafficking as 'a major source of revenue for terrorist and organised criminal networks, particularly groups with a transnational reach' (Gunaratna in Roberts et al. 2005: 2). Similar contributions have been made by the Transform Drug Policy Foundation (Rolles et al. 2006: 9; Rolles 2007), the Canadian Foundation for Drug Policy and the Drug Policy Alliance to name but a few.[4]

---

2   Transnational Institute http://www.tni.org/detail_page.phtml?page=links_drugs-reform, accessed 11/11/2007.

3   Beckley Foundation Drug Policy Programme: http://www.internationaldrugpolicy. net/ accessed 11/11/2007.

4   See the Canadian Foundation for Drug Policy Website: http://www.cjfdp.ca/terror. htm; and the Drug Policy Alliance: Terrorism Website http://www.drugpolicy.org/global/

This list of contributions to recent drug policy debate is indicative rather than complete. Nevertheless, it seems that the conditions that make the problematisation of prohibition possible are undeniably emerging on what Dean (1995: 566) describes as the 'horizons' upon which humans problematise 'being, including their own'. Indeed, it is conceivable that Gary Crooke's 2001 proposal that the Australian Federal government consider options 'previously deemed unpalatable', as a response to the threat posed by drug trafficking to national security, represents a mutation, if not a reversal, of earlier justifications for the outright prohibition of the drug. Moreover, in relation to the treatment debate, for many the question is no longer whether the maintenance spectrum ought or ought not be extended to include heroin – but, how might we govern better through heroin, rather than by simply governing (or trying to govern) its supply?

terrorism/ accessed 11/11/2007.

References

Alcohol and Drug Services Unit (1990), *Policies and Procedures for Methadone Programs in Victoria* (Melbourne: Health Department of Victoria).

Armstrong, D. (1994), 'Bodies of knowledge/knowledge of bodies', in C. Jones and R. Porter (eds.), *Reassessing Foucault: Power, medicine and the body* (London: Routledge), 17-27.

Ashely, R. (1972), *Heroin: The myths and the facts* (New York: St Martin's Press).

Australian Institute of Health and Welfare (2007), 'Alcohol and other drug treatment services in Australia 2005-2006: Report on the National Minimum Data Set', (HSE 53).

Bakalar, J. and Grinspoon, L, (1984), *Drug Control in a Free Society*, (Cambridge: Cambridge University Press).

Bammer, G. and Douglas, R. (1996), 'The ACT heroin trial proposal: An overview', *Medical Journal of Australia,* 164 (June), 690-2.

Bammer, G., et al. (2003), 'What can the Swiss and Dutch trials tell us about the potential risks associated with heroin prescribing?' *Drug and Alcohol Review* 22, 363-71.

Banham, C. and Doherty, L. (2001), 'NCA Calls for Radical Heroin Trial', *Sydney Morning Herald,* 09/08/2001, p. 1.

Barry, A., Osborne, T., and Rose, N. (eds.) (1996), *Foucault and Political Reason: Liberalism, neoliberalism and rationalities of government* (London: UCL Press Limited).

Bassiouni, M.C. (1972), 'A proposal: The international narcotics control system', (United Nations).

Bean, P. (1974), *Drugs and Social Control* (Oxford: Martin Robertson).

Bean, P. and Wilkinson, C. (1988), 'Drug taking, crime and the illicit supply system', *British Journal of Addiction,* 83, 533-9.

Beeching, J. (1975), *The Chinese Opium Wars* (New York: Harcourt Brace).

Bell, J., et al. (2003), 'Clinical guidelines and procedures for the use of naltrexone in the management of opoid dependence', (Canberra: Commonwealth of Australia).

Berridge, V. (1977), 'Opium eating and life insurance', *British Journal of Addiction,* 72, 371-7.

--- (1978), 'War conditions and narcotics control: the passing of Defence of the Realm Act Regulation 40B', *Journal of Social Policy,* 7 (3), 285-304.

--- (1979), 'Morality and medical science: Concepts of narcotic addiction in Britain, 1820-1926', *Annals of Science,* 36, 67-85.

--- (1984), 'Drugs and social policy: The establishment of drug control in Britain, 1900-1930', *British Journal of Addiction,* 79, 17-29.

--- (1990), 'Comments on Stimson's 'AIDS and HIV: The historical perspective'',

British Journal of Addiction, 85, 343-4.

Berridge, V. and Edwards, G. (1987), *Opium and the People: Opiate yse in nineteenth century England,* (2nd edn.; London: Allen Lane).

Bewley-Taylor, D. and Trace, M. (2006), 'The International Narcotics Control Board: watchdog or guardian of the UN drug control conventions?' (Beckley Foundation Drug Policy Programme), 1-12.

Blanken, P., et al. (2005), 'Matching of treatment-resistant heroin-dependent patients to medical prescription of heroin or oral methadone treatment: results from two randomized controlled trials', *Addiction,* 100 (1), 89-95.

Brecher, E.M. (1972), *Licit and illicit drugs: The Consumers Union report on narcotics, stimulants, depressants, inhalants, hallucinogens, and marijuana - including caffeine, nicotine, and alcohol* (Boston: Brown Little).

Bruun, K., Pan, L., and Rexed, I. (1975), *The Gentlemen's Club: International Control of Drugs and Alcohol* (Studies in Crime and Justice Series; Chicago: The University of Chicago Press).

Bull, M. (1991), 'Methadone maintenance: A chemotherapeutic prison', Honours (Australian National University).

--- (1996), 'Power and addiction: the making of the modern addict', *Australian Journal of Social Issues*, 31(2), 191-209.

--- (2002), 'If the answer is methadone what's the question? A genealogy of the regulation of opioids in modern industrialised societies.' (Griffith University).

Bulletin on Narcotics (1951), 'The question of the international opium monopoly', *Bulletin on Narcotics,* (1), 46-58.

Bulmer, M., Bales, K., and Kish Sklar, K. (1991), *The Social Survey in Historical Perspective, 1880-1940* (Cambridge: Cambridge University Press).

Burchell, D. (1995), 'The Attributes of citizens: virtue, manners and the activity of citizenship', *Economy and Society,* 24 (4), 540-58.

Burchell, G., Gordon, C., and Miller, P. (eds.) (1991), *The Foucault Effect: Studies in governmentality, with two lectures by and an interview with Michel Foucault* (Hemel Hempstead: Harvester Wheatsheaf).

Castel, R. (1991), 'From dangerousness to risk', in Graham Burchell, Collin Gordon, and Peter Miller (eds.), *The Foucault Effect. Studies in governmentality* (London: Harvester/Wheatsheaf).

Castel, R. (1994), 'Problematization' as a Mode of Reading History', in J. Goldstein (ed.), *Foucault and the Writing of History* (Cambridge: Blackwell Publishers), 237-52.

CEIDA (1986), 'The methadone controversy', *Connexions: The Journal of Drug and Alcohol Issues,* 6 (7), 1.

--- (1989), 'Dr Stella Dalton - Blockade Pioneer', *Connexions,* September/October, 23-25.

Chartier, R. (1994), 'The chimera of the origin: Archaeology, cultural history and the French Revolution', in J. Goldstein (ed.), *Foucault and the Writing of History* (Cambridge: Blackwell Publishers), 167-86.

Chatterjee, S.K. (1981), *Legal Aspects of International Drug Control* (The Hague: Martinus Nijhoff).

Chouvy, P. (2003), 'Opiate smuggling routes from Afghanistan to Europe and Asia',

Jane's Intelligence Review.

--- (2004a), 'Afghan opium production predicted to reach new high', *Jane's Intelligence Review,* 16 (10), 29-31.

--- (2004b), 'Narco-Terrorism in Afghanistan', *Terrorism Monitor,* 2 (6).

--- (2004c), 'Drugs and the financing of terrorism', *Terrorism Monitor,* 2 (20).

--- (2005), 'The dangers of opium eradication in Asia', *Jane's Intelligence Review,* 17 (1), 26-7.

--- (2006), 'Afghanistan's opium production in perspective', *The China and Eurasia Forum Quarterly,* 4 (1).

Christie, G. and Hil, R. (2000), 'Service users' and providers' perceptions of a methadone maintenance program: A Queensland qualitative pilot study', (Brisbane: Queensland University of Technology).

Cohen, S. (1985), *Visions of Social Control* (Cambridge: Polity Press).

Commonwealth Department of Human Services and Health (1995), 'Review of methadone treatment in Australia, Final Report', (Canberra: Commonwealth Department of Human Services and Health).

Commonwealth of Australia (1985), 'National campaign against drug abuse', *Campaign Document Issued Following the Special Premiers' Conference* (Canberra: Australian Government Publishing Service (AGPS)).

--- (1987), 'National campaign against drug abuse (NCADA)', (Canberra: Australian Government Publishing Service).

--- (1988), 'National methadone guidelines: Guidelines for the use of methadone in treatment programs for opiate dependence,' (Canberra: Canberra Publishing & Printing Co.).

--- (1993), 'National policy on methadone', *National Drug Strategy* (Canberra: Commonwealth Department of Health, Housing, Local Government and Community Services).

--- (1997), 'National policy on methadone treatment', *National Drug Strategy* (Canberra: Commonwealth Department of Health and Family Services).

--- (2007), 'National pharmacotherapy policy for people dependent on opioids', *National Drugs Strategy* (Canberra: Australian Government Department of Health and Ageing).

Cornell, S.E. (2006), 'The narcotics threat in Greater Central Asia: From crime-terror nexus to state infiltration?' *China and Eurasia Forum Quarterly,* 4 (1), 37 67.

Costa, A.M. (2002), 'Counter-narcotics: the silent war in Afghanistan', *Drugs as a cross-cutting issue in Afghan reconstruction: Turning rhetoric into reality* (Wilton Park: UNODCCP).

--- (2005), 'Drugs, crime and terrorist financing: Breaking the links', paper given at Conference on Combating Terrorist Financing, Vienna, 9 November 2005.

Courtwright, D. (1982), *Dark Paradise* (Cambridge: Cambridge University Press).

Cruikshank, B. (1993), 'Self governance and self-esteem', Economy and Society, 22 (3), 327-44.

--- (1994), 'The will to empower: technologies of citizenship and the war on poverty', *Socialist Review,* 23 (4), 29-55.

--- (1996), 'Revolutions within: self-government and self-esteem', in Andrew Barry, Thomas Osborne, and Nikolas Rose (eds.), *Foucault and Political Reason:*

Liberalism, Neo-Liberalism and rationalities of Government (London: University College of London Press), 231-52.

Cullen, M.J. (1975), 'Social statistics and the ideology of improvement in Early Victorian Britain', in M. J. Cullen (ed.), *The Statistical movement in Early Victorian Britain: The Foundations of Empirical Social Research* (Sussex: Harvester Press).

Daley, D.C. (1991), *Kicking Addictive Habits Once and for All: A Relapse Prevention Guide* (Lexington: Lexington Books).

Davies, S. (1986), *Shooting Up* (Sydney: Allen and Unwin).

Dean, M. (1994), *Critical and Effective Histories: Foucault's Methods and Historical Sociology* (London: Roughtledge).

--- (1995), 'Governing the unemployed self in an active society', *Economy and Society,* 24 (4), 559-83.

--- (1999a), 'Risk, calculable and incalculable', in Deborah Lupton (ed.), *Risk and Sociocultural Theory: New Directions and Perspectives* (Cambridge: Cambridge University Press), 131-59.

--- (1999b), *Governmentality: power and rule in modern society* (London: Sage).

Dean, M. and Hindess, B. (eds.) (1998), *Governing Australia: Studies in Contemporary Rationalities of Government* (Cambridge: Cambridge University Press).

Defert, D. (1991), 'Popular life and insurance technology', in Graham Burchell, Collin Gordon, and Peter Miller (eds.), *The Foucault Effect* (Hemel Hempstead: Harvester Wheatsheaf), 221-34.

Department of Community and Health Services (1995), Tasmanian Methadone Program Policy, (Hobart: Department of Community and Health Services).

Dobinson, I. (1994), 'Drug Legalisation: Method or Mayhem', *Current Issues in Criminal Justice,* 6 (2), 221-3.

Dole, V.P. (1970), 'Biochemistry of addiction', *Annual Review of Biochemistry,* 39, 821-40.

--- (1988), 'Implications of methadone maintenance for theories of narcotic addiction', *Journal of the American Medical Association,* 260, 3025-9.

Dole, V.P. and Kreek, M.J. (1973), 'Methadone plasma level: sustained by a reservoir of drug in tissue', *Proceedings of the National Academy of Science,* 70, 10.

Dole, V.P. and Joseph, H.J (1978), 'Long term outcome of patients treated with methadone maintenace', *Annals of the New York Academy of Sciences,* 211, 181-89.

Dole, V.P. and Nyswander, M. (1965), 'A medical treatment for diacetylmorphin (heroin) addiction', *Journal of the American medical Association,* 193, 80-4.

--- (1967), 'Heroin addiction - metabolic disease', *Archives of Internal Medicine,* 120, 19-24.

--- (1968), 'Methadone maintenance and its implication for theories of narcotic addiction', in A Wikler (ed.), *The Addictive State.* (Baltimore: Williams and Wilkins), 359-66.

Dole, V.P. and Nyswander, M. (1980), 'Methadone maintenance, A theoretical perspective', in D.J Lettieri, M. Sayers, and H. W Person (eds.), *Theories on Drug Abuse: Selected contemporary perspectives* (Rockville, Md,: NIDA, US

Department of Health and Human Services).

Dole, V.P., Nyswnader, M., and Kreek, M.J. (1966), 'Narcotic blockade', *Archives of Internal Medicine,* 118, 304-9.

Donzelot, J. (1979), *Policing the Family* (London: Heinemann).

Drug and Alcohol Services Council (1992), 'The public methadone treatment program in South Australia: Policies and procedures', (Parkside, South Australia).

Drug and Alcohol Services Council (1994a), 'Pharmacists handbook on the policy and procedures of the methadone program in South Australia', (Parkside, South Australia: Drugs and Alcohol Services Council and the Public and Environmental Health Services of the South Australian Health Commission).

--- (1994b), 'Private methadone program: Policies and procedures', (Parkside, South Australia).

Drug and Alcohol Services South Australia (2006), 'Guide for Pharmacists: addiction treatment and maintenance pharmacotherapy (methadone and buprenorphine) programs in South Australia', (Adelaide: South Australian Government).

Drugs and Poisons Regulation Group (2006), 'Policy for maintenance pharmacotherapy for opioid dependence', (Melbourne: Department of Human Services).

Duster, T. (1970), *The Legislation of Morality: Law, drugs, and moral judgment* (New York: Free Press).

Eddy, N.B, Hallback, H., and Braeden, O.J. (1957), 'Synthetic substances with morphine-like effect: Clinical experience - potency, side effects, addiction liability', *Bulletin WHO*, 17569-86.

Ewald, F. (1991), 'Insurance and risk', in G Burchell, C Gordon, and P Miller (eds.), *The Foucault Effect: Studies in governmentality, with two lectures by and an interview with Michel Foucault* (Hemel Hempstead: Harvester Wheatsheaf), 197-210.

Eyler, J.M. (1979), *Victorian Social Medicine: The ideas and methods of William Farr* (Baltimore: John Hopkins University Press).

Farrell, G. (1999), 'Drugs and drug control', in United Nations Office of Drug Control and Crime Prevention (ed.), *Global Report on Crime and Justice* (Oxford: Oxford University Press), 171-80.

Farrell, M. and Hall, W. (1998), 'The Swiss heroin trials: testing alternative approaches ', *British Medical Journal,* 316, 639.

Farrell, M., et al. (2001), 'Reviewing current practice in drug-substitution treatment in the European Union', (Luxembourg: European monitoring Centre for Drugs and Drug addiction).

Fay, P.W. (1975), *The Opium War, 1840-1842: Barbarians in the Celestial Empire in the early part of the nineteenth century and the war by which they force her gates ajar.* (Chapel Hill: The University of North Carolina Press).

Fischer, B., et al. (2002), 'Heroin-assisted treatment as a response to the public health problem of opiate dependence', *European Journal of Public Health,* 12 (3), 228-34.

Forster, C. and Hazlehurst, C. (1988), 'Australian Statisticians and the Development of Official Statistics', *Year Book Australia 1988* (Canberra: Australian Bureau of

Statistics), 1-95.

Foucault, M. (1967), *Madness and Civilisation: A history of insanity in the Age of Reason*, trans. R Howard (London: Tavistock Publications Limited).

--- (1972), *The Archaeology of Knowledge* (Tavistock Publications Limited).

--- (1973), *The Birth of the Clinic: An archaeology of medical perception*, trans. A.M. Sheridan (New York: Pantheon).

--- (1977), *Discipline and Punish: The birth of the prison*, trans. A. M Sheridan (London: Penguin).

--- (1979), *The History of Sexuality, Volume 1: An introduction*, trans. R Hurley (London: Allen Lane).

--- (1980), 'The Politics of Health in the Eighteenth Century', in Michel Foucault (ed.), *Power/Knowledge: Selected interview and other writings, 1972-1977* (Brighton: Harvester).

--- (1984a), 'Nietzsche, geneaology, history', in Paul Rabinow (ed.), *The Foucault Reader* (Harmondsworth: Penguin), 76-100.

--- (1984b), 'What is an author?' in Paul Rabinow (ed.), *The Foucault Reader* (Harmondsworth: Penguin), 101-20.

--- (1988), 'Technologies of the self', in L.H. Martin, H. Gutman, and P.H. Hutton (eds.), *Technologies of the Self: a Seminar with Michel Foucault* (London: Tavistock).

--- (1991), 'On governmentality', in G. Burchell, C. Gordon, and P. Miller (eds.), *The Foucault Effect: Studies in governmentality, with two lectures by and an interview with Michel Foucault* (Hemel Hempstead: Harvester Wheatsheaf), 87-104.

Fox, R. and Matthews, I. (1992), *Drugs Policy: Fact, fiction and the future* (Sydney: Federation Press).

Friman, H.R. (1996), *NarcoDiplomacy: Exporting the US war on drugs* (Ithaca: Cornell University Press).

Garland, D. (1985), *Punishment and Welfare: A history of penal strategies*, (Aldershot: Gower Publishing Company Limited).

--- (1996), 'The limits of the sovereign state: Strategies of crime control in contemporary society', *British Journal of Criminology*, 36 (4), 445-71.

Garrenstein-Ross, G. and Dabruzzi, K. (2007), *The Convergence of Crime and Terror: Law enforcement opportunities and perils* (New York: Center for Policing and Terrorism).

Garton, S. (1987), 'Once a drunkard always a drunkard: Social reform and the problem of 'Habitual Drunkenness' in Australia, 1880-1914', *Labour History*, 53 (November), 38-53.

General Assembly (2001a), 'Unprecedented unity prompted by 'Terrible Evil' of 11 September Attack says Secretary-General, as General Assembly Begins Terrorism Debate', *Fifty-sixth General Assembly, Plenary, 12th Meeting (AM)* (GA/9919: United Nations), 1-12.

--- (2001b), 'Speakers call for comprehensive international convention on terrorism, in General Assembly Debate', *Fifty-sixth General Assembly, Plenary 14th Meeting (AM)* (GA/9922: United Nations), 1-9.

--- (2001c), 'General Assembly Fifty-sixth Session', *44th plenary meeting,* (A/56/

pv.44: United Nations), 1-43.

Gerlach, R. (2002), 'Drug-substitution treatment in Germany: A critical overview of its history, legislation and current practice', *The Journal of Drug Issues,* 32 (2), 503-22.

Gordon, C. (1991), 'Governmentality - an introduction', in Graham Burchell, Collin Gordon, and Peter Miller (eds.), *The Foucault Effect: Studies in governmentality, with two lectures by and an interview with Michel Foucault* (London: Harvester Wheatsheaf).

Gossop, M. (1987), *Living With Drugs* (2nd edn.; Aldershot: Wildwood House Limited).

Greenberg, M. (1951), *British Trade and the Opening of China 1800-1842* (Cambridge: Cambridge University Press).

Hacking, I. (1982), 'Biopower and the avalanche of printed numbers', *Humanities in Society,* IV, 279-95.

--- (1986), 'Making up people', in T. C. Heller, M. Sosna, and D. E. Wellbery (eds.), *Reconstructing Individualism: Autonomy, Individuality and the Self in Western Thought* (Standford: Standford University Press), 222-36.

--- (1990), *The Taming of Chance* (Cambridge: Cambridge University Press).

--- (1991), 'How should be do a history of statistics?' in G. Burchell, C. Gordon, and P. Miller (eds.), *The Foucault Effect: Studies in governmentality, with two lectures by and an interview with Michel Foucault* (Hemel Hempstead: Harvester Wheatsheaf).

--- (1992), 'Multiple Personality Disorder and its Host', *History of the Human Sciences*, 5(2), 2-31.

Hall, W., Ward, J., and Hando, J. (1991), 'A review of the research literature of the efficacy of methadone maintenance', *Draft Working Paper Number 8* (Kensington: National Drug and Alcohol Research Centre, The University of New South Wales).

Harding, G. (1986), 'Constructing addiction as moral failing', *Sociology of Health and Illness,* 8 (March), 75-85.

Henry-Edwards, S., et al. (2003), 'Clinical guidelines and procedures for the use of methadone in the maintenance treatment of opioid dependence', (Canberra: Commonwealth of Australia).

Herr, A.C. (1980), 'Historical and theoretical considerations for drug use intervention', in Stanley Einstein (ed.), *The Community's Response to Drug Use* (New York: Pergamon Press), 3-28.

Hindess, B. (2000a), 'The liberal government of unfreedom', *The Ethos of Welfare Symposium* (University of Helsinki), 1-18.

--- (2000b), 'Divide and govern', in R. Ericson and N. Stehr (eds.), *Governing Modern Societies* (Toronto: University of Toronto Press).

Hirst, P. and Thompson, G. (1996), *Globalization in Question: The international economy and the possibilities of Governance* (Cambridge: Polity Press).

Hoffman, J.P. (1990), 'The Historical Shift in the Perception of Opiates: From Medicine to Social Menace', *Journal of Psychoactive Drugs,* 22 (1), 53-62.

Holmes, S. (1995), *Passions and Constraints: on the theory of liberal democracy*

(Chicago: University of Chicago Press).

Hopwood, A.G. and Miller, P. (1994), *Accounting as Social Institutional Practice* (Cambridge: Cambridge University Press).

Hunter, I. (1994), *Rethinking the School: Subjectivity, bureaucracy, criticsim* (Sydney: Allen and Unwin).

--- (1998), 'Unicivil society: Liberal government and the deconfessionalisation of politics', in Mitchell Dean and Barry Hindess (eds.), *Governing Australia: Studies in Contemporary Rationality of Government* (Cambridge: Cambridge University Press), 242-64.

Illich, I. (1975), *Medical Nemesis: The expropriation of health* (London: Calder & Boyars).

Inglis, B. (1975), *The Forbidden Game: A social history of drugs* (London: Hodder and Stoughton).

International Drug Policy Consortium (2006), *The 2006 World Drug Report: Winning the war on drugs?* (Briefing Paper 2, September 2006: IDPC).

International Narcotics Control Board (1998), 'Recommendations by the International Narcotics Control Board: Drug Demand Reduction', <http://undcp.org/adhoc/gass/incb/GA/e/incb-ddr.htm>, accessed 11/12/1999 11.01am.

--- (1999), 'The role of the INCB', <http://www.incb.org/e/erole/menu.html>, accessed 11/12/1999 11.39am.

--- (2003), *The Report of the International Narcotics Control Board for 2003*, (E/INCB/2003: United Nations).

--- (2004), *The Report of the International Narcotics Control Board for 2004*, (E/INCB/2004: United Nations).

Isbell, H. and Vogell, V.H. (1949), 'The addiction liability of methadone (amidone, dolophin, 10820) and its use in the treatment of morphine abstinence syndrome', *American Journal of Psychiatry,* 105, 909-14.

Isbell, H., et al. (1947), 'Tolerance and addiction liability of 6-dimethylamino--4-4-diphenlheptanon-3 (methadone)', *Journal of the American Medical Association,* 135, 888-94.

Jacyna, L.S. (1994), *Philosophic Whigs: Medicine, science and citizenship in Edinburgh, 1789-1848* (London: Routledge).

Janes Yeo, E. (1991), 'The social survey in social perspective, 1830-1930', in M. Bulmer, K. Bales, and K. Kish Sklar (eds.), *The Social Survey in Historical Perspective, 1880-1940* (Cambridge: Cambridge University Press), 49-65.

Johnson, B.D. (1975), 'Righteousness before revenue: The forgotten moral crusade against the Indo-Chinese opium trade', *Journal of Drug Issues,* Fall, 304-26.

Johnson, T. (1993), 'Expertise and the state', in M. Gane and T. Johnson (eds.), *Foucault's New Domains* (London: Routledge).

Joint Committee of the American Bar Association and the American Medical Association on Narcotic Drugs (1958), 'Narcotic Drugs: Interim Report of the Joint Committee of the American Bar Association and the American Medical Association on Narcotic Drugs', (New York).

Joint Secretarial of the Permanent Central Opium Board and the Drug Supervisory Body (1950), 'Note of the Joint Secretarial of the Permanent Central Opium

Board and the Drug Supervisory Body,' *Bulletin on Narcotics,* 2, 55-83.

Kaplan, J. (1983), *The Hardest Drug: Heroin and public policy* (Chicago: Chicago University Press) 247.

Koselleck, R. (1988), *Critique and Crisis: Enlightenment and pathogenesis of modern society* (Oxford: Berg).

Kosten, T. and George, T. (2002), 'The neurobiology of opioid dependence', *Science and Practice Perspectives,* 1 (1), 13-20.

Kreek, M.J. (1973), 'Medical Safety and side effects of methadone in tolerant individuals', *Journal of the American Medical Association,* 223(6), 665-8.

Krishnamoorthy, E.S. (1962), 'Comparative analysis of the Permanent Central Opium board and Drug Supervisory Body and their functions on the one hand, and the future International Control Board and its functions, on the other.' *Bulletin on Narcotics,* 3, 1-19.

Krivanek, J. (1988), *Heroin: Myths and reality* (Sydney: Allen and Unwin).

Latour, B. (1986), 'The Powers of Association', in J. Law (ed.), *Power, Action and Belief, Sociological Review Monograph* (London: Routledge and Kegan Paul), 264-80.

--- (1987), *Science in Action* (Milton Keynes: Open University Press).

Lazarsfeld, P.F. (1961), 'Notes on the history of quantification in sociology - Trends, sources and problems', in Harry Woolf (ed.), *Quantification: A history of the meaning of measurement in the natural and social sciences* (Indianapolis: Bobbs-Merrill Company Inc), 147-203.

Levine, H.G. (1978), 'The discovery of Aaddiction: Changing conceptions of habitual drunkenness in America', *Journal of Studies on Alcohol,* 39 (1), 143-74.

Lintzeris, N., et al. (2006), 'National clinical guidelines and procedures for the use of buprenorphine in the treatment of opioid dependence', (Canberra: Commonwealth of Australia).

Lupton, D. (1995), *The Imperative of Health: Public health and the regulated body* (London: Sage Publications).

Lyall, K. (1997), 'Experimenting with heroin', *Weekend Australian,* 2-3 August 1997, p. 25.

Lynskey, M.T. (1998), 'The comorbidity of alcohol dependence and affective disorders: treatment implications', *Drug Alcohol Dependence,* 52 (201-9).

McCoy, A.W. (1972), *The Politics of Heroin in Southeast Asia,* (New York: Harper & Row Publishers)

--- (1980), *Drug Traffic: Narcotics and organised crime in Australia* (Sydney: Harper & Row Publishers).

--- (1991), *The Politics of Heroin: CIA complicity in the global drug trade* (2nd edn.: Lawrence Hill Books).

McGreggor, O.R. (1957), 'Social research and social policy in the nineteenth century', *British Journal of Sociology,* 8, 146-57.

Makkai, T. (1999), 'Linking drugs and criminal activity: Developing an integrated monitoring system', *Trends and Issues in Crime and Criminal Justice,* 199, (Canberra: Australian Institute of Criminology).

Manderson, D. (1988), 'The first loss of freedom: Early opium laws in Australia',

Australian Drug and Alcohol Review, 7, 439-53.

--- (1993), *From Mr Sin to Mr Big* (Oxford: Oxford University Press Australia).

March, J.C., et al. (2006), 'Controlled trial of prescribed heroin in the treatment of opioid addiction', *Journal of Substance Abuse Treatment,* 31, 203-11.

Marshall, J. (1981) 'Pansies, Perverts and Macho Men: Changing conceptions of male homosexuality', in K. Plummer (ed.), *The Making of the Modern Homosexual,* (Totowa NJ: Barnes and Noble Books), 133-154.

Mattick, R.P., et al. (2004), 'National evaluation of pharmacotherapies for opioids dependence: Report of results and recommendations', *National Drug Strategy* (Canberra: Australian Government Department of Health and Ageing).

May, H.L. (1955), 'The single convention on narcotic drugs: Comments and possibilities', *Bulletin on Narcotic Drugs,* 1, 1-14.

Michels, I.I., Stover, H., and Gerlach, R. (2007), 'Substitution treatment for opioid addicts in Germany', *Harm Reduction Journal,* 4 (5).

Miflin, B., Byrne, D., and Stradley, A. (1995), 'Queensland Methadone Prescribers Manual for Medical Practitioners', (Brisbane: Queensland medial Education Centre).

Miller, P. and Rose, N. (1990), 'Governing economic life', *Economy and Society,* 19 (1), 1-31.

Milligan, B. (1995), *Pleasures and Pains: Opium and the orient in nineteenth century British culture*, ed. K. Chase (Victorian Literature and Culture Series; Charlottesville: University Press of Virginia).

Minson, J. (1997), 'What is an expert?' in C. O'Farrell (ed.), *Foucault: The legacy* (Brisbane: Queensland University of Technology), 405-17.

Morgan, H.W. (1981), *Drugs in America: A Social History, 1800-1980* (Syracuse: Syracuse University Press).

Moynihan, M. (1983), 'Law enforcement and drug trafficking money: recent developments in Australian law and procedures', *Bulletin on Narcotics,* 2, 4-9.

Murdoch, D.W. (1983), 'Drugs of dependence monitoring system: An effective check of the movement of certain drugs in Australia', *Bulletin on Narcotics,* 4, 47-53.

Musto, D. (1973), *The American Disease: Origins of narcotic control* (1st edn.; New Haven: Yale University Press).

Nagler, N. (1984), 'Forfeiture of the proceeds of drug trafficking', *Bulletin on Narcotics,* 4, 21-29.

National Crime Authority (2001), 'Organised crime in Australia', *NCA Commentary 2001* (Canberra: National Crime Authority).

New South Wales Department of Health, Directorate of the Drug Offensive (undated), 'Policies and procedures for the methadone treatment of opioid dependence in NSW', (Sydney).

New South Wales Health Department (2001), 'Pharmacotherapies Accreditation Course – A reference manual for participants', (Sydney: NSW Health Department).

--- (2006), 'NSW opioid treatment program: Clinical guidelines for methadone and buprenorphine treatment of opioid dependence', *Mental Health and Drug and*

Alcohol Office (Sydney: NSW Health Department).

Newman, R.G. (1977), *Methadone Treatment in Narcotic Addiction* (New York: Academic Press).

Noll, A. (1975), 'Drug abuse and its prevention as seen by the international legal profession', *Bulletin on Narcotics,* 1, 37-47.

--- (1977), 'Drug abuse and penal provisions of the international drug control treaties', *Bulletin on Narcotics,* 4, 41-57.

Northern Territory Department of Health and Community Services (2006), 'Poisons and Dangerous Drugs Act, Schedule 8 and Restricted Schedule 4 Substances', *Policy and Clinical Practice Guidelines* (Darwin: Department of Health and Community Services).

O'Brien, S. (2004a), 'Treatment options for heroin and other opioid dependence: A guide for families and carers', (Canberra: Commonwealth of Australia).

--- (2004b), 'Treatment options for heroin and other opioid dependence: A guide for users', (Canberra: Commonwealth of Australia).

O'Malley, P. (1996), 'Risk and responsibility', in A. Barry, T. Osbourne and N. Rose (eds.) *Foucault and Political Reason,* (London: UCL Press Limited), 189-207.

O'Malley, P. (1999), 'Consuming risks: Harm minimization and the government of "drug-users"', in Russell Smandych (ed.), *Governable Places: Readings on governmentality and crime control* (Aldershot: Ashgate).

Oestreich, G. (1982), *Neostocism and the Early Modern State* (Cambridge: Cambridge University Press).

Osbourne, T. (1992), 'Medicine and epistemology: Michel Foucault and the liberatlity of clincial reason', *History of the Human Sciences,* 5 (2), 63-93.

Oscapella, E. (2001), 'How drug prohibition finances and otherwise enables terrorism', *Submission to the Senate of Canada Special Committee on Illegal Drugs* (Ottawa: Senate of Canada Special Committee on Illegal Drugs).

Parssinen, T.M. (1983), *Secret Passions, Secret Remedies: Narcotic Drugs in British Society, 1820-1930* (1st edn; Manchester: Manchester University Press).

Pasquino, P. (1991), 'Theatrum politicum: The genealogy of capital - Police and the state of prosperity', in G. Burchell, C. Gordon, and P. Miller (eds.), *The Foucault Effect: Studies in governmentality, with two lectures and an interview with Michel Foucault* (Hemel Hempstead: Harvester Wheatsheaf), 105-18.

Petersen, A. and Lupton, D. (1996), *The New Public Health: Health and self in the age of risk* (1st edn.; St Leonards: Allen and Unwin).

Peterson, M.J. (1978), *The Medical Profession in Mid-Victorian London* (Berkeley: University of California Press).

Platt, J.J. (1986), *Heroin Addiction: Theory, research and treatment, Vol 1,* 3 vols. (1; Malabar: Krieger Publishing Company).

Porter, R. (1991), 'Reforming the patient in the age of reform: Thomas Beddoes and medical practice', in R. French and A. Wear (eds.), *British Medicine in an Age of Reform* (London: Routledge), 9-44.

Porter, T.M. (1986), *The Rise of Statistical Thinking, 1820-1900* (Princeton: Princeton University Press).

Prescott, J. (1987) 'Issues and priorities in methadone research', *Research Monograph No 2.*, (Kensington: National Drug and Alcohol Research Centre, The University of New South Wales).

Prior, L. and Bloor, M. (1993), 'Why people die: Social representations of death and its causes', *Science as Culture,* 3 (3), 346-75.

Queensland Department of Health (1990), 'Queensland methadone program: Policies and procedures manual', (Brisbane: Queensland Department of Health).

Queensland Health (1994), 'Methadone program: Policies and procedures manual (Draft)', (Brisbane: Queensland Health).

Rehm, J., et al. (2001), 'Feasibility, safety and efficacy of injectable heroin prescription for refractory opioid addicts: a follow-up study', *Lancet,* 358, 1417-20.

Remberg, B.A, Nikiforov, A, and Buchbauer, G (1994), 'Fifty years of development of opium characterization methods', *Bulletin on Narcotics,* 2, 78-108.

Renborg, B.A. (1964), 'The grand old men of the League of Nations: What they achieved, Who they were', *Bulletin on Narcotics,* 4, 1-11.

Ribeaud, D. (2004), 'Long-term impacts of the Swiss heroin prescription trials on crime and treated heroin users', *Journal of Drug Issues,* 34 (1), 163-94.

Rider, B.A.K. (1983), 'The role of the Commonwealth Secretariat in the fight against illicit drug traffic', *Bulletin on Narcotics,* 4, 61-5.

Roberts, M., Klein, A., and Trace, M. (2004), 'Towards a review of global policies on controlled drugs', *The Beckley Foundation Drug Policy Series* (Surrey: The Beckley Foundation Drug Policy Program).

Roberts, M., Bewley-Taylor, D., and Trace, M. (2005), 'Facing the Future: The challenge for national and international drug policy ', *The Beckley Foundation Drug Policy Series* (Surrey: The Beckley Foundation Drug Policy Programme), 1-13.

Rolles, S. (2007), 'After the war on drugs: Tools for the debate', in Steve Rolles (ed.), *After the War on Drugs* (Bristol: Transform Drug Policy Foundation), 1-75.

Rolles, S., Kushlick, D., and Jay, M. (2006), 'After the war on drugs: options for control', in Steve Rolles, Danny Kushlick, and Mike Jay (eds.), (Bristol: Transform Drug Policy Foundation), 1-43.

Rolls, E. (1992), *Sojourners: Flowers and the Wide Sea* (Brisbane: University of Queensland Press).

Rose, N. (1988), 'Calculable minds and manageable individuals: "History" and the psychological sciences', *History of the Human Sciences,* 1 (2), 179-200.

--- (1989), *Governing the Soul: The shaping of the private self* (London: Routledge).

--- (1993), 'Government, authority and expertise in advanced liberalism', *Economy and Society,* 22 (3), 282-99.

--- (1994), 'Medicine, history and the present', in C. Jones and R. Porter (eds.), *Reassessing Foucault: Power medicine and the body* (London: Routledge), 48-72.

--- (1999), *Powers of Freedom: Reframing Political Thought* (Cambridge: Cambridge University Press).

Rose, N. and Miller, P. (1992), 'Political power beyond the State: problematics of government', *British Journal of Sociology,* 43 (2), 173-205.

Rosenbaum, M. and Murphy, S. (1984), 'Always a junkie?: The arduous task of getting off methadone maintenance', *Journal of Drug Issues*, Summer, 527-52.

Rural and Regional Health and Aged Care Services (2006), 'Methadone treatment in Victoria: User information booklet', (Melbourne: Victorian Government Department of Human Services).

Saunders, D. (1997), *Anti-lawyers: Religion and the critics of the law and the State*, (London: Routledge).

Schmidt, A. (2005), 'Links between terrorism and drug trafficking: A case of "Narco-terrorism"?' *The International Summit on Democracy, Terrorism and Security.* (The Madrid Summit Working Paper Series; Madrid).

Scott, J.M. (1969), *The White Poppy* (London: William Heinemann Ltd).

Security Council (2001a), 'Security Council unanimously adopts wide-ranging anti-terrorism resolution; Calls for suppressing financing, improving international cooperation, resolution 1373 (2001) also creates committee to monitor implementation', *Security Council 4385th Meeting (Night)* (SC/7158: United Nations), 1-4.

--- (2001b), 'Security Council requests Secretary-General to establish mechanism for monitoring sanctions against Taliban: Unanimously adopts resolution 1363 (2001)', *Security Council, 4352nd Meeting (PM)* (SC/7110: United Nations), 1-4.

Select Committee on HIV/AIDS Illegal Drugs and Prostitution (1991), 'Second Interim Report: A feasibility study on the controlled availability of opioids', (Canberra: Legislative Assembly of the Australian Capital Territory).

Shafer, R.P. (1973), 'Drug use in America: Problem in perspective', in *US Commission on Marijuana and Drug Abuse* (ed.), (US Congress).

Shyrock, R.H. (1961), 'The history of quantification in medical science', in H. Woolf (ed.), *Quantification: A History of the meaning of measurement in the natural and social sciences* (Indianapolis: Bobbs-Merrill Company Inc), 85-107.

Skocpol, T. (1984), *Vision and Method in Historical Sociology* (Cambridge: Cambridge University Press).

Small, D. and Drucker, E. (2007), 'Closed to reason: time for accountability for the International Narcotics Control Board', *Harm Reduction Journal*, 4 (13).

Spender, D. (1991), *The Diary of Elizabeth Pepys*, (London: Grafton Books).

Stamler, R.T. (1984), 'Forfeiture of the profits and proceeds of drug crime', *Bulletin on Narcotics*, 4, 3-19.

Stamler, R.T., Fahlman, R.C. and Clement, G.W. (1987), 'Cooperation between Canada and other countries and territories to promote counter measures against illicit drug trafficking', *Bulletin on Narcotics*, 1, 78-85.

Starke, J.G. (1937), 'Commentary', *American Journal of International Law*, 31-32.

Steinitz, M.S. (2002), *The Terrorism and Drug Connection in Latin American's Andean Region* (Policy Papers on the Americas: Centre for Strategic and International Studies).

Stimson, G. V. and Metrebian, N. (2003), *Prescribing heroin: What is the evidence* (Water End: Joseph Rowntree Foundation).

Stokes, G., Chalk, P., and Gillen, K. (2000), *Drugs and Democracy: In search of new directions* (Melbourne: Melbourne University Press).

Strang, J. (1994), 'Prescribing Heroin and Other Injectable Drugs', in J. Strang and M. Gossop (eds.), *Heroin Addiction and Drug Policy: The British System* (New

York: Oxford University Press), 192-206.

Sweet, C. (1994), *Off the Hook: How to break free from addiction and enjoy a new way of life,* (London: Paitkus).

Sydney Morning Herald (2001), 'The Medical Problem', *Sydney Morning Herald,* 11/08/2001, p. 36.

Tasmanian Department of Community and Health Services (1995), 'Tasmanian methadone program policy', (Hobart: Department of Community and Health services).

Taylor, A.H. (1969), *American Diplomacy and the Narcotics Traffic, 1900-1939: A Study of International Humanitarian Reform* (Durham, N. C.: Duke University Press).

Thomas, M. and Buckmaster, L. (2007), ''Naltrexone or methadone'? Debates about drug treatments for heroin dependence in the context of drugs policy', in Social Policy Section (ed.), (7; Canberra: Department of Parliamentary Services).

Tuck, R. (1987), 'The 'modern' theory of natural law,' in Anthony Pagden (ed.), *The Language of Political Theory in Early-Modern Europe* (Cambridge: Cambridge University Press), 99-119.

Tuck, R. (1993), *Philosophy and Government, 1572-1651* (New York: Cambridge University Press).

United Nations (1961), 'Single convention on narcotic drugs 1961 as amended by the 1972 Protocol Amending the Single Convention on Narcotic Drugs', (United Nations).

--- (1988), 'United Nations convention against illicit traffic in narcotic drugs and psychotropic substances, 1988', (United Nations).

United Nations Drug Control Program (1999), 'International legal framework', <http://222.undcp.org/international_legal_framework.htm.>,accessed11/12/1999 10.50am.

--- (2000), 'Working with governments and countries: Model legislation', <http://wwww.undcp.org/model_legislation.html>, accessed 14/01/2000 4.13pm.

United Nations General Assembly Special Session on the World Drug Problem (1999), 'Reducing illicit demand for drugs, Fact Sheet No. 4', <http://undcp.org/adhoc/ga/themes/demand-4.htm>, accessed 11/12/1999 10.48.

United Nations International Drug Control Program (1996), *The Social Impact of Drug Abuse* (Technical Series; Vienna: United Nations).

--- (1997), *World Drug Report* (Oxford: Oxford University Press).

--- (1998), 'Reducing Illicit illicit Demand demand for Drugs'drugs', *United Nations General Assembly Special Session on the Drug Problem* (New York: United Nations).

United Nations Office for Drug Control and Crime Prevention (ed.), (2000), *World Drug Report 2000* (United Nations).

United Nations Office of Drug Control (2007), *2007 World Drug Report* (Vienna: United Nations).

United Nations Office on Drugs and Crime Prevention (2006), *2006 World Drug Report*, 2 vols. (1; Vienna: United Nations).

--- (2007), *2007 World Drug Report* (Vienna: United Nations).

Valverde, M. (1996a), 'Governing out of habit: From "habitual inebriates" to "addictive personalities"', *History of the Present* (London: London school of Economics).

--- (1996b), 'Despotism and ethical liberal governance', *Economy and Society,* 25 (3), 357-72.

--- (1998), *Disease of the Will: Alcohol and the dilemmas of freedom* (New York: Cambridge University Press).

Victorian Department of Health and Community Services (1995), 'Victorian methadone program guidelines for providers', (Melbourne: Public Health Branch).

Viroli, M. (1992), 'From politics to reason of state: The acquisition and transformation of the language of politics, 1250-1600,in R. Rorty (ed.) *Ideas in Context* (Cambridge: Cambridge University Press.

Walker, D. (1999), *Anxious Nation: Australia and the Rise of Asia 1850-1939*, St Lucia Queensland: University of Queensland Press.

Ward, Jeff, Mattick, Richard, and Hall, Wayne (1992), *Key Issues in Methadone Maintenance Treatment* (Kensington: New South Wales University Press).

Wardlaw, G. (1988), 'Drug control policies and organised crime', in M. Findlay and R. Hogg (eds.), *Understanding Crime and Criminal Justice* (London: The Law Book Company Limited).

Weeks, J. (1981), 'Discourses, Desire and Sexual Deviance: Some problems in a history of homosexuality', in K. Plummer (ed.), *The Making of the Modern Homosexual*, (Totowa NJ: Barnes and Noble Books), 76-111.

Wells, R. and McKay, B. (1989), 'Review of funding of methadone programs in Australia', (Canberra: Department of Community Services and Health).

Western Australian Alcohol and Drug Authority (1994), 'Methadone program: Polices and procedures', (Perth: Western Australian Alcohol and Drug Authority).

Wiener, M.J. (1990) *Reconstructing the Criminal: Culture, law and policy in England, 1820-1914*, (Cambridge: Cambridge University Press).

Wikler, A. (1965), 'Conditioning factors in opiate addiction and relapse', in D.M. Wilner and G.G. Kassebaum (eds.), *Narcotics* (New York: McGraw-Hill).

Williams, P. and Florez, C. (1994), 'Transnational criminal organisations and drug trafficking', *Bulletin on Narcotics,* 2, 9-24.

Willis, E. (1989), *Medical Dominance: The division of labour in Australian health care* (North Sydney: Allen & Unwin).

Wodak, A. (2007), 'The heroin trial 10 years on; how politics killed hope', *Crikey,* 22 August 2007.

Zwebe, J. and Payte, J. (1990), 'Methadone maintenance in the treatment of opioid dependence', *Western Journal of Medicine*, 5, 588-99.

Index

Note: Numbers in brackets preceded by *n* refer to footnotes.